D1130879

MIRACLES IN DISPUTE

Miracles in Dispute

A Continuing Debate

by Ernst and Marie-Luise Keller
translated by Margaret Kohl

FORTRESS PRESS
PHILADELPHIA

Translated by Margaret Kohl from the German
Der Streit um die Wunder
Gütersloher Verlagshaus Gerd Mohn, Gütersloh, 1968

CONTENTS

PREFACE

Is the question of miracle still a live one? For a long time one was inclined to think that the matter was finished with – that the ground had been thoroughly gone over and the matter talked out for educated people. Today it seems that this assumption was too hasty. Unrest has developed at the points of contact between man's everyday awareness and theology.

Nothing in the Bible makes a more alien impression than the alleged workings of a supernatural power. Under the influence of such impressions, 'rational' and 'enlightened' people had once concluded that these things were entirely out of date and a matter of indifference, and that they could give way to other problems; but now this attitude is being superseded by a new interest in factors which might possibly prove to be relevant. Even in quarters where a rigid and monotonously anti-religious attitude once held sway, people are now cautiously considering what the Christian tradition might perhaps have to contribute to a better understanding of the present situation and its problems. Complaints are heard about the 'monopolization of Jesus' by Christian congregations and the corresponding diminution of his significance for other spheres of intellectual life. 'Jesus' cultural restoration' seems desirable.[1] The feeling is abroad, and rightly so, that there must be objective facts, that these must be known and considered before any opinion is given, and that there must be no pressure towards any particular profession of faith. Information, not proclamation, is needed. 'I believe nothing which has not been explained to me'[2] – this principle expresses precisely the standard by which the quality of theological statement is to be gauged.

But how do miracles fit into this framework? Are there any 'facts' at all here? Of what kind are these facts supposed to be and what do they mean? Whenever questions of this kind are even touched on in Christian

[1] Leszek Kolakowski, in *Almanach 1 für Literatur und Theologie* (Wuppertal, 1967), p. 156.
[2] Erich Kästner.

7

circles, opinions diverge diametrically. Did Jesus rise bodily from the tomb? Does physics once again allow the possibility of miracle? Must a Christian believe in miracles? This is the other front in the continuing battle over the miraculous. It is quite impossible to speak of a satisfactory solution, either within the Church or outside it. How, then, are we to proceed?

Anyone who takes up the problem soon makes a welcome discovery. We are not alone in our reflections and criticisms; there is a considerable tradition of investigation. The controversy over miracle is nearly two thousand years old, and has brought to light many new insights and discoveries. But the results have received far too little notice, shut up as they are between the covers of scholarly books, absorbed by the further progress of research, silently assigned by specialists to the material pigeon-holed as being a matter of course; either that, or they have been simply forgotten. Our first task is to collect, view, publicize and make generally available what lies hidden in our archives.

What is the purpose of a historical approach? Albert Schweitzer's *Quest of the Historical Jesus* has shown this impressively. How much we owe to this work will be repeatedly clear in the first part of our book. Like the various attempts of liberal theologians to go behind the Church's dogmas and to grasp and depict Jesus' life 'as it really was', the various suggestions about the way in which the question of miracle is to be solved are connected in a highly instructive manner. From the very beginning, they were formulated in the course of controversy, and were worked out with the passionate desire to bring to light some aspect of truth which had up to then been ignored. It would be surprising indeed if all these attempts had been completely fruitless. Although it is impossible to incorporate the gropings of the past in their original form into a changed present, they still represent steps of insight, stages of perception, approaches to truth. And the impulse, the will to knowledge which moves them, cannot become obsolete at any period, however late, as long as a living interest in the discovery of truth remains.

The history of the question of miracle is a history of the evolution of constantly new perspectives and points of view. No other Christian subject in modern times has set people thinking to such an extent, even outside the Church; nor has anything else so challenged the theologians, in the interests of their cause, to be self-critical and to maintain their ground against the attacks of the spirit of the age through the presentation of new and fruitful ideas. These ideas – often formulated in extreme form through the exigencies of controversy – should not be smoothed over in a modern account. If our knowledge today is more complete and our judgments more adequate, it is thanks to them. The obvious course, therefore, is to allow the authors of these ideas to speak for themselves. Who is more competent to describe and defend a point of view than the man who developed it and made it a talking-point?

We shall therefore look at these ideas as they arise in history. The reader is invited to listen to voices from the past and to examine for himself what, for instance, Hermann Samuel Reimarus or Carl Friedrich Bahrdt had to urge against belief in miracles. He will discover that the difficulties they found in the material are our difficulties as well – only they seem to us to have become much more complicated, so that we often fail to summon up the courage to make definite statements at all. It is no longer possible for us to pick out and depict with the same direct simplicity what is so closely interwoven and entangled in the contemporary consciousness; we are frequently no longer able to give reasons for what has long seemed to us a matter of course. The language of the older writers is clear. They go thoroughly into a few particular things and explain with precision every step of their thinking. In many respects they are a better introduction for the reader who wants to start from rock bottom than a general survey in our abstract contemporary style – in spite of their apparent ceremoniousness, an occasionally comic elaboration of expression and old-fashioned spelling. All the other things which give these documents their historical freshness and add to their factual arguments – the enthusiasm at the discovery of a new insight, the vigorous combating of error, the moral seriousness and the solemnity of uncompromising truthfulness, the courage to speak the dangerous word – all these are hard to convey indirectly.

Finally, a word about how this book may be used. Each chapter deals with a particular subject; the chapters are more or less self-contained and of varying difficulty. The reader can pick out some and leave others on one side at will. Some overlapping and repetition is unavoidable. Part of our purpose in writing the book was the practical one of gathering together, in manageable amounts, material for discussion, which could be used by study groups of all kinds, as well as in schools.

Marburg *Ernst and Marie-Luise Keller*
October 1967

PART ONE

HISTORICAL TRENDS

1 The Biblical View of Miracle and Belief in the Supernatural

With God all things are possible

What is a miracle? Anybody who sits down to consider this question finds himself in a difficulty. We are living in the twentieth century and miracles today are somewhat of a rarity. Personal experience will hardly provide much of a guide for anyone in search of a provisional definition.

We shall, rather, have to turn to a literary example, for example, 'Father Malachy's miracle', in Bruce Marshall's novel of the same name. In this book a Scottish priest decides to perform a miracle, with God's help, in order to prove God's undiminished power to unbelieving humanity, and in particular to the sceptical vicar of the Anglican church opposite. His brother priests view the plan with the greatest reserve: ' "Sure," said Father Neary, "and miracles are intoirely out of fashion these days. If one were to take place in His Lordship the Bishop's bedroom the Right Riverend ould gint would be after hushing the indaicency up." '[1]

But Father Malachy refuses to be diverted; and on a cold December night at 11.30 sharp his prayer causes the translation of an obnoxious dance hall from an Edinburgh street to the Bass Rock in the Firth of Forth. Instead of bringing renown to himself and his church, however, the miracle is merely a source of embarrassment. Far from strengthening belief in God, it becomes material for the popular press and all kinds of publicity, so that all its edifying effects are destroyed. Even the police, who are called to the scene immediately, are angry over the breach of the peace. But since there is no law forbidding miracles, no action can be taken. Father Malachy's own superiors – even the pope himself – are far from pleased at the demonstration. 'A pretty kettle of fish,' says the bishop. The attempt to perform a miracle in the twentieth century is,

[1] Bruce Marshall, *Father Malachy's Miracle*, rev. ed. (London, 1947), p. 41.

spiritually speaking, a dire failure. For it is in fact impossible for people today to imagine God as the author of manifestations of this kind.

'I do not think that if I say to a mountain "Be thou removed into the midst of the sea" that the mountain will budge an inch. I do not think so for the very simple reason that it is against the natural law that mountains should, to use the Psalmist's phrase, skip like rams.'[1]

Probably all Christians today share, consciously or unconsciously, the opinion of the sceptic in Bruce Marshall's novel, though they may not always ask themselves whether things were once different and whether events of this kind really did take place in earlier times.

The theory in Marshall's novel – a theory which makes a pious explanation for the failure possible – is that in earlier times there were, of course, miracles, but what it pleased God to do then has ceased to be an appropriate expression of his power today and therefore no longer takes place. Is this an acceptable theory?

We do not want to take up a hard and fast attitude to the problem too hastily, but will try to do justice to all views and attempts at interpretation. So first, let us attempt to consider and understand how miracles are explained by those who – in earlier times as well as today – are convinced of their historical truth.

The Book of Genesis tells a remarkable story about Abraham, whom the New Testament calls the father of all 'men of faith'. When Abraham was ninety-nine years old and still without heirs, the Lord God appeared to him and said: 'Behold, my covenant is with you, and you shall be the father of a multitude of nations. ... I will make you exceedingly fruitful; and I will make nations of you, and kings shall come forth from you. ... As for [Sarah] your wife ... I will bless her ... and she shall be a mother of nations; kings of peoples shall come from her.' The story goes on: 'Then Abraham fell on his face and laughed, and said to himself, "Shall a child be born to a man who is a hundred years old? Shall Sarah, who is ninety years old, bear a child?"' (Gen. 17.4–17). And Sarah laughed also. But 'the Lord visited Sarah as he had said, and the Lord did to Sarah as he had promised'. The heir of the promise was born and they called him Isaac. 'And Sarah said, "God has made laughter for me; every one who hears will laugh over me"' (Gen. 21.1–7).

Similar stories may be found elsewhere in the Old Testament and the theme is found again at the beginning of the Gospels, in the account which preceeds the birth of John the Baptist. An angel promises the

[1] *Ibid.*, pp. 32f.

elderly priest Zechariah a son, for whom he prophesies a great part in the salvation of Israel. But Zechariah answers the angel, 'How shall I know this? For I am an old man, and my wife is advanced in years' (Luke 1.18). Faced by a no less astounding promise, Mary asks, 'How can this be?' (Luke 1.34)

How can this be? That is the question of all those whose everyday lives are pierced by the impossible. And they find to their astonishment that the impossible can actually happen. How? The narrators of the miracle stories have an answer: 'Is anything too hard for the Lord?' (Gen. 18.14) And 'With God nothing will be impossible' (Luke 1.37).

The astonishing event, or miracle, comes about as God's act of power. And what is possible for God is possible in his name for those who have received his commission – the prophets, Jesus and Jesus' disciples and apostles.

All things are possible to him who believes (Mark 9.23).

If you have faith as a grain of mustard seed, you will say to this mountain, 'Move hence to yonder place,' and it will move; and nothing will be impossible to you (Matt. 17.20).

These sentences are attributed to Jesus. And, as a corollary, though mountains are not removed, still, the winds and waves are subdued at a word, fish gather themselves obediently into the fisherman's net, water becomes wine, and bread and fish multiply in the most astonishing way. The blind see, the lame walk and the dead are raised. And just as at Jesus' birth the heavens are opened and the songs of angels are heard, so at the hour of his death the sun is eclipsed, the earth shakes and the veil of the temple is torn in two.

It seems probable that all these miracle stories had a deep significance for the minds of the early narrators and first readers, a significance which is not immediately evident today. We shall have to go into the question of significance later in more detail; but leaving that on one side, we can at least be certain that most of the narrators were convinced, as a matter of course, that the miracles actually happened. They may describe the astonishment – even in many cases the offence – which the marvellous event produces; but for them the offence is swept aside by the explanation that God was at work here. How can such a point of view be explained?

Everyone has a certain conception of the reality surrounding him. From his particular experience of everyday life, and from his association with the features of his environment, he forms something like a total impression of what is and what is possible. For example, he discovers that when he lets go the stone which he holds in his hand, it falls down and does not fly up. (If it does fly upwards, then it was not in fact a stone at all but perhaps a sparrow – as in Grimm's story of the brave little tailor, where it is only the stupid giant who is deceived.) If, now, a man hears that something is supposed to have happened which is inexplicable on the basis of his previous and normal experience, he can only believe in the event if he assumes that it has been brought about by unknown forces which are hidden from him.

For example, he knows from experience that it is impossible to walk on water; if, in spite of this, walking on water has actually occurred, then other forces must have been at work; and if these cannot have been the forces of nature (as would be the case if the water were frozen into ice), then the forces must be superior to nature, i.e., *supernatural* forces. So ran the argument. The origin of these forces does not need to be immediately determined; it is enough that they are effective *in* nature.

If it is now claimed that *divine* power which has manifested itself in this supernatural event, then the supernatural forces are divine in origin and the event is classed as a miracle of God.

'A miraculous act is a happening or deed which can be effected by no natural cause, being above the settled and recognized laws of nature; and which can hence only be attributed to God, the creator and lord of nature: for example, the resurrection of a dead body.' This is the way in which a German Dictionary of Christian Faith and Morals,[1] published in 1786, defines what is important for the concept of miracle. Let us look at two of the leading ideas:

1. Miracles are 'above nature'.
2. Miracles count as acts of God.

Apparently the early Christians found no difficulty in accepting the possibility that supernatural forces could be active in the world; the same is true of the other religions with which Christianity was in contact. In the Old and New Testaments it is evidently assumed that not only can God and his plenipotentiaries perform miracles and signs, but so can the devil and his demonic angels, and even false prophets and the Antichrist. Hence the first Christian theologians spent a great deal of time in trying to distinguish true Christian and divine miracles from pagan and demonic ones. An important factor in the decision was the *purpose* to be served by the miracles, when these were performed by human agency. True

---

[1] *Lexikon der christlichen Glaubens- und Sittenlehre.*

miracles, says the Dictionary quoted above, 'serve . . . no evil or vain purpose, for example, the satisfaction of curiosity; they have some important purpose such as befits the deity'. One can follow the Early Church Fathers and say simply that they serve the salvation of mankind; in addition, by their very unusualness, they aim at drawing attention to something which comes directly from God.

The world in which supernatural forces of this kind are active is not fixed or self-contained, but is open at all times to influences both from a heavenly world above it and from a demonic world below. Such an interpretation of the world, according to which miracles do not represent anything basically impossible because the natural world is overshadowed by another and mightier supernatural reality, is generally called the 'supernatural' view; and those who believe in miracles without reservation, because they are convinced that supernatural forces are at work in the world, are known as 'supernaturalists'.

Since the first century most Christians have undoubtedly been supernaturalists, though they have not given themselves this title; the technical-theological expression derives, significantly, only from a time when the supernatural view had already become open to question. This is easy to understand. As long as all Christians were united in the matter there was no need for a special term to describe their conviction; it only became necessary once critical voices had been raised and parties formed.

Apparently there was no criticism of this kind in the primitive era of Christianity or at the time of the Early Church, at least not among Christians. It is true that when a theologian had to deal with a miracle in a sermon or in doctrinal teaching he did first list the witnesses who vouched for the genuineness of the tradition; but apart from that there was no problem. Since the historical truth of the miracle was presupposed, one could proceed immediately to an edifying interpretation of the story.

For the purpose of this interpretation, in which the significance of the biblical passage for the contemporary Church was to be shown, use was frequently made of an artificial hermeneutical method which grew up in the world of Hellenism and was especially cultivated and disseminated by the teachers of the Christian catechetical school in the Egyptian city of Alexandria, one of the cultural centres of the Greek world. This method was that of allegorical interpretation. The Greek word *allegorein* means 'to express something in a different way'; for example, one may bring out the meaning of something by telling a symbolic story through which the hearer may penetrate in order to find the real significance. If one interprets a story allegorically, one therefore assumes that behind the direct narrative lies a hidden meaning which can be worked out by the art of interpretation, or hermeneutics. In that case, a distinction is made between a literal and an allegorical meaning. The latter can be further divided, according to the dimensions of meaning which are believed to be discernible, into a moral interpretation, a spiritual interpretation, an ecclesiastical interpretation, etc. We can still see this in the exegetical works of sixteenth-century writers.

Allegorically interpreted, the marriage at Cana, for example, is an image of the inner joy and blessedness to which Christ leads the souls of believers; and the wine which he miraculously bestows on the guests is the wine of his spirit.

The story of Peter's 'miraculous draught', which ends with Jesus' saying, 'from henceforth you will be catching men', is interpreted in an ancient hymn (attributed to Clement of Alexandria, c. AD 200) in the following way:[1]

Σῶτερ 'Ιησοῦ –	Jesus, Saviour of our race; . . .
'Αλιεῦ μερόπων	Fisher of men, whom Thou to
Τῶν σωζομένων	life dost bring;
Πελάγους κακίας	From evil sea of sin,
'Ιχθῦς 'αγνοὺς	And from the billowy strife,
Κύματος ἐχθροῦ	Gathering pure fishes in,
Γλυκερῇ ζωῇ θελεάζων	Caught with sweet bait of life. . . .

Although allegorical interpretation often went to fantastic lengths, like all theories of a multiple literary meaning it was fed by a correct intuition: that the significance of many biblical stories, and especially the miracles, is not exhausted by the surface narrative; today we say that such stories have a particular 'significance', which is open to discovery. For example, it is not mere chance that the stories and parables of Jesus often speak of marriage-feasts and banquets and the miraculous feeding of multitudes; in Jewish tradition, the marriage-feast with all its lavishness was in fact interpreted as a symbol of the highest joy and blessedness – it was an image of the fulfilment of all earthly hopes in the end-time.

These examples show that such an interpretation of biblical stories can leave quite untouched the historical question of whether the miracles actually took place. The allegorical method could be used to exclude, or

[1] Quoted in H. Olshausen, *Biblischer Commentar über sämmtliche Schriften des Neuen Testaments*, 2nd ed. (Reutlingen, 1834), vol. 1, pp. 285f.; ET in Clement of Alexandria, *Writings*, trans. by W. Wilson (Edinburgh, 1867), vol. 1, p. 343 (trans. of this particular passage by W. L. Alexander).

at least to push aside or play down, a realistic reading at particularly difficult points, for example, the story of the temptation. One can find this in the Alexandrian theologians Clement and Origen, but the possibility is seldom exploited because there were no serious objections to miracles in the Church itself.

Critical questions of a really basic kind seem first to have cropped up when Christian theologians saw themselves confronted by an alien intellectual world – the world of the late Greek Enlightenment and its philosophy – and began to try to come to terms with it.

From its beginnings, Greek thought showed particular interest in the world as *nature*, whereas biblical thinking was far more tied – in fact almost exclusively so – to *historical* experience. The early Greek world saw the beginnings of the natural sciences; here and there natural processes were already being precisely observed, considered and traced back to regularities by the process of abstract reasoning; whereas Israel's wisdom served a religious and practical purpose only:

> Behold, the fear of the Lord, that is wisdom;
> and to depart from evil is understanding (Job 28.28).

But Greek thought had a religious interest in its objects of study as well: it revered God in the ordered revolutions of the heavenly bodies, indeed the whole marvellous *order* of nature *per se* had for the Greeks the character of the beautiful and the divine. The arbitrary actions of the God of the Bible, who caused the sun to stand still at will, or even to go backwards (Josh. 10.12ff.; Isa. 38.7f.) and who frequently interfered with the natural order in sundry miracles, must have appeared to the Greek as appalling irregularities, sacrilegious interference with the cosmic harmony. Although simple people throughout the ancient world gave themselves up to a fantastic belief in the marvellous far surpassing anything in the Bible, in educated circles superstition was mocked at, and the proclamation of miracles by the Christian Church must inevitably have represented an impossible obstacle to the strictly philosophical mind.

Consequently all the great theologians of the Early Church and in the Middle Ages – now familiar with Greek learning themselves – saw the necessity of justifying the Christian belief in miracles before the forum of reason and, if possible, of reconciling that belief with reasoned thinking. Is this possible? It may well be asked. The following pages may help us to find an answer.

2 Augustine and the Problem of Miracle

God does not act contrary to nature but only contrary to the order of nature known to us

'We say all portents are contrary to nature (*contra naturam*), but we are deceived. For how can that be against nature which is effected by the will of God, the Lord and Maker of all nature?' Such is the answer of the fourth-century Church Father Augustine (354–430) to the reproach which seems to hover over all serious discussions between the Christian creed and Hellenistic philosophy. Augustine is not willing to accept an absolute contradiction between nature and miracles, because nature (the revered cosmos of the Greeks) is also according to the creed of the Bible, the work of God and bears the stamp of his divine will, just as do miracles. God cannot contradict himself – that is a cogent argument, both logically and theologically. If, then, the contradiction cannot be either real or ultimate, it must be merely superficial and apparent. It may possibly be based on a false subjective impression, or perhaps on man's imperfect knowledge. This is in fact what Augustine thinks. A portent, therefore, is not against nature, but against the order of nature known to us.[1]

Long after Augustine this sentence gave rise to a noteworthy type of argument: when we know more about nature we shall be able to explain miracles. But Augustine would hardly have been able to admit this conclusion, for what he here calls nature and contrasts with 'the order of nature known to us' is in its very essence not open to explanation by the methods of the probing intellect. What does this mean?

It would be generally agreed that miracles are events which give rise to amazement because they are 'incomprehensible'. They are incomprehensible because we do not know their causes. It may well be that certain events which appear to be marvellous become explicable once their

[1] Cf. *The City of God*, trans. by John Healey, ed. by R. V. G. Tasker (London, Everyman's Lib., 1945); xxi. 28, p. 329.

causes are discovered; but this is only true of events whose causes really are to be found among created things. And even here Augustine makes an important qualification. In his doctrine of creation he puts forward the highly remarkable and interesting theory that the powers or seeds which God gave to the elements at the creation of the world are not yet exhausted; there are hidden seeds (*semina occulta*) or combinations of seeds (*seminariae rationes*), which still await development; the world is, as it were, pregnant with the causes of things unborn.[1] If these hidden aptitudes and possibilities are to be recognized and brought to fruition, specially endowed natures are necessary – Augustine is thinking of divine and demonic powers even among men – who, like the farmer who prepares the field, are capable of bringing the seed into favourable conditions. The forms which duly develop from these germs are also viewed by men as miracles because of their unusual character. But in the case of these phenomena we are dealing only with what is *relatively* miraculous, not absolutely so, since they proceed from natural predispositions. Augustine does not seem to think that the discovery of such hidden causes is a function of the eye of reason in the usual sense.

Miracles in the real and true sense, however, are completely inaccessible to reason because their causes lie directly and solely within the will of God.

> God has hidden causes for certain events within himself, which he has not put into created things and which he does not allow to become reality by virtue of the providence by which he calls nature into being, but by virtue of that providence by which he rules the world according to his will – that same world which he created according to that will.[2]

These independent acts of the almighty God, acts not based on nature, are miracles in the real and absolute sense; and it is from this that Augustine justifies the sentence that they 'are contrary to what we know of nature' or that they 'transgress the rules of nature which are familiar to us'. 'We admit that what is contrary to the ordinary course of human experience is commonly spoken of as contrary to nature.' He follows this up, however, with a decisive qualification: 'But God, the Author and Creator of all natures, does nothing contrary to nature; for whatever is

---

[1] '*Sicut matres gravidae sunt foetibus, sic ipse mundus est gravidus causis nascentium*' (*De trinitate*, III. 9).
[2] *De genesi ad litteram*, IX, § 33.

done by him who appoints all natural order and measure and proportion must be natural in every case.'[1]

In the Epistle to the Romans, ch. 11, Paul gives an indication of where in the sphere of Christian faith one might justly and rationally speak of an experience 'contrary to nature'. The theme with which he is dealing is the burning question arising from the course of salvation history: how was it possible and reconcilable with God's plan of redemption for the people of Israel (in whom God originally planted his saving promise) to have been blind to redemption when it appeared, so that the Gentiles had now become the heirs of salvation? Paul expresses in an image what was for the devout Jew, the 'seed of Abraham', an apparently paradoxical experience: Israel is the cultivated olive tree, planted by God, the rich root of his promise; but certain branches have now been broken off, because of their unbelief; in their stead God has set others 'cut from what is by nature a wild olive tree and grafted, contrary to nature (*contra naturam*), into a cultivated olive tree'. 'Note, then, the kindness and the severity of God,' says the apostle to the Gentile Christians, 'otherwise you too will be cut off. And even the others, if they do not persist in their unbelief, will be grafted in, for God has the power to graft them in again' (Rom. 11.17–24).

This passage serves Augustine as an example of God's power to do something which at first seems to historical man contrary to reason, but which a deeper insight into God's plan of salvation may show to be meaningful and in line with a higher purpose – as Paul shows in the whole argument of Rom. 11. This higher purpose and the whole over-riding divine conception of the world and world-history which it reveals is also called by Augustine (following the terminology of Hellenistic philosophy) 'nature' or 'the laws of nature'. He sees all the more justification for this term as – also according to the Epistle to the Romans – God's revelation in history has the purpose of opening up for man the opportunities for true knowledge of God, for a reasonable divine service, and for right conduct and right use of his worldly goods, all of which had been already given to him at the creation. Hence Augustine is able to say that what God does is part of nature, or, summing up:

> There is, however, no impropriety in saying that God does a thing contrary to nature, when it is contrary to what we know of nature. For we give the name nature to the usual common course of nature; and

[1] *Contra Faustum Manichaeum*, XXVI. 3; ET in Augustine, *Works*, vol. 5: *Reply to Faustus the Manichaean*, ed. by Marcus Dods, trans. by R. Stothert (Edinburgh, 1871–1876), pp. 508–509.

whatever God does contrary to this, we call a prodigy or miracle (*magnalia vel mirabilia*). But against the supreme law of nature, which is beyond the knowledge both of the ungodly and of weak believers, God never acts, any more than he acts against himself. As regards spiritual and rational beings, to which class the human soul belongs, the more they partake of this unchangeable law and light, the more clearly they see what is possible and what impossible; and again, the greater their distance from it, the less their perception of the future, and the more frequent their surprise at strange occurrences.[1]

In the last analysis, for the perception of the believer, all contradictions are dissolved; and Augustine is anxious that the believer should not merely gaze in astonishment at miracles but should understand them. Through the physically unusual nature of their appearance they rouse the man who is only reachable through his senses out of the dullness of his everyday jog-trot, just as one might wake someone from sleep in order to announce some message from God. But 'our Lord Jesus Christ desired that what he did physically should be understood spiritually. For he did not perform miracles as an end in themselves but in order that what he did should be marvellous for those that saw and true for those that understood.'[2]

Now Paul's example (in the Epistle to the Romans) of a divine action apparently contrary to nature does not, properly speaking, mention any non-natural miracle – one standing in contradiction to natural laws – at all; for the basis is in fact Paul's entirely non-miraculous experience of history – an experience which merely runs counter in a puzzling way to religious hopes and expectations. This 'spiritual' contradiction is to be overcome through faith. What, however, is the position as regards the miracle actually contrary to nature, such as the virgin birth, the changing of water into wine, the feeding of the five thousand, etc.?

Augustine may be right in seeing here merely various physical reflections of one and the same fundamental saving process, that God acts contrary to man's expectations by choosing the insignificant and creating something out of nothing – as one may read in Paul. But is the 'physical' contradiction which these miracles present to the reason also to be resolved through faith?

That is the question. Augustine answers it in the affirmative. And since he is greatly concerned – even in the interests of reason – to eliminate unendurable antinomies, he declares all biblical miracles, lock,

---

[1] *Ibid.*, p. 509.   [2] *Sermones*, XCVIII, § 3.

stock and barrel, as not contrary to nature but only contrary to nature as it is known to us. He transfers, broadly speaking, his theological and religious judgment – that 'we men cannot know what is against nature and what is in accordance with it' – into the sphere of physics. And here it becomes plain that Augustine, like nearly all his contemporaries, including those for whom he was writing, really had no standards whereby to distinguish between what is possible in nature and what is not. All biblical miracles took place precisely as they are related, including Jesus' birth from the virgin womb of his mother and the passing of the risen Christ through closed doors. He holds that various miracles performed by pagan gods also really happened, for example, that the figures of the *Penates*, the Roman household gods, moved from one place to another. All kinds of curiosities from the animal world in which people then believed are to serve to make biblical miracles appear less incredible: bees do not receive the seed of their offspring through copulation but gather it with their mouths when flying over the earth; in Cappadocia, we are told, mares even conceive by the wind and the fruits of this conception only live for three years; there are other cases where animals are born without the mating of parents, both during the course of creation and later, for example, worms in fruit or snakes in rotten wood (consequently the transformation of Aaron's staff and the staff of the Egyptian magician in Ex. 7.8–12 is not contrary to nature); etc.

Augustine only makes much of miracles to his miracle-loving contemporaries in order to stress the uniqueness of the Son of God. And in his interpretations of the great miracles of Christ one constantly sees him at pains to play down the element of the marvellous by letting miracles appear as natural as possible or, alternatively, by making natural phenomena as miraculous as may be.

> The miracle indeed of our Lord Jesus Christ, whereby he made the water into wine, is not marvellous to those who know that it was God's doing. For he who made wine on that day at the marriage-feast, in those six water-pots, which he commanded to be filled with water, the self-same does this every year in vines. For even as that which the servants put into the water-pots was turned into wine by the doing of the Lord, so in like manner also is what the clouds pour forth changed into wine by the doing of the same Lord. But we do not wonder at the latter, because it happens every year: it has lost its marvellousness by its constant recurrence.[1]

[1] Augustine, *Works*, vol. 10: *Lectures or Tractates on the Gospel According to St. John*, ed. by Marcus Dods, trans. by J. Gibb, p. 113.

What therefore took place in that act of the miraculous transformation of water into wine really represents – so Augustine suggests – something approximating to an 'accelerated natural process'.[1] This explanation is quoted approvingly centuries later.

'The one true view of this event [the miracle at Cana] is certainly that whereby we assume a real power which only expresses itself in accelerated form. The Fathers of the Church already rightly remind us that here nothing came to pass which we may not see year for year in the vines, though there it develops more slowly.' So writes Hermann Olshausen (a professor of theology who taught at Königsberg after the time of Kant) in his *Biblical Commentary* published in 1834.[2]

Augustine has a similar explanation for the miraculous feeding of the five thousand:

> He made bread from nothing. For whence came so great a quantity of food to fill so many thousands? The source of the bread was in the hands of the Lord. That need not surprise us. For he that made from five loaves bread to fill so many thousands was the same who daily prepares mighty harvests in the earth from but a few grains. For this too is a miracle of God, although we have ceased to wonder at it because it comes about day by day.[3]

These two passages show clearly once more how important to Augustine was the bracketing of God's actions in history with his actions in creation: the same God acts in a twofold and yet similar way. God cannot contradict himself. It is not only a logical and theological problem which is here under discussion; concealed in this problem is a difficulty springing from the historical situation in which Augustine sees himself set: on the one hand, Greek experience of life as the experience of whatever happens according to law and rule and whatever naturally determines the background of everyday life; on the other hand, Christian historical experience as the experience of single and unique, completely undeducible events, in which the believer recognizes spiritually the meaning of his life – how do these two fit in with one another? Contradiction in principle would condemn to schizophrenia the man whose life is simultaneously determined by the two experiences, historically and day by day; and this would be intolerable to both reason and faith. The Christian experience of history, however, expresses itself historically

---

[1] cf. *De genesi ad litteram*, VI. 13.
[2] H. Olshausen, *op. cit.*, vol. II, p. 74.
[3] *Enarrationes in Psalmos* XC; *Sermones* I, § 1.

in these non-natural miracles and seems therefore to assert a basic contradiction.

Here for the first time the difficulty emerges which was later to develop into 'the problem of miracle'. In Augustine it is still completely undeveloped; it is merely hinted at, as his constant concern to smooth out contradictions suggests some touch of dissatisfaction.

Were Augustine's attempts successful? Augustine was *the* great teacher of the Early and Mediaeval Church. All later utterances about miracles draw on his treatises on the Gospel of John, his expositions of the Psalms and his sermons. Even in Thomas Aquinas and Luther there are constant references. There is hardly an idea on the subject which was not already touched on by Augustine; it is only the emphasis which changes here and there.

From the time of Augustine onwards a distinction was made between two kinds of events: those which correspond to the usual order of things and those which run counter to it. God acts in a twofold manner: sometimes he acts through the indwelling laws of the created world; sometimes through direct supernatural intervention, i.e., miracles. From the time of Augustine, people were accustomed to see the contradiction between nature and miracles as being reconciled in God. The alliance between reason and faith was so secure and firm on this point that later one could even afford to stress the extra-natural, anti-natural or supernatural nature of the miracle (*praeter – contra – supra facultatem naturae*) and to classify miracles generally according to the degree to which they were opposed to nature, as the thirteenth-century Thomas Aquinas does in a central passage of his chief work.[1] The distinction between God's two modes of activity now came more to the fore and was depicted with mechanistic precision.

> God is the prime mover who established the natural order and set the machine of the world in motion. If he wishes to perform a miracle he causes the world mechanism to stand still, performs the miraculous act, and sets it in motion once more. Hence a miracle can only take place if it breaks through the natural order.[2]

Such is a simple attempt to characterize the intellectual pattern through

[1] *Summa Theologiae*, part I, qu. 105, arts. 6–8, cf. *Summa Theologiae*, Latin text and English translation . . ., ed. by Thomas Gilby and others (London and New York, 1964 –), vol. 14.

[2] *Biblisch-theologisches Handwörterbuch zur Lutherbibel*, 2nd ed. (Göttingen, 1959), col. 713.

which Aquinas introduced the miraculous activity of the God of the Bible into the rational scheme of Aristotelian physics.

How can this obvious contradiction on the level of nature still be overshadowed by and subordinated to Augustine's programmatic declaration that God, the founder and creator of all natural existence, does nothing against nature?[1] How can we explain the fact that such a synthesis proved acceptable to reason and was able to maintain itself, almost unopposed, for more than a thousand years? Two main reasons may be suggested:

1. 'Who can deny to God, the unlimited Lord of nature, the power to impede the laws of that which he himself has made and to perform miracles? "Let us confess that God can do more than we are in a position to understand. For in respect to the marvellous the whole cause of their performance is the power of him that performs them," says St Augustine. And again: "Just as it was not impossible for God to ordain the natures he desired, it is likewise not impossible for him to alter what he has ordained into what he wills." And yet again: "If the cause of God's works is concealed from man, yet he must not forget that he *is* man; and let him not ascribe lack of wisdom to God because he himself does not understand the wisdom of the same." '

With God all things are possible. This ancient biblical argument lies behind all the statements of the dictionary of 1786 which we have just quoted (see also above, p. 16). The limitless might or almighty power of God is, theologically speaking, the magic formula which can always demolish any doubts about miracles which may arise. It is the precise counterpart of man's inadequacy, or incapacity for knowledge.

It is apparent that here thinking and argument starts from 'above', from God, beginning with the idea of the almighty Creator and Director of all earthly things. By very definition it follows that God may do with his world what he wants and that there is nothing which he cannot do.

2. This idea comes up against certain difficulties. On the natural level and wherever one becomes conscious of the problem (as originally with Augustine and later in modern times), the concept of nature has to be so tempered and made so flexible that it offers no contradiction to the idea of God's almighty power. A concept of nature which is not disturbed when a body passes through closed doors, or when a substance changes in a trice and without the addition of anything else, or when a particular quantity abruptly extends itself into a vast amount without altering its state of aggregation, etc. – such a concept is not indicative of that stable

[1] *Summa Theologiae*, part 1, qu. 105, art. 6.

structure of the world which is called nature both in Greek philosophy and later in modern times. Augustine could proceed in this way because in his particular historical situation the natural world of nature was still almost completely undiscovered and hence positively teemed with oddities of all kinds – we can only touch the fringe of all the things which he thought were possible in nature – so that the biblical miracles were not nearly so remote from the general world picture as they are today. The main reason why Augustine and all his spiritual heirs were completely convinced of the possibility of miracle, however, was because they thought that nature as it is known to us is at all times open to intervention from a supernatural world, and that the activity of supernatural forces in the natural world was an incontrovertible experience.

To sum up: A dominant supernatural faith combined with an undeveloped knowledge of the natural world-processes – these two general conditions of the outlook of the ancient world guaranteed the long endurance of the theological synthesis of nature and miracles and did not permit a 'problem of miracle' to enter the consciousness in any radical form.

But what is the impression made in a later period by Augustine's arguments, which were continuously repeated by the Church? What, for example, does the reader today make of the philosophical considerations with which Father Malachy would like to commend the ancient supernatural faith to modern times?

And so, as the train went clanging through time and space, he pondered the mystery of miracle and of how absurd it was that men should deny to the Creator the power of doing what he would with his creation. For it was surely evident that he who had ordered the tides should also, if the caprice should take him or if there were souls to be saved that way, be able to disorder them and that he who had commanded the sun to move should be able to command it to stand still. Nay, more, was not the miracle of sequence more marvellous than the miracle of the interruption of the same sequence? Was it not more marvellous that, when one woke in the morning, one's coat was still hanging over the back of the same chair than it would have been if, during the night, God had caused it to be transferred to a scarecrow in Russia? More marvellous and more kind. . . . *Omnia*, as Saint Thomas Aquinas had pointed out, *exibant in mysterium*.[1]

[1] Marshall, *op. cit.*, pp. 5f.

3 Spinoza and the Naturalistic Viewpoint

Nothing happens which is contrary to nature

We are told in the Gospel of John that at a marriage-feast at Cana in Galilee, when the wine was running short, Jesus changed the water in six great stone jugs into wine. According to our measurements there must have been about thirty to forty gallons. What are we to make of this story? Is an event of this kind in any way explicable?

In the last chapter we met a view of history which the Early and Mediaeval Church found convincing and dogmatically correct: why should not God, the Lord of nature, be able to do in a moment what he does every year in the vines? According to this viewpoint God can act in two different ways. On the one hand, he acts according to the usual natural order, for example, when, every year, he allows corn to ripen in the fields and grapes to ripen on the vines. But in addition he has reserved to himself the possibility of interrupting the normal course of things and then acts through direct intervention; he acts in this way in the providence which guides the world, in the mystery of grace and, particularly noticeably, in the events which we call miracles. Miracles therefore count as visible proofs of the power of God and of Christ's divine nature; they confirm the truth of Christianity.

The technical-theological name for this view is the 'supernatural' explanation, because it assumes the possibility of direct intervention in nature. Does it offer a satisfactory solution? Are miracles which interrupt the course of nature possible?

As may be imagined, the supernatural view did not remain undisputed. Early Church writers became conscious of the beginnings of opposition to it, and this opposition raised its voice unmistakably in the seventeenth and eighteenth centuries, starting in England, Holland and France. Let us see what objections the earliest critics and contesters of supernatural faith had to urge against miracles.

29

We can scarcely wonder that of the old religion nothing survives but its outward forms ... and that faith has become a mere compound of credulity and prejudices – aye, prejudices too, which degrade man from rational being to beast, which completely stifle the power of judgment between true and false, which seem, in fact, carefully fostered for the purpose of extinguishing the last spark of reason. Piety, great God! and religion are become a tissue of ridiculous mysteries; men, who flatly despise reason, who reject and turn away from understanding as naturally corrupt, these, I say, these of all men, are thought, O lie most horrible! to possess light from on High.[1]

These sentences are noticeably different from anything said previously about the question of miracles. They can be read in the preface to an anonymously published theological-political treatise which came out in 1670. Its author was the Dutch lens-grinder and philosopher Benedictus Baruch de Spinoza (1632–1677).

What changes have come about? Religion is 'a tissue of ridiculous mysteries'. Reason is said to be fundamentally despised. The earlier harmony of reason and faith has seemingly been shattered. Reason has discovered the ridiculous in faith and has criticized it. Faith has replied with contempt and rejection of reason. To what does reason, in whose name Spinoza speaks, object?

As men are accustomed to call Divine the knowledge which transcends human understanding, so also do they style Divine, or the work of God, anything of which the cause is not generally known: for the masses think that the power and providence of God are most clearly displayed by events that are extraordinary and contrary to the conception they have formed of nature ... they think that the clearest possible proof of God's existence is afforded when nature, as they suppose, breaks her accustomed order, and consequently they believe that those who explain or endeavour to understand phenomena or miracles through their natural causes are doing away with God and his providence.[2]

Reason objects to religion's preference for what is extraordinary in nature; for what is extraordinary is incomprehensible – incomprehensible because its causes are not known.

---

[1] Spinoza, *Tractatus theologico-politicus*, trans. by R. H. M. Elwes, rev. ed., 2 vols. (Bohn's Philosophical Library, London, 1900), Preface, p. 7.
[2] *Ibid.*, p. 81 (ch. VI: 'Of Miracles').

The masses then style unusual phenomena 'miracles'; and partly from piety, partly for the sake of opposing the students of science, prefer to remain in ignorance of natural causes, and only to hear of those things which they know least, and consequently admire most.[1]

Has reason anything better to offer? What Spinoza expounds here, on the basis of his observation of contemporary faith, contains a new theory of miracles, or rather, an interpretation of them from a new angle. The people, he says, see the power of God particularly in the extraordinary. They cling to miracles and adhere obstinately to their faith in supernatural powers, even when new opportunities are given of explaining the inexplicable – miracles – on a natural basis.

What has given rise to this new opportunity on which Spinoza's criticism of popular belief in miracles is founded? It was discovered by the people who study the natural sciences. A process was beginning which was to set the treatment of the question of miracles on a new basis: things which were earlier thought to be the inscrutable effects of supernatural forces could now be explained by natural causes. An important event of the year 1752 may serve to illustrate the point at issue – the discovery of the nature of lightning and the invention of the lightning conductor by the American printer, scientist and politician, Benjamin Franklin (1706–1790).

There is something uncanny about thunder and lightning. Unsophisticated man feels himself helpless and at the mercy of inexplicable powers. Consequently, from time immemorial thunderstorms were thought to be manifestations of power on the part of mighty gods or demons. In antiquity, the power to send down lightning was reserved to the chief of the gods, Zeus or Jupiter, Donar or Thor. In the Old Testament we are told that it was in the midst of thunder and lightning that God revealed himself to Moses as the law-giver in the clouds of Mount Sinai.

> The Lord also thundered in the heavens,
>   and the Most High uttered his voice,
>   hailstones and coals of fire.
> And he sent out his arrows, and scattered them;
>   he flashed forth lightnings, and routed them (Ps. 18.13f.).

These are the words of a psalm of thanksgiving for victory which celebrates the deliverance of David from the hands of his enemies.

---

[1] *Ibid.*, p. 81.

In the Christian Middle Ages the only question was whether thunder-storms were caused by God or the devil. The popular creed conceived the middle air as being thronged with demons who went in for all kinds of destructive activities. Useful defences were prayer and the ringing of church bells to disperse the demons, as well as the bloody persecution of poor wretches who were believed to have a covenant with the devil and to influence the weather through witchcraft. In each instance, thunder and lightning was thought to be the wrathful judgment of God and hence to issue from the divine will.

Benjamin Franklin was not concerned with what superstition and Christian theology thought about storms. He had observed that electric sparks which struck the ground like lightning could be produced by friction, and he suspected that lightning was the unloading of vast quantities of electricity. Experiments which he subsequently carried out confirmed his hypothesis. He constructed a kite with a metal point and a thin wire running parallel to the string and ending just above the ground. This he sent up into storm clouds. The contrivance attracted the light-ning and drew it to the earth. The experiment showed that storms are unloadings of the electricity in the atmosphere. At the same time it sug-gested to Franklin that buildings could be protected from lightning if a similar metal conductor were attached to their highest points. In this way the lightning conductor was invented – a method whereby man could protect himself against the blind forces of nature and one which could be scientifically explained and technically directed into the appropriate channels.

The philosophical consequences were immense. The atmosphere was de-demonized and human impotence was ended. 'Knowledge is power,' said Francis Bacon, the sixteenth-century scientist and philosopher, characterizing the result of proceedings of this kind. It is true that many Christians viewed lightning conductors as an impious intervention in God's sphere of influence and many of the clergy refused to equip their churches with what were popularly termed in Germany 'Heretic Rods'.

But these were rearguard battles. G. C. Lichtenberg, a professor of physics who had a lightning conductor attached to his summer house in 1780, wrote to a friend:

So that is that. Lightning so fierce that everyone within ten square miles breaks softly into 'A Safe Stronghold' allows itself to be conduc-ted lamb-like to a wire and is led away, entirely disarmed, through golden wires. This may clarify what one has to do. One must only avoid believing that the conductor is dangerous. Fashion makes fools but everything is profit to the wise man. I have always found this a golden rule.[1]

In Lichtenberg's *Sudelheften* we find: 'Lightning conductors on churches are not unnecessary because sermons are preached within.'[2] Yet there was implicit here a hard problem for the Church at the beginning of modern times. Something which had counted from time immemorial as a manifestation of God's power was now debatable; and moreover something in the Bible had been contradicted by human research. The Church itself – for fifteen hundred years a sacred authority in matters of faith and knowledge – was now ceasing to be recognized as the source of authoritative teaching in important questions. No wonder that it bitterly defended every inch of its claims, or that it proceeded against what it thought to be a denial of God with the terrible weapon of the Inquisition, supported by the laws on blasphemy issued by authority of the state.[3]

But the process of explaining the world naturalistically could no longer be held back by means of force. And what were the first results it had to offer as regards the possibility of miracle? Are there events which are demonstrably *contra naturam*, against nature?

'Whatever comes to pass, comes to pass according to laws and rules which involve eternal necessity and truth.'[4] This is Spinoza's considered judgment on the basis of the new view of nature presented by mathematics and physics. For him non-natural or supernatural miracles are

[1] To Ramberg, May 20, 1782.
[2] See also Lichtenberg's essay 'Über Gewitterfurcht und Blitzableitung', *Göttinger Taschenkalender* (Göttingen, 1795).
[3] It is a proof of blasphemy, and blasphemy of the most extreme kind, when anyone 'disgracefully slanders Almighty God, hence the most holy Trinity or one of the three divine Persons directly by word or deed, attributing to God what is unfitting or diminishing one of his attributes'. The punishment is 'the tearing out or cutting off of the tongue if the blasphemy has been by word of mouth, the cutting off of the hand if it has been by deed; and in both cases burning alive. According to the nature of the case, if there are particularly aggravating circumstances, the judge may order the additional application of red-hot pincers, and drawing and quartering.' So run some regulations from the fifty-sixth Article of the 1769 *Constitutio Criminalis Theresiana*, the criminal code of the Empress Maria Theresia, a code which was thought to be mild and humane compared with its predecessors. The whole Article on blasphemy is printed in Heinrich Fuchss, *Hat die Bibel recht?* (Leipzig, Jena, 1957), pp. 221ff. The book offers a 'historical survey of the struggle of theology against scientific progress'. Although one-sided in its interpretation, it contains much useful information.
[4] Spinoza, *op. cit.*, p. 83.

'a mere absurdity'.[1] If they really existed, they would do away with all certainty in human affairs.

The latter argument is clear enough. A man who has to reckon with the possibility that at any moment the most extraordinary things may take place before his very eyes – the man who cannot be sure that, for example, the sun will rise or that spring will be followed by summer – cannot plan ahead or build on any sure foundation. He would be a helpless being at the mercy of chance. And if a God actually stood behind such disorderly events, as a kind of heavenly trouble-maker, he would be a monster, the embodiment of caprice and meaninglessness. Such a conception of God is impossible. Anyone who so thinks denies him, says Spinoza.

With this the philosopher and scientist goes over to the attack as theologian. What, then, is nature? It is the work of God and hence the expression of his reason, his will and his divine nature.

> Hence, any event happening in nature which contravened nature's universal laws, would necessarily also contravene the Divine decree, nature, and understanding; or if anyone asserted that God acts in contravention to the laws of nature, he, *ipso facto*, would be compelled to assert that God acted against his own nature – an evident absurdity.[2]

It is for religious reasons as well as because of his considered observation of nature that Spinoza sees himself forced to reject miracles. It is the particular characteristic of enlightened piety to see and reverence God above all in the fixed, immutable and wisely ordained order of nature, not in pointless and irregular mysteries. Thus miracles now become a hindrance to faith instead of one of its supports.

> If, therefore, anything should come to pass in nature which does not follow from her laws, it would also be in contravention to the order which God has established in nature for ever through universal natural laws . . . and, consequently, belief in it would throw doubt upon everything, and lead to Atheism.[3]

God cannot contradict himself – this argument led Augustine to the dogmatic assertion that miracles did not therefore offend against nature and to questionable attempts to declare that events such as the turning of water into wine were possible within the bounds of nature. In Spinoza,

[1] *Ibid.*, p. 87.   [2] *Ibid.*, p. 83.   [3] *Ibid.*, p. 87.

the same principle leads to the abandonment of miracles, because neither a scientific nor a dogmatic harmonization is possible any longer. Why not? Apparently because man is beginning to investigate exactly and methodically what nature really is and because such investigations develop a new consciousness of nature as a fixed complex of natural causes and effects which recognizes no arbitrary interventions and abolitions.

A second reason lies in the experience that many phenomena which were once inexplicable and were therefore thought to be miraculous show themselves to be natural as soon as they are analysed with understanding and method.

What is to be inferred from this about the miracles in the Bible? Up to now Spinoza – unlike the theologians and exegetes – has based his argument on reasons deriving from his present knowledge of reality. Now he proceeds to an examination of Scripture based on reason.

> We may, then, be absolutely certain that every event which is truly described in Scripture necessarily happened, like everything else, according to natural laws; and if anything is there set down which can be proved in set terms to contravene the order of nature, or not to be deducible therefrom, we must believe it to have been foisted into the sacred writings by irreligious hands; for whatsoever is contrary to nature is also contrary to reason, and whatsoever is contrary to reason is absurd, and, *ipso facto*, to be rejected.[1]

But no-one immediately thinks of rejection. There is a much better alternative. Rather than to ascribe nonsense to Scripture it is much easier to suppose that it is only our false interpretation which causes us to find absurdities in it. False interpretation must therefore be replaced by a better and more appropriate one. How is this to be done?

In the principles which follow, Spinoza anticipates fundamental recognitions of modern biblical exegesis. His basic principle is that one should have an eye for the individual characteristics of the biblical writers. First of all, one must notice the way in which the Jews expressed themselves. It is a peculiarity of Hebrew writings, says Spinoza, to attribute everything that happens in the course of nature to God. Wind and fire are called God's messengers and servants; when it rains heavily they say that God is opening the windows of heaven; when Pharaoh obstinately opposes Israel's plans they say that God has hardened his heart, etc. 'Whence it appears that the Bible seems to relate nothing but miracles, even when speaking of the most ordinary occurrences.'[2]

[1] *Ibid.*, p. 92.　　　　[2] *Ibid.*, p. 95.

But one may go still deeper and compare the way in which a miracle is reported in different places. Take, for example, the miracle at the Red Sea. In one passage, at God's command a way opens for the Jews through the sea because an east wind blows hard all night; in another passage we are told that the sea rose at a mere gesture from Moses – there is no mention of the wind. In this latter report, therefore, the *natural accompanying circumstance* is passed over so that the miracle appears all the greater.

> If, therefore, events are found in the Bible which we cannot refer to their causes, nay, which seem entirely to contradict the order of nature, we must not come to a stand, but assuredly believe that whatever did really happen happened naturally. This view is confirmed by the fact that in the case of every miracle there were many attendant circumstances, though these were not always related, especially where the narrative was of a poetic character.[1]

How can we explain this curious method of expression? The Scriptures, says Spinoza, do not teach natural causes and frequently pass them over because they are concerned with something different. The object they have in view is to bring the people to obedience and the fear of God.

> Therefore [Scripture] speaks inaccurately of God and of events, seeing that its object is not to convince the reason, but to attract and lay hold of the imagination. If the Bible were to describe the destruction of an empire in the style of political historians, the masses would remain unstirred, whereas the contrary is the case when it adopts the method of poetic description, and refers all things immediately to God.[2]

Behind sentences like this is the view – which is substantiated in detail in another passage of the treatise – that the Scriptures, and particularly the central section of the prophetic writings, are not aiming at a scientific description of nature and history but have an entirely different purpose. They are concerned with morals, with what Kant was later to call the sphere of 'practical reason'. They teach how man ought to behave in his world. They teach, mainly, love and obedience. The realm of faith and obedience is completely different from the realm of reason; they have equal rights and are parallel to one another, not mutually contradictory; they comprise different human potentialities.

Scripture therefore does not think it important to investigate natural

---

[1] *Ibid.*, p. 90.   [2] *Ibid.*, pp. 91f.

causes accurately, because its concern is different. It speaks poetically or figuratively and – as Spinoza sees quite clearly – according to the viewpoints and capacity for understanding of its own time.

Thus in order to interpret the scriptural miracles and understand from the narration of them how they really happened, it is necessary to know the opinions of those who first related them, and have recorded them for us in writing, and to distinguish such opinions from the actual impression made upon their senses, otherwise we shall confound opinions and judgments with the actual miracle as it really occurred.[1]

According to Spinoza, therefore, two things must always be distinguished: what is reported and what really happened; the story and the real event behind the story. No-one forces us to assume that the events really happened word for word as they are related. Indeed experience teaches us that people seldom simply describe things as they happened; they incorporate their own views into what they tell. 'When they see or hear anything new, they are, unless strictly on their guard, so occupied with their own preconceived opinions that they perceive something quite different from the plain facts seen or heard.'[2]

Spinoza illustrates the philosophical bias of the narrator from a story from Israelite history. When at evening Joshua, the people's leader, was on the point of victory against the two native kings of Canaan, we are told that he abjured the sun:

> Sun, stand thou still at Gibeon,
> and thou Moon in the valley of Aijalon.
> And the sun stood still, and the moon stayed,
> until the nation took vengeance on their enemies (Josh. 10.12f.).

So the narrator reports. Spinoza concludes:

In the time of Joshua the Hebrews held the ordinary opinion that the sun moves with a daily motion, and that the earth remains at rest; to this preconceived opinion they adapted the miracle which occurred during their battle with the five kings. They did not simply relate that that day was longer than usual, but asserted that the sun and moon stood still, or ceased from their motion – a statement which would be of great service to them at that time in convincing and proving by experience to the Gentiles, who worshipped the sun, that the sun was under the control of another deity who could compel it to change its

[1] *Ibid.*, p. 93.   [2] *Ibid.*, p. 92.

daily course. Thus, partly through religious motives, partly through preconceived opinions, they conceived of and related the occurrences as something quite different from what really happened.[1]

The cardinal importance of the question of interpretation of Scripture in Spinoza's time becomes clear when one remembers that this verse from the Book of Joshua served the Church for centuries as confutation of the new Copernican doctrine. Even in Luther there is an unwilling notice of 'a certain new astrology' which would like to prove that it is the earth that turns, not sun and moon.

> But that is the way of it: he that would appear wise may not recognize what others think true; he must make something new for himself, as does the man who designs to overthrow the whole astrology. But even if he should turn it upside down I would yet believe the Holy Scriptures. For Joshua commanded the sun to stand still and not the earth.[2]

We must therefore also be familiar with the views which were conditioned by their period, because otherwise we may perhaps confuse things which were merely imagined, merely prophetic ideas, with real facts.

> For many things are narrated in Scripture as real, and were believed to be real, which were in fact only symbolic and imaginary. As, for instance, that God came down from heaven . . . and that Mount Sinai smoked because God descended upon it surrounded with fire; or, again, that Elijah ascended into heaven in a chariot of fire, with horses of fire; all these things were assuredly merely symbols adapted to the opinions of those who have handed them down to us as they were represented to them, namely as real.[3]

These ideas to a later age seem to be conditioned by their period because thought has withdrawn from such conceptual forms and has built up a new way of looking at reality. 'All who have any education know that God has no right hand nor left; that he is not moved nor at rest, nor in a particular place, but that he is absolutely infinite and contains in himself all perfections.'[4] One does not therefore have to conceive God as a physical presence or as a royal ruler who has his throne in heaven beyond the stars. Spinoza concludes: 'To these and similar opinions

---

[1] *Ibid.*, p. 93.

[2] Martin Luther, *Werke, Kritische Gesamtausgabe* (Weimar, 1883ff.), T 4, 412, 32ff., Nr. 4638.

[3] Spinoza, *op. cit.*, p. 93.   [4] *Ibid.*, pp. 93f.

very many narrations in Scripture are adapted, and should not, therefore, be mistaken by philosophers for realities.'[1]

Spinoza, who wrote this chapter 'Of Miracles' in 1670, was expelled from his Jewish community and banished because of 'frightful heresies which he practised and taught'; more precisely, because of 'abominable blasphemies against God and Moses'. His book was forbidden by the government four years after publication; for a time it passed secretly from hand to hand in a few reprints under a false name, but after 1700 it practically disappeared. It was only a hundred years after its first appearance, when times were freer, that it received due honour among the German theologians of the Enlightenment. It gave them the cue for their own method of interpreting miracles: the naturalistic explanation.

[1] *Ibid.*, p. 94.

4 Hermann Samuel Reimarus and the Viewpoint of Reason

Blind faith is to be rejected

See, then, since no way remains open to sound reason whereby she may, under the name of Christian, revere God according to her own lights, she has been finally compelled to declare herself and to state directly: no, it is true: we do not believe what Christianity today demands that we believe, and cannot do so for good cause; and yet we are not disreputable men, but try to honour God humbly according to our reasonable knowledge of him, to love our neighbour truly and actively, to fulfil honestly the duties of an upright citizen and to walk virtuously in all respects.[1]

A hundred years after an anonymous tract had for the first time raised a protest in Holland against certain 'ridiculous mysteries' in religion, a series of similar writings appeared in Germany, published by Lessing. From 1770, Gotthold Ephraim Lessing (1729–1781) was librarian of the ducal library in Wolfenbüttel. There he was allowed to print a periodical which the duke freed of censorship. In two contributions to this periodical Lessing printed anonymously parts of a larger work which he mendaciously alleged he had found among the library's manuscripts, extracts which he called 'Fragments by an Unknown Hand'. Lessing said of them:

They are written with the greatest freedom but also with the greatest earnestness. . . . The enquirer never forgets his own dignity. Levity does not seem to be one of his faults and he never permits himself ridicule or buffoonery. He is a true and sober German, both in his style and in his opinions. He states his opinion plainly and scorns all petty arts whereby to cheat applause out of his readers.

[1] *Von Duldung der Deisten*, in Lessing, *Sämtliche Schriften*, ed. by K. Lachmann, vol. 12 (Berlin, 1897), p. 256.

As Lessing very well knew, although he had good reason for concealing the fact, the author was Hermann Samuel Reimarus (1694–1768), teacher of oriental languages at the Hamburg grammar school.

What does 'sound reason', in whose name the writer pleads, actually object to?

> Men are to believe before they are capable of the smallest understanding, judgment or examination of what they believe. They are to believe what is beyond reason before they have any comprehension of what can be grasped by reason. How can a religion, or knowledge of God, be implanted without any clear concepts and without any means whereby it may be comprehended? How can a mysterious faith come into being if it is not built on the foundations of a rational religion? From this only a blind faith can evolve, since men themselves do not know what they believe or why they believe it.[1]

The inner situation which forced the author to write can be gathered from his reproachful questions. Christian faith (and by that he means, basically, that faith in the miraculous which the Church then taught) seems to 'the man of reason' so ridiculous that he could only accept it without, or in spite of, his own assenting judgment – that is to say, blindly.

This is a new situation compared with the Middle Ages or even the Reformation period. For the Early and Mediaeval Church there was nothing objectionable about faith, even faith in miracles, because it was a matter of course to ascribe to God the creator the right to do with his world whatever he wanted. Since reason conceived of God as being 'above' the world, and since the idea of God was inseparable from the notion of his limitless power, there was no cause for opposing the concept of miracles.

Even Luther (1483–1546) had no objection to miracles, although in his mind reason and faith were already beginning to diverge and although he occasionally thundered in no uncertain terms against scholastic reasoning. He is not in the least concerned with the question of whether miracles are possible, because, for theological reasons, he is not interested in external miracles at all. For Luther, the contemplation of Jesus Christ's *one* great miracle – that he conquered sin and death through his suffering and crucifixion and gives righteousness and eternal life to them that believe – was far more important than the question of whether he performed this or that miraculous sign. From this angle Luther could

[1] *Ibid.*, pp. 266f.

criticize miracles vigorously, though not because of their natural impossibility but because of their lack of conclusive force, spiritually speaking. He says, for example:

> I have never desired that a sign might be granted for doctrine's sake. For I am certain that nothing would be achieved thus and that this perverse generation of hypocrites would ascribe it all to the Devil. For me, it is enough that they are convinced through the power of truth itself and that they are forced to condemn themselves through their own consciences.[1]

To a man like Reimarus two hundred years later, the situation looks very different. Reimarus was a universal scholar, as well versed in mathematics and the natural sciences as in history, languages, theology and philosophy. Why does he find miracles unacceptable?

> If we now consider one kind of miracle alone – that Jesus cast out the Devil, indeed seven devils, from Mary Magdalene, and a whole legion, that is several thousand, from other men: since such apparitions have now been quite expelled from the rational world, the rest must also be considered open to suspicion and must be put down to the score of the superstition and credulity of the time.[2]

Belief in miracles is superstition. By superstition Reimarus means such beliefs as can now be explained away by our superior knowledge and can be ranked with the illusions to which people obstinately cling in the face of all attempts to convince them otherwise. At the time of Reimarus fuller knowledge of the nature of things was no longer gained, as in the Middle Ages, from the study of the sacred writings of the past – the Bible, the Early Church Fathers and the other doctrinal authorities of the Church; it was to be won by precise observation of the natural phenomena themselves, as these present themselves directly to the eye. The new knowledge was better, because it no longer rested on mere faith, but on a deliberately unbiased investigation, which went to work experimentally and methodically and could show demonstrable results.

The following event is said to have taken place in Hamburg in 1729, that is to say, at the time of Reimarus:

[1] Luther, *op. cit.*, 38, 601, 35–602, 20, as quoted in the *Luther Lexikon*, ed. by K. Aland (Berlin, 1956), pp. 434f.
[2] Quoted by D. F. Strauss in his book, *Hermann Samuel Reimarus und seine Schutzschrift für die vernünftigen Verehrer Gottes* (Leipzig, 1862), pp. 193f.

A woman showed in their acutest form all the signs of being possessed by the devil. Exorcism, preaching and the application of holy water, etc. brought no improvement. The doctors of the town intervened and ordered the use of such gentle remedies as the mediaeval science of the time allowed. None the less, in the end the patient died. An official autopsy, in the presence of fifteen doctors and a notary, showed that the woman supposedly so possessed had suffered from chronic encephalitis and had apparently died as a result of the disease.[1]

The Mediaeval Church tried by exorcism and by sometimes cruel physical procedures to drive the devil out of those possessed – people who, according to modern medicine, were in fact suffering from nervous disorders, particularly schizophrenia and epilepsy. But the same must have been true of the 'possessed' in the Bible, as might be deduced by a comparison of the cases described in the Scriptures with the symptoms of insanity in contemporary times. Altogether, the new knowledge differed from the old faith in that devils, demons or supernatural forces in general were no longer considered to be the cause of particular phenomena, natural causes having been discovered. This was so in the case of illness but was also, for example, true of atmospheric conditions such as hail, thunder and lightning, which people had earlier believed to have been caused by God, or by the devil and his demons, or even by witches. There are natural reasons for many occurrences which at first seem marvellous: this is the daily experience of a scientist like Reimarus. Could the same thing perhaps be true of the miracles in the Bible?

The feeding of the hungry in the wilderness with manna and quails is a famous miracle of the early Israelite period:

And the Lord said to Moses, 'I have heard the murmurings of the people of Israel; say to them, "At twilight you shall eat flesh, and in the morning you shall be filled with bread; then you shall know that I am the Lord your God." '

In the evening quails came up and covered the camp; and in the morning dew lay round about the camp. And when the dew had gone up, there was on the face of the wilderness, a fine, flake-like thing, fine as hoarfrost on the ground (Ex. 16.11ff.).

As desert travellers know, manna is a secretion of certain Arabian bushes round about harvest time.

[1] H. Fuchss, *Hat die Bibel recht?* (Leipzig, Jena, 1957), p. 154.

It may well be, therefore, 'that if the Israelites reached the shrubby part of the desert round about harvest time, they found a sweet manna on the leaves which they collected daily, as long as it lasted, using it to make their bread, biscuit, etc. more palatable, as if it were honey'; but that, with some exceptions, they lived entirely from manna during the whole of their forty years in the desert is impossible.

This is the way in which David Friedrich Strauss (who had seen the complete unpublished manuscript) described Reimarus' interpretation. He goes on:

Moses, having been often in the desert previously, knew well that manna was of natural origin; yet he presented it to the people as food miraculously conferred on them by God, using the people's nonsensical notion that it fell from heaven; and the historians of later times increasingly elaborated the story into a miracle. 'For it was at all times the characteristic of the Hebrews, ever since they had learnt to believe themselves a people chosen of God, to impose upon all natural things and events in their history the flavour of the divine, the great, the supernatural and the marvellous.'[1]

The quails incident is similar:

At certain seasons they pass over the Red Sea and Egypt in great flocks, after their long flight falling to the ground in great numbers so that they can be gathered up without much ado. But now this fortunate chance 'which is to be entirely explained by the nature of the quails and the association of circumstances, is built up into a miracle by the exaggeration of the historian'. First the people are made to grumble over a lack of meat, which cannot possibly have been the case (because they had their own cattle with them); then the quails are produced by supernatural means, whereas their arrival was entirely natural. Finally the number and the ease with which they could be captured is exaggerated to the point of nonsense, in that, within a circumference of three to four miles and to a depth of two ells high, they are said to have lain so still for two days and a night that they merely had to be raked together into the baskets. Reimarus reckons on the basis of the text that during the whole month that the quails were present, every Israelite would have had 288 quails to eat every day. 'Then gorge, till the meat chokes you,' he adds angrily.[2]

[1] Strauss, *op. cit.*, pp. 98f.   [2] *Ibid.*, pp. 101f.

So much for what Strauss has to say about Reimarus.

But a great many miracles are lacking in any natural basis. Some of them are, morally speaking, so detestable – for instance, the story of the Ark of the Covenant, at the sight of which people are stricken with sickness or fall dead – that Reimarus remarks:

> We honour God more when we do not believe them than when, assuming them to be true, we form from them the notion of a bogy figure of cruel power.

> If miracles themselves are so monstrous, turning the nature of things upside down without either enlightening the understanding or conferring any benefit, they belong to the nightmares of the world of fantasy, which do not deserve serious confutation. If, however, they even diminish our reverence for God and his perfections, or offend against the laws both of nature and of men, then they belong to the realm of the devil and are the inventions of the most lying and evil people who ever lived.[1]

Anyone today who is shocked by these occasionally biting flings at popular superstition and the trickery of domineering priests should try to think himself back into Reimarus' own time. Conditions must have been unbearable indeed if they drove so serious and so morally sensitive a scholar to such outbreaks. His criticism of miracles is always tantamount to criticism of the Church of his day because the Church forbade any rational investigations of its own concerns (though investigation was in all other sectors a matter of course for the scientific spirit of the eighteenth century) and went on demanding blind faith. But blind faith, says Reimarus, must be condemned not only from a rational standpoint but even from a religious and moral point of view:

> Men are simply to believe, without reason, and thereby to become pious Christians; but it is only because he is a rational being that man is, alone of all the animals, capable of religion and capable of being moved to goodness on rational grounds; how, then, can one expect those to be Christians who are not yet become men?[2]

The worst feature, however, is the external pressure to which the voice of reason is subjected by blindly believing churchmen, in association with the powers that be.

[1] *Ibid.*, pp. 120, 241.
[2] *Von Duldung der Deisten*, Lessing, *op. cit.*, p. 267.

For the vulgar believe so firmly that they would doubtless die for their faith and would as willingly slay others who do not believe the same. So they set up for the suppression of rational religion a whole army of terrible champions and the authorities, as the guardians of faith, must now forbid free-thinking writings in the bookshops on pain of heavy punishment and must cause such writings to be burnt at the hand of the executioner; if, upon his discovery, the writer is not also dismissed from office, imprisoned or miserably banished.[1]

Reimarus himself thought it useless to publish his ideas during his lifetime. Nor could he resolve to give up his solid livelihood as teacher and scholar and to endanger his family, especially since he believed that such a sacrifice would be premature and would benefit very few. But the constant concealment of his deepest convictions oppressed him.

The hypocrisy by which many Christians must help themselves, to their secret chagrin, witnesses against the theologians, who hinder a free confession of rational religion through fear and coercion. For who would in so serious a matter act publicly against his own convictions in a way he loathes and despises? Who would wish constantly to conceal his true opinions from friends and kindred, although he has no grounds to be ashamed of them? Who would wish to send his children to schools where they will be led into what his notion of true religion condemns as a blind and pernicious superstition? But he is forced to do all this because he fears to lose his whole temporal prosperity. Our noble preachers may be sure that an honest man does no small violence to his feelings when he is compelled to dissemble and dissimulate all his life long. But what is he to do, since the priests have filled the greater number of those among whom he lives with hatred and malice against those who do not believe? He would be refused friendship, trust, intercourse, trade and traffic, indeed all the services of kindness, and would be avoided as a profligate and abominable evil-doer.[2]

Reimarus challenges the representatives of the Church to a theological discussion by appealing to Jesus against them. 'Are our revered theologians right in using faith to repress and smother reason and rational religion? The example of their great teacher Jesus is not on their side. For he preached naught but a reasonable and practical religion.'[3] Many Protestant theologians were later to follow Reimarus in this criti-

[1] *Ibid.*, p. 257.   [2] *Ibid.*, pp. 257f.
[3] *Von Verschreyung der Vernunft auf den Kanzeln*, Lessing, *op. cit.*, p. 307.

cal appeal from the contemporary form of faith to its origins. He himself, prejudiced and undoubtedly unjust in certain respects, viewed both the past and his own time with gloomy pessimism. But he was certain that in the future things would improve:

> It was always easy to dazzle the superstitious with miracles and this is still true of the mob. And it is easier still to invent miraculous facts or to exaggerate innocent events with tongue and pen and to give them the guise of miracles. . . . Time later increasingly shrouds the true circumstances in the impenetrable darkness of shadowy antiquity, and the blind religious zeal of priests and people then forbids these now hallowed errors to be violated or exposed; until a sound philosophy raises men's spirits and gives them the courage to reflect on the alleged facts.[1]

Why did Lessing publish parts of this work, although he did not find himself in entire agreement either with rational religion or with the results of Reimarus' criticism of miracle? Why did he take upon himself everything that followed: the indignation of the Church, violent theological warfare, the imposition of a strict censorship and even prohibition of publication at the instigation of the consistory? Nearly a century later, when Strauss undertook to write a book in honour of Reimarus, he gave as his reason the following:

> What so much appealed to me about Reimarus was not this or that opinion, not this or that individual gift or characteristic, but the whole man. In Reimarus I saw a living characterization of free and rational thinking in the matter of religion, the earnestness of his striving and the courage of his investigation making amends even for his mistakes of judgment.[2]

Today we could give similar reasons for concerning ourselves with Reimarus, who might be called the father of Protestant critical theology. His thinking is of fundamental importance, confronting every Christian and every theologian with the question whether the application of reason to the Christian faith is permissible or not. He demonstrates the freedom of the man who, without concern for the consequences, can answer this question with an unequivocal 'yes'.

[1] Strauss, *op. cit.*, p. 243.   [2] Strauss, *op. cit.*, p. v.

5 David Hume and Sound Judgment

*A wise man proportions his belief
to the evidence*

I

There is a story that round about 1700 a sick man came to William III and begged the king to cure him by laying his hands on him. The king, a devout Calvinist, found it hard to reconcile this request with his conscience. However, he laid his hands on the man, expressing the hope that God would heal his infirmities and improve his understanding. This anecdote might be said to be characteristic of the English attitude to miracles: a certain scepticism combined with a reluctance to offend the other by too bluntly expressed an opinion. Of course a great deal more than this (some of it very different in kind) was thought and said about miracles in England. Let us look in some detail at the important contribution to the subject made by the great philosopher David Hume (1711–1776).

Hume's ideas had curiously little influence on continental theology. There is Kant's famous remark that Hume awakened him from his 'dogmatic slumber';[1] but this honourable mention is almost all that is known about the English philosopher in Germany. We also gather from Kant that Hume's most important service was his attack on traditional metaphysics.[2] And if we look at the first section of Hume's epistemological work, *An Inquiry Concerning Human Understanding*,[3] we shall see that there he does in fact talk about the obscurity of a profound and abstract philosophy called metaphysics which, he claims, is not really a science at all but arises 'either from the fruitless efforts of human vanity, which

[1] Immanuel Kant, *Prolegomena zu einer jeden zukünftigen Metaphysik, die als Wissenschaft wird auftreten können, Vorwort* (1783).

[2] *Ibid.*

[3] *An Inquiry Concerning Human Understanding*, Section I (1748); we quote from the edition in vol. 4 of *The Philosophical Works of David Hume* (Edinburgh, 1826). For a selection of Hume's writings on religion see R. Wollheim (ed.), *Hume on Religion* (London and Glasgow, Fontana, 1963).

would penetrate into subjects utterly inaccessible to the understanding, or from the craft of popular superstitions, which, being unable to defend themselves on fair ground, raise these entangling brambles to cover and protect their weakness.'[1] Obscurity, says Hume, is painful to the mind. He wants to wage war on the 'brambles' of philosophical speculation and dogma with the 'spirit of accuracy'. 'Accurate and just reasoning' is the panacea to subvert metaphysical jargon and to liberate the mind once and for all from questions 'utterly inaccessible to the understanding'.[2] And what method ought reason to take in order to achieve its purpose? A serious enquiry 'into the nature of human understanding' will show how that understanding works, the nature of its powers and capacities, and the things for which it is hence really fitted and competent. At an important point in the framework of this enquiry Hume introduces a little treatise 'Of Miracles', as a subject for advanced pupils, so to speak – a particularly difficult test-piece for the enlightened understanding. Let us look more closely at the way in which the understanding, correctly used (in Hume's sense), proceeds in this field and what results it has to show at the end.

II

'I should not believe such a story were it told me by Cato!' This old Roman saying meant that some stories are so incredible that even the most trustworthy authority (the wise Roman statesman Cato, for instance) would not be sufficient to persuade us to believe them. Why not? The answer is that they are *palpably* untrue.[3]

These are emotional judgments arrived at by common sense; we can hear them every day. But on what grounds can they be justified? What makes us decide one way or the other, with an almost instinctive sureness of touch? It would seem that our minds have an unconscious evidential canon at their disposal which allows us to decide almost immediately whether an alleged fact can be considered as a fact at all, at least provisionally, whether it perhaps needs further investigation, or whether we can exclude it from the realm of fact entirely. But how can we explain the circumstance that this canon apparently differs from person to person – as we can see, for instance, from the history of opinion about miracles? And how, in such cases, can a control be introduced or any certainty be achieved?

Essential questions of this kind were first raised by Hume's essay 'Of

[1] Hume, *op. cit.*, p. 10. [2] *Ibid.*, pp. 10f.
[3] *Ibid.*, Section X, pp. 132, 144.

Miracles' and they mark a new approach to the question of miracles: a striving towards 'sound judgment'.

Let us therefore look at one particular miracle story from the Bible. Let us choose the 'miracle of miracles', the subject of most discussion in eighteenth-century England: the story of Jesus' rising from the dead after three days. Although it is open to various interpretations, this story (which, as everyone knows, consists of different fragments varying in kind) contains at least one clear assertion of fact. The proof offered is the empty tomb and the discarded grave clothes. The story is in certain respects contrary to reason. What method can we use to test its veracity?

First, it is worth pointing out what was no longer a possible method at Hume's period. It was useless to assert that the sacred writers who wrote down the story were inspired by the Holy Ghost; that the Holy Ghost was incapable of error; and that therefore the story was true. Such an argument was theologically useless because it is full of premises which were no longer accepted as a matter of course in the eighteenth century and because it did not answer the new questions of the age. The change of intellectual attitude had historical grounds. At the beginning of the colonial era the outlook was widening beyond the borders of the familiar religious culture. Accounts of 'the religion of the heathen and their errors'[1] or of 'all the religions in the world'[2] were already appearing in the seventeenth century, written by widely travelled men. And soon entirely new questions arose about the 'truth' (and that increasingly meant the 'reasonableness') of Christianity.[3] The Christian religion became relativized; men became conscious of its relationship to other popular religions of the ancient world and this affinity roused the criticism and antipathy of enlightened minds. How far is Christian doctrine the one true teaching? How far is it a divine message? This had to be constantly demonstrated anew by the Christian apologists. And the only proof that occurred to them was the ancient miracles! For since reason – even in the opinion of enlightened Christians – cannot determine the divinity of an asserted revelation, it is bound to rely on credentials open to the senses.[4]

[1] Lord Herbert of Cherbury, *De religione gentilium errorumque apud eos causis* (1663).

[2] Alexander Ross, *Pansebeia or a View of All the Religions in the World* (1653).

[3] The title of John Locke's book, *The Reasonableness of Christianity* (1695), is characteristic.

[4] 'To know that any revelation is from God, it is necessary to know that the messenger that delivers it is sent from God, and that cannot be known but by some credential given him by God himself . . .

But since the speculative and learned will be putting of cases which never were, and it may be presumed never will be; since scholars and disputants will be

Hence miracles acquired a key position within Christian doctrine which they had never enjoyed before. To them was shifted the whole burden of proof as to the truth of revealed religion. It is therefore clear that when a thinker like Hume directs his criticism to the subject of miracles, it is the equivalent of an attack on the foundations of a whole religious system. Hume himself is fully aware of this.[1] It is also clear that all immanental Christian arguments such as those indicated above have ceased to have any cogency and that this kind of assumption can no longer be presupposed.

But if a theological argument no longer comes into question, the only possibility left is the profane and sober view. According to this we are considering a historical document like any other. A historical fact is being asserted. Such a fact must be examined according to the standards which we usually apply in such cases. What happens or has happened in the world cannot be decided *a priori*, by pure processes of thought – Hume has gathered together detailed reflections on this point in an earlier section of his *Inquiry*.[2] We cannot, by the pure processes of thought, even answer so simple a question as whether the sun will rise tomorrow; for the one alternative is as conceivable as the other. There must be something else which supplies us with material for our reflections. We must know a considerable amount before we can reflect on it. And we acquire this knowledge, says Hume, simply through experience. 'Experience' is the most important concept, as well as the characteristic instrument, of the new philosophy which begins beyond the old religion and metaphysics. How far experience can be used as a criterion is to be demonstrated on the basis of difficult and unusual subjects like the miracle stories. A correct judgment about the resurrection of Jesus, then, would be a judgment based on general human experience. But how can experience be a guide here?

---

raising of questions where there are none, and enter upon debates whereof there is no need; I crave leave to say, that he who comes with a message from God to be delivered to the world, cannot be refused belief if he vouches his mission by a miracle, because his credentials have a right to it. For every rational man must conclude as Nicodemus did, "We know that thou art a teacher come from God, for no man can do these signs which thou doest, except God be with him." '
John Locke, *A Discourse of Miracles* (1706), reprinted in *The Reasonableness of Christianity, etc.*, ed. by I. T. Ramsey (London, 1958), pp. 80–82.

[1] See the reasoning with which he introduces his section on miracles (pp. 128f.), as well as his summing up (p. 150) and his ironical closing passage (p. 154).

[2] Hume, *op. cit.*, Section IV, pp. 32f.

III

Everyone builds up a store of conceptions and combinations of conceptions through the constant learning process of experience. He learns through experience and is ultimately in a position to draw general conclusions from that experience. He brings his store of experience into play when he is faced with the necessity of forming a correct judgment about new data which have entered his field of vision. . . . Deliberations of this kind are among the preliminary studies which Hume carries out before he turns to the question of miracles. And the matter seems very simple, for the advice given by experience seems to be clear enough as long as it is only a question of whether the sun will rise or whether one season will follow another. But if the evidence which experience offers us is not clear, what then? And what if it is even contradictory?

This is the problem which Hume analyses philosophically, during his slow advance towards the question of miracles. Patience is needed if the reader is to follow Hume's process of thought. He begins once more – with the weather!

> Though experience be our only guide in reasoning concerning matters of fact, it must be acknowledged that this guide is not altogather infallible, but in some cases is apt to lead us into errors. One, who in our climate, should expect better weather in any week of June than in one of December, would reason justly and conformably to experience; but it is certain, that he may happen, in the event, to find himself mistaken.[1]

We must be cautious in drawing conclusions from experience. Not all facts within the sphere of human experience are equally unambiguous: 'Some events are found, in all countries and all ages, to have been constantly conjoined together: Others are found to have been more variable, and sometimes to disappoint our expectations. . . .' The inference is that our judgment about facts does not always have the same 'assurance'; there are varying degrees of assurance or certainty.

The important thing, then, in forming a judgment is to weigh up the 'evidence' of the data correctly. The rule is as follows:

> A wise man, therefore, proportions his belief to the evidence. In such conclusions as are founded on an infallible experience, he expects the event with the last degree of assurance, and regards his past

[1] *Ibid.*, Section X, p. 128.

experience as a full *proof* of the future existence of that event. In other cases, he proceeds with more caution: He weighs the opposite experiments: He considers which side is supported by the greatest number of experiments: to that side he inclines with doubt and hesitation; and when at last he fixes his judgment, the evidence exceeds not what we properly call *probability*.[1]

The last point is particularly important. What is here being developed is really something like a new morality[2] – the morality of sober judgment. One avoids the hasty verdict, the over-simplified Yes or No, Everything or Nothing, the false assurance. Nor is the finally accepted conviction credited with any greater conclusive force than is permitted by its grounds in experience. Typical of the description of such rules of judgment given by Hume and those like him are the notions of balancing, calculating and weighing up:

A hundred instances or experiments on one side, and fifty on another, afford a doubtful expectation of any event; though a hundred uniform experiments, with only one that is contradictory, reasonably beget a pretty strong degree of assurance. In all cases, we must balance the opposite experiments, where they are opposite, and deduct the smaller number from the greater, in order to know the exact force of the superior evidence.[3]

The reader who, in the midst of these abstract arguments, tries to conjure up real, concrete cases may think of a number of situations. One plans a holiday. X has had a lot of rain for the last three years running. But before that it is said to have had largely fine weather. So what do we think the weather will be this year? And so on. However sophisticated in its presentation, does not this method of arriving at a judgment make a totally unscientific impression, even though it is practical and comprehensible? Hume seems to think just like a farmer who calculates how big his potatoes are likely to be after a particular kind of weather; and this does not seem very philosophical. But Hume would not have been insulted if anyone had pointed out the similarity to him. On the contrary, he would have accepted it as praise, as a virtue; for the philosophy which avoids all such banalities in favour of metaphysical speculation would have roused his deepest mistrust.

[1] *Ibid.*, Section X, p. 129.
[2] See Van A. Harvey, *The Historian and the Believer* (New York, 1966; London, 1967), ch. 2.
[3] *Ibid.*

IV

Let us look at the matter more closely and apply Hume's principle to human testimony; for miracles do not meet the investigations of reason directly but only through the medium of human witnesses. Here then is a whole series of circumstances to be taken into consideration. 'We frequently hesitate concerning the reports of others. We balance the opposite circumstances which cause any doubt or uncertainty; and when we discover a superiority on any side, we incline to it, but still with a diminution of assurance, in proportion to the force of its antagonist.' This 'contrariety of evidence' can have different causes: 'We entertain a suspicion concerning any matter of fact, when the witnesses contradict each other; when they are but few, or of a doubtful character; when they have an interest in what they affirm; when they deliver their testimony with hesitation, or, on the contrary, with too violent asseverations.' The following factor is even more important: 'Suppose . . . that the fact which the testimony endeavours to establish partakes of the extraordinary and the marvellous, in that case, the evidence resulting from the testimony admits of a diminution, greater or less, in proportion as the fact is more or less unusual.'[1] The reader now sees plainly enough where this is leading him. The rare fact, or the fact to which there is only one witness – so Hume apparently assumes – has the whole span of common experience against it, experience in which this extraordinary phenomenon was not observed, but in which things were seen to proceed according to a regular course. Such a testimony therefore displays its own dubiousness 'upon the very face of it', as Hume says. It contains an inherent contradiction. This argument also seems a cogent one at first sight. Do we not react in exactly this way to the report of some unheard-of event? Do we not quickly run through the knowledge that we have built up from our own experience, being inclined to mistrust anything that departs from the norm? But is this not precisely the point at which we can make a gigantic mistake? Is a calf with two heads not occasionally born after all?

Hume was very well aware of the possibility of error and illustrated it from a story which roused great contemporary interest. The story runs briefly as follows: an Indian prince, hearing for the first time reports of how rivers in northern countries freeze, simply refused to believe such absurd tales. His reasoning was correct, says Hume. So how can the result none the less be false?

[1] *Ibid.*, Section X, p. 131.

Unfortunately Hume only made a few observations on this particular case. But his opponents in the camp of ecclesiastical orthodoxy pounced joyfully on the argument and used it as a weapon against Hume's whole argument. The prince argued according to his experience, in which such an event did not occur. And is his judgment not a striking example of the inadequacy of experience as a criterion – the pattern case of narrow-minded misjudgment?

> Vulgar minds, who judge of every thing by their own narrow no-tions, and by what they themselves have seen, are often apt to reject and disbelieve a thing, that is not conformable to their own particular customs or experience. But wise men and those of more enlarged minds judge otherwise: and provided a thing comes to them suffi-ciently attested and confirmed by good evidence, make its being un-usual no objection at all to its credibility.[1]

This is a typical comment. It derives from John Leland, who undertook an account and refutation of 'the principal Deistical writers' of the seventeenth and eighteenth centuries. And are his objections not well-founded? Does the story of the Indian prince not go to show the limita-tions of any individual's mental orbit and how little his subjective expe-rience is capable of judging what happens in the large areas of reality which are unknown to him? Are not important qualifications necessary before the concept of experience can serve as a really useful criterion?

Hume has no intention of sliding over the difficulty. If he had, he would have never taken this example, which is apparently anything but favourable to his cause. Was the prince's argument, which led to so false a conclusion, then not quite sound after all, in Hume's sense? This is in fact the case. 'The inhabitants of Sumatra have always seen water fluid in their own climate, and the freezing of their rivers ought to be deemed a prodigy: But they never saw water in Muscovy during the winter; and therefore they cannot reasonably be positive what would there be the consequence.'[2] Indians can form a definite judgment about the possible freezing of their own rivers, if they look back over the experience of centuries; but they cannot judge an event which took place under entirely different circumstances. Conclusions based on the analogy of a similar experience therefore only apply in the sphere where the natural conditions are exactly the same.

[1] John Leland, *A View of the Principal Deistical Writers* (1754–56) vol. I, Letter XVIII. We quote from the 4th ed. (1764), p. 291.
[2] Hume, *op. cit.*, Section X, p. 133 note.

If a lesson is to be drawn from this test case, it is that at least three qualifications must be made to Hume's criterion of experience, as precautions, so to speak, against common misunderstandings and misuse:

1. If the criterion is to serve as more than a purely private standard of reference – if it is to be raised to the rank of a generally applicable standard – the individual's personal knowledge derived from experience must be extended to the general level of knowledge of mankind. The criterion is not reliable when based on a narrow, private point of view.

2. Even with this extension it can prove inadequate in areas which are insufficiently known to mankind. It is therefore only applicable where the natural conditions of a phenomenon are completely known; and that means for us today, where they have been scientifically investigated and are secured by law and rule.

3. Science must be called in if certainty is to be achieved. For one problem in Hume's method of exposition occasionally raises a slight doubt in the reader's mind. Does this calculating, reckoning and weighing up of the evidence not end in a curiously vague result? A hundred cases against fifty, or a hundred against one – do such quantitative, statistical investigations really say anything satisfactory about the qualitative value or the factual correctness of a single one of the 'evidences'? Can we content ourselves, especially in important questions, with a statistical enquiry of this kind? In view of the contrary indications of experience, must we not press on to the root of the matter and find out exactly the reason for the contradiction, and hence the uncertainty, in experience? In a later passage Hume compares his method of proof with the reasoning of a judge 'who supposes that the credit of two witnesses, maintaining a crime against any one, is destroyed by the testimony of two others, who affirm him to have been two hundred leagues distant at the same instant when the crime is said to have been committed.'[1] Who would be satisfied with such a decision? And in principle, cannot one person still be right in the face of many?

Hume himself seems to be conscious here and there that his criterion of judgment demands greater precision.[2] Even in the case of the Indian prince he admits in a lengthy footnote that the conclusion from analogy

[1] *Ibid.*, Section X, p. 142.
[2] He recommends that a problematical case should be referred back to the philosophers, for example: 'It is evident that our present philosophers, instead of doubting the fact, ought to receive it as certain, and ought to search for the causes whence it might be derived' (p. 151). For a closer examination of the logical problems in Hume's argument, *see* Antony Flew, *Hume's Philosophy of Belief* (London, 1961), pp. 166–213.

does not always follow where the event is apparently an extraordinary one, but that scientific, preferably experimental, observations make a well-founded judgment possible.

It must be confessed, that, in the present case of freezing, the event follows contrary to the rules of analogy, and is such as a rational Indian would not look for. The operations of cold upon water are not gradual, according to the degrees of cold; but whenever it comes to the freezing point, the water passes in a moment, from the utmost liquidity to perfect hardness . . .[1]

'One may sometimes conjecture from analogy what will follow,' says Hume, 'but still this is but conjecture.' Conjecture: this is a pre-scientific yet indispensable way of finding one's bearings, a method which was for thousands of years the only one open to mankind.

One may here interpose a question. Does Hume's philosophy, with its determination to turn its back on the obscure mysteries of traditional metaphysics and to address itself to 'the examination of common life',[2] not itself give the impression of being a journey of discovery in unexplored territory?

This part of philosophy, it is observable, had been little cultivated either by the ancients or the moderns; and therefore our doubts and errors, in the prosecution of so important an inquiry, may be the more excusable, while we march through such difficult paths without any guide or direction. They may even prove useful, by exciting curiosity, and destroying that implicit faith and security which is the bane of all reasoning and free enquiry.[3]

V

It is only a short step from an extraordinary event to the miracle, but the transition is full of pitfalls. 'In order to increase the probability against the testimony of witnesses, let us suppose that the fact, which they affirm, instead of being only marvellous, is really miraculous. . . .' What does miraculous mean? There is a 'uniform experience' of such similarity and unalterability at all times and all places that in the minds of men it has coalesced as natural law. An event which is contrary to these established laws of nature is called by Hume a miracle.

[1] Hume, *op. cit.*, Section X, p. 133 note.
[2] *Ibid.*, Section VIII, p. 120. [3] *Ibid.*, Section IV, p. 33.

Why is it more than probable that all men must die; that lead cannot, of itself, remain suspended in the air; that fire consumes wood, and is extinguished by water; unless it be that these events are found agreeable to the laws of nature, and there is required a violation of these laws, or, in other words, a miracle to prevent them?

A miracle is a violation of the laws of nature.[1]

A law is the regulation of a process and allows of no exception. Hume does not concern himself further with the logical problem of how even a long series of similar data drawn from experience can become a 'law'. Experience is in principle unfinished. From its uniformity in the past one can deduce at most a law of probability for the future, a law which in principle allows of exceptions. 'It is a miracle, that a dead man should come to life; because that has never been observed in any age or country.'[2] Is this a stringently compelling argument? Kant and the scientists have developed new ways of thinking which go beyond Hume here[3] and which can only be spied on the very horizon of Hume's thought, where he speaks of 'unalterable experience' and of the laws of nature. But when one uses terms like these the inference must be drawn that so uniform an experience rises beyond mere probability to the rank of proof and that 'there is here a direct and full *proof*, from the nature of the fact, against the existence of any miracle'.[4]

Here we have finally arrived at the peak of the argument. The upshot is that the miracle has no chance of recognition in the face of an otherwise unalterable experience. This might be said to be the ultimate conclusion, for what more do we need than a 'full proof'? But, someone might say, somewhere the argument must be unsound. Something has been overlooked. If the evidence were really as clear as this, how could there be any controversy about miracles at all?

The objection is a just one. Hume could in fact only arrive at his 'full proof' by altering his perspective for a moment: he judged the question of miracles in isolation, apart from the fact that miracles come to us *via* human testimony. If one now looks at the facts as a whole, there can be no question of an absolute uniformity of experience, since numerous accounts of miracles do, after all, exist. The diversity of testimony cannot be simply disregarded if we are to arrive at a considered judgment.

[1] *Ibid.*, Section X, p. 133.   [2] *Ibid.*, Section X, p. 134.
[3] See the discussion about law and causality in A. Flew, *op. cit.*, pp. 187, 200f., 204–209.   [4] Hume, *op. cit.*, Section X, p. 134.

How, then, do people over and over again come to tell miracle stories? The sober thinker, at least, cannot simply assert *a priori* that all this was pure invention or mere figments of fantasy.

It is after all conceivable (and it is even conceded by Hume) that a testimony of this kind, taken by itself and critically examined according to all the rules otherwise applicable to the examination of human testimony, might be found to be completely credible, therefore achieving the status of a 'full proof'. Why should all these witnesses be liars? 'In that case there is a mutual destruction of arguments, and the superior only gives us an assurance suitable to that degree of force which remains, after deducting the inferior.'[1]

Here we are in fact faced with a dilemma, a dilemma which Hume expounded with lucidity and precision: this is the way in which thoughtful people who were also convinced Christians saw the Enlightenment, torn between two equally convincing chains of reasoning; their intellect rejected miracles and yet could find no reason to doubt the witnesses of the Bible, the evangelists and apostles. Were these not men of unquestionable sincerity, far above any suspicion of fraud? Were they not the supporters of a cause which brought them no personal advantage, which indeed could cost them their lives? Did they set themselves up in opposition to the closed front of a politically powerful religious philosophy and suffer persecution and death merely for the sake of a chimera? One can see from John Leland why Christians found no reason to suspect the first preachers of their faith, men whose teaching seemed to them in all its other parts to be entirely worthy of belief and divinely inspired; why they therefore remained conservative and closed their ears to the voice of free-thinking criticism.[2]

It would seem that Hume did not feel this dilemma personally, for his attitude to the Bible does not bear the traces of intense engagement or a passionate coming to terms with the content of the Scriptures; it makes a detached impression. Hume seems to be almost indifferent. No signs of any convincing experience – of the truth of Jesus' teaching, for instance – can be discovered in his writings. He is therefore in a position to unfold the dilemma in abstract terms, lucidly, cleanly and with detachment, drawing the appropriate conclusions as is fitting for an unprejudiced, rational and sober thinker.

What would happen if it actually came to the point that one proof stood over against another – which is the more unlikely, that the

---

[1] *Ibid.*, Section X, p. 135.
[2] cf. Leland, *op. cit.*, Letter XVIII, pp. 298–302.

apparently trustworthy witness was after all a deceiver, or that the apparently improbable testimony was after all true? According to Hume:

> When anyone tells me that he saw a dead man restored to life, I immediately consider with myself whether it be more probable that this person should either deceive or be deceived, or that the fact which he relates should really have happened. I weigh the one miracle against the other; and according to the superiority which I discover, I pronounce my decision, and always reject the greater miracle. If the falsehood of his testimony would be more miraculous than the event which he relates, then, and not till then, can he pretend to command my belief or opinion.[1]

Here Hume reaches the heights of theoretical clarity and the thinking person cannot escape his argument. The play on the word miracle which Hume here permits himself incidentally shows that 'miracle' at this stage of the discussion simply means the preposterous, the absurd and the utterly improbable – an interpretation which fills a staunch defender of the Bible like John Leland with grief and indignation.[2]

VI

In theory Hume's judgment on miracles is now complete. But his opinion about particular miracle stories of tradition is still missing. Among all the varied mass of testimonies, is there any which passes the test? That is to say, is there any of which it can be said that its falsity would be even more miraculous (or improbable) than the improbable thing which is asserted? How about the 'miracle of miracles', for example, the resurrection of Jesus?

This kind of question can no longer be answered by pure processes of thought, for now historical details have to be considered. For this Hume needs a (considerably longer) second section. However, our summing up can be brief, for the conclusion is very simple.

'When anyone tells me that he saw a dead man restored to life, I immediately consider with myself. . . .' What, then, is the correct view of the case in question? Hume's answer is on the following lines:

> Suppose that all the historians who treat of England should agree, that on the first of January 1600, Queen Elizabeth died; that both before and after her death, she was seen by her physicians and the

---

[1] Hume, *op. cit.*, Section X, p. 135.   [2] Leland, *op. cit.*, p. 298.

whole court, as is usual with persons of her rank; that her successor was acknowledged and proclaimed by the Parliament; and that, after being interred for a month, she again appeared, resumed the throne, and governed England for three years; I must confess that I should be surprised at the concurrence of so many odd circumstances, but should not have the least inclination to believe so miraculous an event. I should not doubt of her pretended death, and of those other public circumstances that followed it: I should only assert it to have been pretended, and that it neither was, nor possibly could be real. You would in vain object to me the difficulty, and almost impossibility of deceiving the world in an affair of such consequence; the wisdom and solid judgment of that renowned Queen; with the little or no advantage which she could reap from so poor an artifice: All this might astonish me; but I would still reply, that the knavery and folly of men are such common phenomena, that I should rather believe the most extraordinary event to arise from their concurrence, than admit of so signal a violation of the laws of nature.

But should this miracle be ascribed to any new system of religion; men, in all ages, have been so much imposed on by ridiculous stories of that kind, that this very circumstance would be a full proof of a cheat, and sufficient, with all men of sense, not only to make them reject the fact, but even reject it without further examination. . . . As the violations of truth are more common in testimony concerning religious miracles than in that concerning any other matter of fact; this must diminish very much the authority of the former testimony, and make us form a general resolution, never to lend any attention to it, with whatever specious pretence it may be covered.[1]

In this fantastic story (whose apparent irreverence gave offence to a number of sensitive souls) Hume's standpoint is summed up: his opinion of miracles in general and human testimony in particular – and, not least, though in concealed form, his quite definite verdict on the resurrection of Jesus.

What, is that all? The Christian reader may ask in disappointment. For cannot we now reasonably expect the biblical stories to be considered individually and concretely? Cannot we expect Hume, the historian who was capable of writing a voluminous 'History of England', to give the biblical story a fair trial as well, and to cross-examine the witnesses of the resurrection? And what are we offered instead? Merely a feeble

---

[1] Hume, *op. cit.*, Section X, pp. 151f.

substitute in the form of a gross fantasy. 'Mr Hume is pleased here to put the case in a very loose and general way.'[1] Why so veiled and roundabout an approach? And is this sneering suspicion of all religious testimony as a whole supposed to be a sober judgment?

Two questions arise here. First, why does Hume choose this indirect form of approach? And secondly, what argument really has decisive weight? Both questions receive an unequivocal answer, if one probes the various arguments in the second part of Hume's essay, in which he himself puts the question: is there in the whole world one single, valid testimony to a miracle? A testimony so incontrovertibly sure that it can justly be made the basis and support of a whole religious system?

Hume, the historian, sees a great many reasons for scepticism. He does not find as much as one miracle in the whole of history 'attested by a sufficient number of men, of such unquestioned good sense, education, and learning, as to secure us against all delusion in themselves. . . .'[2] In addition, he sees in human nature a suspicious tendency eagerly to accept the absurd and the miraculous because the emotions of surprise and wonder are felt to be agreeable stimuli.

> With what greediness are the miraculous accounts of travellers received, their descriptions of sea and land monsters, their relations of wonderful adventures, strange men, and uncouth manners? But if the spirit of religion join itself to the love of wonder, there is an end of common sense. . . . A religionist may be an enthusiast, and imagine he sees what has no reality: He may know his narrative to be false, and yet persevere in it, with the best intentions in the world, for the sake of promoting so holy a cause. . . . His auditors may not have, and commonly have not, sufficient judgment to canvass his evidence: What judgment they have, they renounce by principle, in these sublime and mysterious subjects.[3]

Even more weighty is the fact that stories of this kind are to be found in profusion chiefly 'among ignorant and barbarous nations'.

> When we peruse the first histories of all nations, we are apt to imagine ourselves transported into some new world, where the whole frame of nature is disjointed, and every element performs its operations in a different manner from what it does at present. Battles, revolutions, pestilence, famine, and death, are never the effect of those

---

[1] Leland, *op. cit.*, p. 298; this is Leland's opinion throughout.
[2] Hume, *op. cit.*, Section X, p. 135.
[3] *Ibid.*, Section X, p. 137.

natural causes, which we experience. Prodigies, omens, oracles, judgments, quite obscure the few natural events that are intermingled with them. But as the former grow thinner every page, in proportion as we advance nearer the enlightened ages, we soon learn that there is nothing mysterious or supernatural in the case. . . . *It is strange*, a judicious reader is apt to say, upon the perusal of these wonderful historians, *that such prodigious events never happen in our days!* But it is nothing strange, I hope, that men should lie in all ages.[1]

And so on. Hume has by no means come to the end of his objections. What he here gathers together in the way of argument on a few pages of terse and pregnant brevity would seem to provide enough material for generations of theologians. At that time arguments of this kind were in the air. A century later writers like Ludwig Feuerbach and David Friedrich Strauss were still busy with them.

Hume's final conclusion is almost self-evident: not a single reliable testimony is, under these circumstances, to be found in religion, and certainly none of the kind we are seeking, testimony which, taken by itself, is of so reliable a nature that it even remotely balances out the immense improbability of miracles, or could even raise a question in the mind of the rational thinker. There is therefore no point in discussing a biblical miracle such as the resurrection in detail – quite apart from the fact that it is irksome and disagreeable to grapple with the statements of people who have lost their powers of reasoning! The Christian reader therefore need not expect anything of this kind from Hume.

The only case which could really be of interest to a thinker like Hume would be the following: Let us imagine a completely believable testimony about a completely unbelievable miracle; on the one hand, that is to say, we have every conceivable degree of trustworthiness and on the other complete improbability. We weigh up the evidence. And what then?

This is Hume's dilemma in undiluted form – the dilemma which actually faces the devout Christian – and here we have arrived once more at Hume's daring hypothetical case. Given that all experts in English history were at one, given the ideal conditions – the enlightened period, the presence of doctors and scholars (i.e. the representatives of science), a stage set at the focal point of public life, not in some remote corner, and at the centre of the event a person quite above suspicion. What would then tip the scales and what form would sound judgment then take?

[1] *Ibid.*, Section X, pp. 138f.

'In that case there is a mutual destruction of arguments, and the superior only gives us an assurance suitable to that degree of force which remains after deducting the inferior.'[1] If we look at this decision in practice, it appears that the casting vote is given simply by the marvellous nature or complete impossibility of the event: anything – delusion, folly, knavery – would be more likely than 'so signal a violation of the laws of nature'.[2] And which contemporary reader would in all honesty dispute Hume's judgment in his hypothetical case of Queen Elizabeth?

There is inevitably a limit to what human credulity can be expected to accept. It is Hume's contribution to the debate on miracle to have made this clear. Since Hume, controversy may be usefully confined to the question where to draw the dividing line between the extraordinary event and the miracle in any given case. Precisely speaking it is no longer a principle which is in dispute; it is now a matter of sober, scientific investigation. But a few not unimportant questions remain to be considered.

VII

At the end of the enquiry the reader may still feel somewhat dissatisfied. He was perhaps inclined to attach a high value to Hume's theory of judgment-formation, because of its caution, discretion and justness – in short, because of what we have called its morality; but is he not sometimes considerably astounded by Hume's opinions in practice? We must not conclude our survey of Hume's view of miracles without mentioning at least one interesting case, because it shows what traps are still hidden in the material, even if the theory is clear. Here, for example, is 'one of the best attested miracles in all profane history', the miracle which the Roman historian Tacitus reports of the Emperor Vespasian, 'who cured a blind man in Alexandria by means of his spittle, and a lame man by the mere touch of his foot; and in obedience to a vision of the god Serapis, who had enjoined them to have recourse to the Emperor for these miraculous cures.'[3]

Here all the circumstances seem to confirm the weight of the testimony – 'the gravity, solidity, age, and probity of so great an Emperor' as well as the character of the historian, 'noted for candour and veracity, and withal, the greatest and most penetrating genius perhaps of all antiquity . . .'; yet Hume does not think it necessary to enter into an

[1] *Ibid.*, Section X, p. 135.   [2] *Ibid.*, Section X, p. 152.
[3] *Ibid.*, Section X, p. 142.

examination of the incident, or even to look at the sources; for in his opinion it is nothing more than a 'gross and . . . palpable' falsehood. But what if Hume was in fact wrong? Even the exact words of the Tacitus passage can disconcert the reader, as Antony Flew rightly points out in his philosophical commentary on Hume's *Inquiry*.[1] For Tacitus reports that the emperor, being undecided, first demanded the opinion of the doctors as to 'whether such blindness and paralysis could with human help be cured?' The doctors were hopeful. 'In the one case the power of sight was not destroyed, and with the removal of obstructions would return; and in the other the crippled joint could be healed, given an access of healthy strength.' On hearing all this Vespasian, convinced that anything was possible if he was fortunate, with a cheerful face performed the act that was asked of him. 'And immediately the hand could be used again and the blind man was able to see once more.' What can be deduced from this example? One should apply to the expert! In the judgment of the doctors of the ancient world, the healing was not impossible. And modern doctors confirm that such healings can be achieved in an apparently miraculous way through symbolic actions and a powerful influence on the mind of the patient. Hume may be excused, for his opinion corresponded to the general opinion of his time. And yet – does he not fall a victim to the same error as the Indian prince? Even in the case of the famous miracles of healing of Abbé Pâris, who was almost a contemporary of Hume and whom he yet condemned as fraudulent,[2] there is today a juster evaluation, the beginnings of which could already be noticed in Hume's own time.[3] One conclusion, at least, emerges from the case for the man who, like Hume, wants to learn 'from experience': the only thinker who is more or less safe from mistaken judgments is the man who is undogmatic and flexible. This means, for example, that he has a mind open for future scientific developments and that his opinions are marked, not by an aura of omniscience, but rather by the laborious search for impartiality.

But – and this is the last point – people other than Tacitus have a right to expect impartiality from the historian: for example, the biblical narrators. That these were all knaves and cheats or crazy fools is not, after all, a thesis which commends itself to the reader's understanding either. Adequate concepts for this kind of story have evidently not yet

---

[1] A. Flew, *op. cit.*, pp. 183f. The Tacitus reference in Hume is incorrect and should read *Histories*, Book IV, Chapter 81. The translation is taken from Flew, with the exception of the last sentence.

[2] Hume, *op. cit.*, Section X, p. 145 note.

[3] See A. Flew, *op. cit.*, pp. 195–198.

been found. The final word about miracles has still to be spoken. To this problem a new group now addresses itself, sometimes more one-sidedly than Hume, sometimes less well-considered, but with devotion and a close attention to detail: the German theologians.

6 Carl Friedrich Bahrdt's Rationalistic Explanation of Miracle

Everything happened quite naturally

O friends! that I might engrave these thoughts deep in your hearts, that I might show you that the supernatural and belief in the same is never of any profit; for it robs a man of all personal concern and private endeavour, taking from him all enduring zeal for good. It entangles him in many difficulties, shutting off the light of reason, making his soul a slave dependent on priests whom he must allow to say what he is to think, believe, cherish, wish, do and avoid; so that a man can neither think nor will with any desire or pleasure, since thinking and willing is but blind obedience; and that he hence does not learn to love the truth, since he does not discover it by his own reason but is accustomed only to echo the forms that he has learnt to know . . .

It is in such naïvely uplifting tones that Carl Friedrich Bahrdt (1741–1792), a German theologian of the Enlightenment period, appeals to his readers in his series of *Letters on the Bible in the Language of the People* and *Letters to the Reader seeking Truth*.[1]

I have long observed that a too frequent contemplation of the miracles in the Bible robs readers of the profit which they might have from the study of Holy Writ. For the marvellous has the character of

---

[1] *Briefe über die Bibel im Volkston. Eine Wochenschrift von einem Prediger auf dem Lande* were first published anonymously in Halle from 1782 onwards. From 1784 Bahrdt published his little essays in Berlin, now calling them *Ausführung des Plans und Zweks Jesu. In Briefen an Wahrheit suchende Leser*, because the first series was to have explained the 'plan of Jesus' life'. The new series comprised 129 'Letters' 'designed as a handbook for preachers and as a general book of devotion for thoughtful Christians'. The whole work contains over 3,500 pages. We cite the numbers of the various letters. Other works of this now forgotten but once well-known and prolific writer include: *Die neusten Offenbarungen Gottes in Briefen und Erzählungen verdeutscht durch D. Carl Friedrich Bahrdt* (1773/74), a

drawing a man's attention to itself and away from the moral teaching, especially in the case of those in whom the fantasy is stronger than an acute reflection; the more so since most men pay in any case but little attention to the moral aspect of the biblical narratives (since they believe that they already know sufficient), gaping rather at the marvellous and ruminating over this.

Hence, it is my opinion that the preacher should also take this fact for his guide in teaching the people and should pass over the miraculous in the stories of the Scriptures, in as far as this is present, and should treat the stories merely as ground for edification. That is to say, he should so expound them that hearers in our present time should be led to profitable principles and reflections. For what is miraculous is not profitable at all for the multitude. It was merely a necessity in the time of our Lord Jesus and the Apostles, because men were then used to such things and would not have hearkened to the teaching of our Lord Jesus if its presentation and its form had had nothing to enflame their fantasies and to fill them with a feeling of greatness and solemnity. It is not in fact at all necessary for belief in the truth and divinity of the teaching of Jesus, apart from the circumstances of the time. For – I know not, brethren, if you are like-minded – I at least believe, cherish, reverence and follow the teaching of Jesus Christ not because of the miracles which were done in the service of that teaching, but because of its inner truth and excellence. And if everything that the New Testament tells us of the author of Christendom only belonged to the *natural* course of human affairs, I should not therefore doubt for a single moment the truth of Christianity or our duty to obey its tenets. And should not preachers also win the common people to love and honour the teaching of the Lord Jesus because of its inner goodness and excellence rather than because of the miraculous nature of the events through which it was first proclaimed?

There is yet another important reason why it should be a duty to leave out all talk of the marvellous from the teaching of the people:

---

translation of the complete New Testament in four volumes, with paraphrases which attempt to explain the meaning of the biblical text as Bahrdt understood it; *System der moralischen Religion | zur endlichen Beruhigung für Zweifler und Denker. Allen Christen und Nichtchristen lesbar* (Berlin, 1787); *Würdigung der natürlichen Religion und des Naturalismus in Beziehung auf Staat und Menschenrechte* (Halle, 1791); and *Dr Carl Friedrich Bahrdts Geschichte seines Lebens, seiner Meinungen und Schicksale, Von ihm selbst geschrieben*, four parts (Berlin, 1790/91, rev. ed. Berlin, 1922). On Bahrdt see A. Schweitzer, *Quest of the Historical Jesus* (ET, London, 1954[3]), pp. 38–44. The above quotation is taken from the 65th Letter of the *Ausführung*.

this is that the miraculous is itself subject to such grave doubts. Hence the more that a teacher grounds the faith of his hearers on miracles, the more does he expose them to the danger of being shaken by doubt. Whereas our faith in the Gospel is unshakable if we do but found it on the inner tokens of its divinity.[1]

Thus Bahrdt declares his intention of explaining away everything supernatural and 'marvellous' in the biblical narrative. When one thinks of the space taken up by miracles in the New Testament, this seems a bold, if not a hopeless, task. Can such an undertaking be seriously carried out without tricks or sleight of hand or rash argumentation? Let us look at one example of Bahrdt's method, applied to a story which he himself regards as a problematical one. Having neatly explained a number of miracle stories in his own particular way, he turns in the 69th Letter to the story of Jesus' walking on the water:

But the walking on the water? What are we to say to this? Was this natural also? Brethren, first agree that if a scene *can* receive a natural explanation, sound reason compels us to prefer this explanation to all others. Grant this and you will soon cease to believe in any miracles at all.

With this introduction, Bahrdt first encourages himself and his readers and then begins his explanation. The relevant passage in the Gospel of Matthew reads as follows:

Then he made the disciples get into the boat and go before him to the other side. . . . And after he had dismissed the crowds, he went up into the hills by himself to pray. When evening came, he was there alone, but the boat by this time was many furlongs distant from the land, beaten by the waves; for the wind was against them. And in the fourth watch of the night he came to them, walking on the sea. But when the disciples saw him walking on the sea, they were terrified, saying 'It is a ghost!' And they cried out for fear. But immediately he spoke to them, saying, 'Take heart, it is I; have no fear.' And Peter answered him, 'Lord, if it is you, bid me come to you on the water.' He said, 'Come.' So Peter got out of the boat and walked on the water and came to Jesus; but when he saw the wind, he was afraid, and beginning to sink he cried out, 'Lord, save me.' Jesus immediately reached out his hand and caught him, saying to him, 'O man of little faith, why did you doubt?' (Matt. 14.22–31).

[1] *Briefe über die Bibel*, 3rd Letter.

69

How is Bahrdt going to explain this highly mysterious event naturally?

This, too, that Jesus walked on the sea and came towards the terrified Peter, who took him for a spirit – for this, too, there is more than one explanation with which one may be contented and whereby one may avoid the supernatural.

The disciples' ship was near the shore during this event (John 6.21). Do you now find it impossible to believe that one or more pieces of timber lay on the shore or that one of these pieces of timber was floating in the water? May we not suppose that this piece of timber was by chance floating near the ship? We can easily imagine that Jesus, on the shore, might have seen this and Peter can as easily be supposed to have overlooked it. We may well believe that Jesus, as the ship was near land, stepped on to the wood, felt that it bore his weight and approached the ship or boat on it, clambering in beside the disciples. Is it not easy to believe that the disciples, who never viewed anything clearly but always saw more than was really to be seen, were terrified by the figure whom they saw walking towards them, that Peter cried out, imagining a spirit and – that now the worthy folk passed on to the posterity the story of Jesus' journey on the hundred-ell cedar wood as if the waves themselves had borne up their master.

Or do you find it unworthy of belief that Jesus called Peter to come to him; that Peter, with his dream-filled fantasy, imagined naught but waves under his feet and, at the first sinking of the beam, began to stagger in the water, crying out for help in the fear of death, but springing back into the boat as soon as he was caught by Jesus?

Let me enquire whether there is anything unworthy of belief in these suppositions? And is this not a way whereby every man of sound sense may extract the miraculous from the story?

That the worthy disciples could not do so is very natural. For their prejudices held their reason prisoner (Mark 6.52).[1]

Bahrdt's explanation is amusing to read and is by no means so wide of the mark. Why should the event not have taken place more or less in this way? The explanation is at least worthy of consideration. If one is looking for counter-arguments one will say at once that there is nothing about pieces of wood in the Bible. The hundred-ell-long piece of timber is a pure invention of Bahrdt's. But this is not a refutation, for Bahrdt would immediately agree. Nor would he maintain that the event *must* have

[1] *Ausführung*, 69th Letter.

happened in exactly this way, but only that the explanation makes it at least *possible* to view the event in reasonable terms. Against this there is really nothing that can be said. Bahrdt invents the piece of timber quite deliberately because a link is missing in the story – a natural cause which turns the walking on the water into a believable event. Anyone who wants to turn miracle stories into natural happenings is forced into similar inventions or assumptions. The miracle story can only be accepted as such because it lacks a natural cause; if it is to stop being a miracle, the gap must be filled and the missing link found. Bahrdt's suggested addition is not the only one possible; other theologians with similar intentions have thought out other hypotheses: for instance, that Jesus was wading in the shallow water at the edge of the lake; or that he was walking on the shore, the disciples completely misinterpreting this fact because it was foggy; or that he was able to tread water!

If one is looking for further objections, the following might be urged: according to the Gospel accounts (except for John 6.21, which Bahrdt quotes but which actually purports to relate a miraculously sudden change of place) the disciples' ship was not near the shore at all but had long since sailed out into deep water and was in the middle of the lake. It is hard to conceive that pieces of wood were floating about there; and how, in any case, could Jesus have reached them? Above all, why did Jesus' disciples (some of whom were fishermen and consequently experienced sailors) fail to notice the pieces of wood? Why did they cry out in fear of spirits? Bahrdt is ready with an explanation: they were 'held prisoner' by the prejudices of their own miracle-believing age and – with constantly inflamed imaginations – always saw more in phenomena than was there in reality; above all, they disregarded the natural causes of things.

But in this case it was only their limited knowledge which made the disciples assume a miracle: the miracle is a mere illusion. *We*, Bahrdt would say, are no longer subject to this limitation; we know better. It is out of the question for a man to walk physically on water without being subject to the law of gravity. It is a principle that the laws of nature do not allow of any exception. This recognition (which continually won new confirmation during the Enlightenment from the scientific observation of nature) is as unshakable for Bahrdt as it had already been for Spinoza and Leibniz and Reimarus. Everything that happens in the world has a cause in that world: this is the fundamental principle.

Everything that is and happens is a web of causes and effects, so closely woven that no part of the fabric can stand in any other place or can act or be acted upon at any other time. Everything has its fitting place, its own particular moment. If the geese on Capitol Hill had stood in another place or if they had cackled one moment later, that which happened would not have happened. If the earth altered its distance from the sun but a very little, there would be a general alteration and disorder in Nature. In short, all things are so linked and bound together that no one thing can alter its position or time once these have been assigned to it in the fabric of the whole.

Take, for example, twenty-four balls and lay them next to one another in a circle so that each touches its neighbour. Imagine that a machine has the function of making these balls constantly revolve in this circle, so that the one drives the next forward. Would you in such a case take out one ball or add another? Impossible. For as soon as you remove one, the rest cease to drive one another onwards. And as soon as you force another ball in between, the size of the whole circle is altered. See, brethren, even so impossible is it to remove or add one link in the great chain of universal happening or in the marvellous web of causes and effects made by the Creator in his adorable wisdom. Grant this, and then consider the notion of a miracle and see whether you can still admit it. A miracle either introduces a new link into the chain or removes one already present. For as soon as God effects a thing directly, something comes into being which has no connection, as effect to cause, with anything else that already exists; otherwise it were no miracle but a natural event. Therefore something new comes into existence. In consequence it must be fitted into the whole. The point, therefore, where it is inserted must be conceived of as being between other, already existent things. This insertion must consequently effect an alteration in the position and time of those things between which it is now set. But no such alteration is possible in Nature because everything that is and happens has its proper place and its proper moment, so that in another place and at another moment it can neither itself be acted upon nor can it perform what it is called upon to perform. Hence miracles are inconceivable . . .

The laws of Nature are eternal and unalterable. Miracles suspend them. Therefore miracles are impossible.[1]

There is no doubt that this is a clear position. And it is one that can hardly be disputed if one starts from the same presupposition. But how

---

[1] *Ausführung*, 16th Letter.

does Bahrdt come to ascribe to the disciples' 'inflamed' and 'dream-filled' fantasies? 'Their prejudices held their reason prisoner.' They 'never viewed anything clearly'. With regard to the healing of the sick, Bahrdt gives a kind of religious-psychological explanation which brings out his point of view even more drastically:

In fact, brethren, it is very noticeable that these healings of the sick only owe the name of miracle to the ignorant narrators. For when one takes together all the attempts to heal the weak-minded with which Jesus himself in lamentable tones so often reproaches his disciples; and if one remembers the ruling Jewish tendency to ascribe everything new, rare, inexplicable to an invisible divine power or to a demon; it then becomes highly understandable that the disciples of Jesus, as Jews and as in fact weak men incapable of deep thinking, noticed only the marvellous aspect of Jesus' deeds and saw *nothing else*. Consequently they related everything in such a way that the only circumstances which appeared were those which gave the matter a strange and marvellous aspect, while the natural features were entirely lost.[1]

What justification has Bahrdt for these remarkable insinuations? He bases them on a contemporary experience belonging to the Enlightenment which we have already discussed at greater length: phenomena which were earlier held to be inexplicable and hence due to supernatural, divine and demonic, powers could not be clarified by rational and scientific observation and proved to have entirely natural causes. From the standpoint of a later and superior knowledge, the old supernatural faith was bound to appear as dream-like and fantastic – rather like belief in ghosts; it seemed like the superstition which fancies that something more and something different lies behind things than is really the case.

Bahrdt's programme of natural explanations is thus drawn from an experience typical of his time and it is explicable on this basis; it is not a virtuoso display of mental agility. For Bahrdt it is a matter of course that the knowledge which reason acquires in real life (such as knowledge of a coherent pattern of things ruled by law) is equally applicable to the Bible. Unlike the upholders of supernatural theology then and now, Bahrdt does not think of permitting Jesus Christ special laws in this respect. He is at one with the majority of modern scholars in his acceptance of the principle that: 'The sacred history is subject to the same laws as all other views of the past.'

[1] *Ausführung*, 66th Letter.

Scientific thinking only becomes possible when one abandons pious preconceptions. Piety is not the appropriate attitude in the quest for truth. Traditional judgments have no claim to acceptance merely because of their venerability. The only things that count in the claim to truth are demonstrable reasons. Bahrdt lays great stress on these presuppositions. And if a further consideration of his explanations of miracle shows that they do not offer a satisfactory solution to the problem, the presuppositions, at least, subsequently remained uncontested and can basically no longer be abandoned.

In Bahrdt, as with all 'enlightened' theologians, moral and religious arguments join the scientific objections. From a religious point of view, he says, miracles are valueless and even harmful.

For no man has any certain token whereby he may divide true divine miracles from deceit and fantasy on the one hand and from the effects of unknown natural powers on the other, so that he is able to take them as certain proof or testimony of a divine envoy: yes, instead of establishing us in our faith, they entangle us in dangerous superstition and *accustom* men to hold as true things which rest merely on strange witnesses and which not only lack the support of reason but are directly contrary to it.[1]

What does a miracle prove? 'What are men supposed to believe on the grounds of these so-called miracles? That the teaching of our Lord Jesus was *true*? Impossible. For a thousand miracles can neither make false teaching true nor true false.'[2] For faith, miracles have no conclusive force, because a spiritual or moral truth like the teaching of Jesus can neither be proved nor disproved by inexplicable facts in the external course of nature. This can be demonstrated, for example, from Jesus' command to love one's neighbour. Whether we take the summons to love as obligatory for us all or whether it satisfies us as being a justifiable demand is completely independent of the question of whether we believe that Jesus also performed miracles. Indeed, miracles can be a positive distraction from the real point at issue and can establish faith on the shaky ground of uncertain, chance events instead of on a truth convincing to the mind. Bahrdt found Jesus' teaching cogent 'because of its inner truth and excellence'.

It is from his conviction that the real truth of Christian doctrine is independent of allegedly miraculous events that Bahrdt gains the freedom for his fearlessly radical reinterpretation and naturalistic remould-

[1] *Ibid.*   [2] *Ibid.*

ing of the biblical miracles. He does not avoid doing violence to the text, as we have seen from his explanation of Jesus' walking on the water; Bahrdt is never at a loss for an explanation and his imagination shows itself master of every difficulty. Take his interpretation of the stilling of the storm, for example. We are told that, when the disciples thought themselves to be in danger from the storm, they broke into cries of fear; and that Jesus, wakened from sleep, cried, 'Peace! Be still!', telling the others reproachfully that they ought to be ashamed of being so afraid of a few passing storm clouds. Since at the same moment the wind chanced to drop, the disciples took it that the command to be still had been addressed to the wind instead of to themselves; and it became obvious to them that Jesus could rule even the wind and the sky. In the story of the Gadarene swine (the two thousand pigs possessed by demons which rushed into the lake), it was not demons that were responsible (since demons do not exist): the sick in their excitement rushed among the pigs so that the animals panicked, rushed down the slope and were for the most part drowned in the lake. When Jesus raised the dead, for example, the young man of Nain or Jairus' daughter, or even Lazarus in the Gospel of John, he was, of course, reviving people who were unconscious and only apparently dead, the skilled eye of the great judge of souls and wise physician recognizing the traces of life that remained. 'Jesus saves from premature burial' is the chapter-heading added later by one of Bahrdt's sympathizers.

Two miracles – the changing of water into wine at the marriage at Cana and the feeding of the four thousand – cause Bahrdt such difficulty that he cannot have Jesus performing them by himself. For these he needed some assistants, and since they are not mentioned in the text, Bahrdt promptly invents a kind of secret organization to make the alleged miracles possible – he calls them 'Brethren of the third degree'. The activity of this group was unknown even to Jesus' other disciples. At the marriage at Cana, one of these 'brethren' at Jesus' command secretly replaced the water in the pitchers with wine. Before the feeding of the four thousand, these disciples even hid a large quantity of provisions in a cave only known to themselves and then distributed basketsful to the crowd without the people noticing the manipulation. Thus the whole proceeding was bound to appear miraculous.

Let me enquire whether you here feel *bound* to believe in a miracle? The only enquiry which the unprejudiced reader may put is: where can Jesus have acquired the bread that was necessary to fill the mouths of so many? For it is not said that he broke up only the bread which he received from the disciples. It is said merely that the *disciples* gave him but five loaves. And this means only that so plenteous a provision could not have come from the *disciples* and that these, and in consequence the evangelists who tell the tale, *knew* nothing of the presence of a great provision. By no means does it follow that *Jesus had* no such provision . . .

Will you conclude that because no man can with certainty discover the natural means whereby Jesus received the necessary provision, those means must have been supernatural? Would this not be as foolish a conclusion as if a farmer seeing an aerostatic machine for the first time should decide that its ascent must have a supernatural cause because he can *name* no natural one? It is indeed true that men have always concluded thus, and the priests of the people have sought to confirm their flock in such conclusions, since on them rests all faith in the supernatural and the mysterious which must necessarily be the staff of priestly rule and the source of priestly revenue. But shall we, brethren, hold fast to this superstition because the world has held fast to it for thousands of years? Are we never to put away childish things and be men?

In short, you see well enough that even from the report of the evangelists no miracle is demonstrable: and that it is more reasonable to think of the thousand possibilities whereby Jesus could have sufficient reserve of bread and by dispensing the same could put the despondency of the disciples to shame, than to believe in a miracle . . .

Do you find it unbelievable that Jesus had secret disciples (of whom even the evangelists make mention – disciples who came to Jesus by night), who were privately zealous for his cause? Do you find it unbelievable that Jesus should seek out divers caves in the country of the Jews (of which there are a countless number, and so large that David had room in one for three thousand men) where he sometimes met together with the brethren of the third degree, where he kept his secret possessions, where he hid himself to escape from the press of the multitude and to enjoy solitude and quietness, and where his disciples had no entry, except that they might come into its foremost part? Imagine that when Jesus said that he would feed the multitude he was standing in front of such a cave, in which his friends had, days before, gathered plenteous provision. Imagine that he was trying his disciples to see what they would say; and that now, as they despondently brought him the five loaves, declaring his plan to be impossible, he took the bread with purposeful mien and told them to cause the people to sit down – he would feed them. Suppose that he thereupon caused one basket after another to be brought from the cave and to be distributed; until finally twelve baskets of what remained were gathered together. What? You find this impossible? Yet you do not find it impossible that God should cast aside the laws of Nature, which he has made in his wisdom, and should transform the hunger-stilling property of five loaves into that of two thousand? Where is your reason, that you cast aside so simple a possibility and rather flee to what is at least half an impossibility? Have you the slightest ground for the supernatural acts of God? Are these more than barely possible? And if I can choose between two possibilities (for instance the possibility that Jesus had secret provision and the possibility that God performed a miracle), does not sound common sense bid me to choose the possibility which is the most comprehensible and inclines most closely to Nature?[1]

If one seeks for a counter-argument to these reinterpretations, there is only one that is convincing, namely, that the *meaning* of the New Testament stories of miracle is turned upside down by such manipulations. What would Matthew, Luke or Mark have said to rationalistic adaptations of this kind? They would have felt themselves hopelessly misunderstood, for what they are aiming to tell is the very miracle story which Bahrdt explains away through his 'improved' explanation. And what actually emerges from Bahrdt's method? What, for example, remains of the stilling of the storm when the miraculous features have been extracted from it? A perfectly ordinary story of a stormy voyage during which Jesus – most improbably – shows a better knowledge of weather conditions than the disciples. One might even say, a boring everyday occurrence not worth telling. What is left of the strange account of Jesus' walking on the water, with its tale of horror, terror and faith? A rather trivial joke played by Jesus on his frightened disciples – also highly improbable and hardly worth telling.

We can see that if the miracle is removed from the text, nothing is left – or at least nothing worthy of report. Something is wrong. But where does the fault lie?

The biblical texts contain accounts of miracles – that is the starting point. But miracles contradict the laws of nature and are therefore impossible. So far we can follow Bahrdt. If, therefore, there is anything

[1] *Ausführung*, 68th Letter.

true in the story, then it must have happened – as it does everywhere else in the world – naturally and not miraculously. This conclusion is also incontrovertible. How can the result of the argument, then, still be false? Is Bahrdt perhaps starting from a false premiss – hence his lack of success in attempting an explanation? He says:

> If I therefore deny miracles or recognize them to be impossible, yet I do not desire to deny the facts themselves, the circumstances which are related in the Bible as if they were miraculous. I merely contest the way in which these circumstances are said, according to the common view, to have taken place. Hence you have no need to fear that I shall bring under suspicion the historical truth of the Gospel history. For it is rather one of the purposes of these Letters to defend the story of Jesus against all doubts and objections, and to show that all that the evangelists themselves tell of Jesus and what they *could themselves know* is historically true.[1]

Bahrdt, therefore, does not doubt for a moment that the miracle stories are the reports of historical facts. And the supernaturalists, Bahrdt's theological opponents, whom he is really trying to refute, maintained precisely the same thing. It is here, therefore, that the main problem lies. If the path which Bahrdt takes on the basis of his premiss does not lead any further than this, then we are faced with an inescapable question: is the assumption of the historicity, the historical truth, of miracles tenable?

A further step is obviously needed to bring us out of this dilemma, but it is a step which Bahrdt and his contemporaries were not in a position to take. Belief in miracles has become involved in difficulties which are not really removed by Bahrdt's somewhat comic reconstructions. Many people will feel that this is merely to go from bad to worse. The undertaking which began so promisingly ends in confusion.

But whatever objections critical theologians may later have justifiably levied against Bahrdt, they are at one with him in his basic intention:

> O brethren, may no teacher ever find it necessary to rise among you and dispute so baseless a faith as faith in miracles. May you once and for all have done with an article of faith which does not make you one whit wiser, one whit more enlightened or one whit more settled in your religion: which rather leads you into a thousand difficulties; exposes your convictions to every mocker who has intellect enough

[1] *Ausführung*, 16th Letter.

to spy out their nakedness and to reproach you with it; an article of faith which dishonours reason, the true Spirit of God, and takes from you the satisfaction, independent of all priestly authority, of seeing truth, loving the truth which you yourselves have discovered, and following it with a joyful spirit.[1]

[1] *Ausführung*, 68th Letter.

7 David Friedrich Strauss and the Mythical Viewpoint

Was Jesus able to walk on the water? Did it really happen?

Until the nineteenth century there were two answers to this question. The first answer was: yes – because Jesus possessed supernatural powers and with God all things are possible. Moreover, we cannot doubt the truth of the story, because the evangelists received it word for word, as direct inspiration, from the Holy Spirit. The second answer was: yes and no. Yes – the story may have happened; but no – not in the form in which it is reported. It is inconceivable that Jesus' body was not subject to the force of gravity; to believe in a miracle here is impossible. But we are not in fact obliged to do so. This was a mistaken impression on the part of the disciples who, with their undeveloped rational powers and credulous imaginations, saw miracles where none existed. Jesus walked naturally on logs of wood which were floating in the water.

Can we not content ourselves with the second answer, if not with the first? But is the point of the New Testament story supposed to be that Jesus deceived his disciples through a slightly odd performance of this kind? The story cannot have been told for the sake of such improbable trivialities; the whole point of it was the miracle – so much is certain; and it is by this that the story stands or falls. But is there a better explanation? There seems to be only one possibility left. If the story can neither have happened supernaturally nor naturally, then it did not happen at all; it must have been *invented*.

In 1835 the most sensational work of Protestant theology during the whole of the last century appeared: *Das Leben Jesus, kritisch bearbeitet von Dr. David Friedrich Strauss*.[1] The writer,[2] a clever young man from

---

[1] The work made its impact on the English public in George Eliot's translation (anonymously published): *The Life of Jesus*, 3 vols. (London, 1846); the English version is translated from the 4th German edition; we quote from the 5th English ed. in one volume (London, 1906).

[2] David Friedrich Strauss (1808–1874).

Württemberg, was a theological and philosophical scholar at Tübingen University. He was only twenty-seven years old, a pleasant young man, we are told, though rather shy. The book brought him fame, but also immediate dismissal from his Tübingen post. It ruined his budding scholarly career, and turned him into a lonely and hated outsider. But it was a milestone in the history of biblical criticism. 'A new opinion, which aims to fill the place of an older one, ought fully to adjust its position with respect to the latter.' Strauss' book offers a logically ordered summing up of previous attempts to explain miracles, the writer working methodically at each point through the stages of super-natural and naturalistic interpretation, 'but, as becomes a valid refuta-tion, with an acknowledgment of what is true in the opinions combated and an incorporation of this truth into the new theory.'[1]

Strauss' treatment of the feeding of the five thousand is a good illus-tration of his method:

> When it was evening, the disciples came to him and said, 'This is a lonely place, and the day is now over; send the crowds away to go into the villages and buy food for themselves.' Jesus said, 'They need not go away; you give them something to eat.' They said to him, 'We have only five loaves here and two fish.' And he said, 'Bring them here to me.' Then he ordered the crowds to sit down on the grass; and taking the five loaves and the two fish he looked up to heaven, and blessed, and broke and gave the loaves to the disciples, and the disciples gave them to the crowds. And they all ate and were satisfied. And they took up twelve baskets full of the broken pieces left over. And those who ate were about five thousand men, besides women and children (Matt. 14.15–21).

The story of the miraculous feeding of the multitude seemed so impor-tant to the evangelists that they relate it six times in all, with slight varia-tions. The authors of the Gospels found it in two different versions in the tradition which they used, which is why Matthew and Mark faith-fully repeat it twice. In one case five thousand people, five loaves and two fish are involved; in the other four thousand people, seven loaves and a few small fish. In the one version twelve basketful are left over and in the other version seven. In both cases the scene is a mountain or lonely place near the lake. Why was this story so particularly important? Strauss first of all examines the conservative view, which adheres to

[1] Strauss, *op. cit.*, Preface to the First German Edition, pp. xxx–xxxi.

the miracle, maintaining that this was merely an accelerated natural process.

> The most correct view of the matter, then, is undoubtedly this, that under the hands of the Saviour, and by his Divine power, an increase of the means of food must be held to have taken place. As, by the touch of his hand, he healed and blessed, so in the same way he *made*. Along with this, however, the idea is still to be firmly retained, that these appearances were merely natural processes, extremely hurried forward in point of time . . .[1]

So writes Hermann Olshausen, in Strauss' time the most influential representative of a modernized supernatural interpretation, which endeavoured to smooth away the contradiction between the miracle and natural law. 'That which comes to pass in the space of three quarters of a year, from seed-time to harvest, was here effected in the minutes which were required for the distribution of the food; for natural developments are capable of acceleration, and to how great an extent we cannot determine.'[2] This is the argument. But Strauss has a reply:

> It would, indeed, have been an acceleration of a natural process, if in the hand of Jesus a grain of corn had borne fruit a hundred-fold, and brought it to maturity, and if he had shaken the multiplied grain out of his hands as they were filled again and again, that the people might grind, knead, and bake it, or eat it raw from the husk in the wilderness where they were; – or if he had taken a living fish, suddenly called forth the eggs from its body, and converted them into full-grown fish, which then the disciples or the people might have boiled or roasted, this, we should say, would have been an acceleration of a natural process. But it is not corn that he takes into his hand, but bread; and the fish also, as they are distributed in pieces, must have been prepared in some way, perhaps . . . broiled or salted. Here, then, on both sides, the production of nature is no longer simple and living, but dead and modified by art: so that to introduce a natural process of the above kind, Jesus must, in the first place, by his miraculous power have metamorphosed the bread into corn again, the roasted fish into raw and living ones; then instantaneously have effected the described multiplication; and lastly, have restored the whole from the natural

---

[1] H. Olshausen, *Biblischer Commentar*, 2nd ed. (1834); ET, *Commentary on the Gospels*, Clark's Foreign Theological Library X (Edinburgh, 1848), vol. II, p. 187.

[2] Strauss, *op. cit.*, pt. II, ch. 9 § 102, pp. 511–512.

to the artificial state. Thus the miracle would be composed, first, of a revivification, which would exceed in miraculousness all other instances in the Gospels; secondly, of an extremely accelerated natural process; and thirdly, of an artificial process, effected invisibly, and likewise extremely accelerated, since all the tedious proceedings of the miller and baker on the one hand, and of the cook on the other, must have been accomplished in a moment by the word of Jesus.[1]

The expression 'an accelerated natural process', which sounds so plausible to the believer, is therefore a delusion. And how is one to visualize Jesus' method of increasing the food at his disposal?

> We may ... endeavour to represent the matter to ourselves in two ways: first, we may suppose that as fast as one loaf or fish was gone, a new one came out of the hands of Jesus, or secondly, that the single loaves and fishes grew, so that as one piece was broken off, its loss was repaired, until on a calculation the turn came for the next loaf or fish.[2]

It is necessary to look really closely into the matter for, as Strauss rightly remarks:

> This miracle belongs to the class which can only appear in any degree credible so long as they can be retained in the obscurity of an indefinite conception: no sooner does the light shine on them, so that they can be examined in all their parts, than they dissolve like the unsubstantial creations of the mist. Loaves, which in the hands of the distributors expand like wetted sponges, – broiled fish, in which the severed parts are replaced instantaneously, as in the living crab gradually, – plainly belong to quite another domain than that of reality.[3]

If the supernatural explanation will not hold water, perhaps the naturalistic or, as Strauss calls it, the rationalistic explanation, is a possibility.

> What gratitude, then, do we owe to the rationalistic interpretation, if it be true that it can free us, in the easiest manner, from the burden of so unheard-of a miracle? If we are to believe Dr Paulus [of Heidelberg], the evangelists had no idea that they were narrating anything miraculous. ... As ... the multitude appear to have consisted for the greater part of a caravan on its way to the feast, they cannot have been quite destitute of provisions, and probably a few indigent persons

[1] *Ibid.*, p. 512.   [2] *Ibid.*, pp. 512–513.   [3] *Ibid.*, p. 513.

only had exhausted their stores. In order, then, to induce the better provided to share their food with those who were in want, Jesus arranged that they should have a meal, and himself set the example of imparting what he and the disciples could spare from their own little store; this example was imitated, and thus . . . the whole multitude was satisfied.[1]

But the text offers no evidence at all for the supposition that the people had food with them and distributed it among themselves.

The natural explanation falls into especial embarrassment when it comes to the baskets which, after all were satisfied, Jesus caused to be filled with the fragments that remained. [More seems to have been left over than was there at the beginning.] Here, therefore, the natural expositor is put to the most extravagent contrivances in order to evade the miracle. . . . Here, therefore, the natural explanation once more fails to fulfil its task: the text retains its miracle, and if we have reason to think this incredible, we must enquire whether the narrative of the text deserves credence.[2]

The new question, therefore, is: are there grounds which justify us in holding the story as a whole to be unhistorical? What standards can we apply in order to arrive at a scientifically based and non-arbitrary judgment in individual cases? Strauss devotes a special section to this important question, calling it 'criteria by which to distinguish the unhistorical in the Gospel narrative'.

That an account is not historical – that the matter related could not have taken place in the manner described is evident;
First. When the narration is irreconcilable with the known and universal laws which govern the course of events . . .
Secondly. An account which shall be regarded as historically valid, must neither be inconsistent with itself, nor in contradiction with other accounts.[3]

In a later version of his book, *Das Leben Jesus für das deutsche Volk* (1864), Strauss describes in more detail how a historian proceeds to test the historical accuracy of a text:

If, upon the strength of evidence, we are to look upon an event as having really taken place, we, of course, first test the credibility of that

[1] *Ibid.*   [2] *Ibid.*, pp. 514–515.   [3] *Ibid.*, Introduction § 16, p. 88.

evidence. We consider whether it rests upon the declaration of eye-witnesses or persons at a distance, of many persons or of few, whether these agree in their declarations, whether they are to be looked upon as honest, truth-loving men, whether the author who tells us of the event was himself an eye-witness or not, and so forth. But supposing even that the evidence satisfied all the demands which we could make upon its credibility, still the question would remain as to the character of the event testified to by it. The Romans had a proverb: I would not believe the story even were it told me by Cato: which means that there may be things so incredible in themselves that this incredibility would invalidate the evidence of a witness in other respects the most credible of men.[1]

Strauss takes as an example the well-known Old Testament story of Balaam's ass: 'Then the Lord opened the mouth of the ass, and she said to Balaam, "What have I done to you, that you have struck me these three times?" ' (Num. 22.28)

Supposing (Hume might have used this example) the 22nd chapter of the fourth Book of Moses [Num.] were really written by Moses, or by Balaam himself; supposing even that we had been present when he had just dismounted from his ass, and told the story in all its freshness of the ass having spoken to him in human words, and had been well known to us as an honest man; all this would do no good, but we should tell him downright that he is trifling, that he must have dreamt it, even if we did not lose our opinion of his honesty and accuse him of absolute falsehood. In our own minds we should balance the two probabilities, considering which was the greater, that a witness apparently the most credible should nevertheless have deceived us, or that an event should have happened contradicting all previous experience. . . . There are examples of testimony, even the most credible, given by eye-witnesses, by honest men, and so forth, having been false. These instances may be rare, but still there have been such. But, with the exception of the cases where credibility is in question, there are no instances of events demonstrably contradicting the laws of Nature. And on this point there is a quality assumed on the part of the evidence which does not belong to any of our evangelical accounts of miracles, not one of which has been recorded by an eye-witness, but on the contrary by those who received them from the

---

[1] D. F. Strauss, *New Life of Jesus*, ET, 2 vols. (London, 1865), vol. I, p. 199.

tradition of others, and who show, by the whole tendency of their writings, that they were disposed to do anything rather than to try the tradition they received by a critical test.[1]

When the evangelists passed on the traditions about Jesus, they were not interested in historical correctness; their aim was the proclamation and glorification of their subject. This is what Strauss means by his final remark.

If, having considered the standards to be applied to history in general, we now return to the feeding of the five thousand, it is easy to see which possibility has the casting vote. The different accounts certainly contradict one another in detail. The Gospel of John introduces certain features which do not appear in the other three Gospels. But the decisive factor is the inconceivable character of the miracle, which becomes all the more obvious through the efforts of the supernaturalists; for Strauss, it is no less inconceivable than the story of Balaam's ass. The only possibility left, therefore, is to declare that the story is unhistorical – an invention.

But then the interpreter is immediately faced with a new question. Why was a story of this kind invented at all, and who invented it? Are there any pointers in the stories themselves, or in the framework surrounding them, to show what meaning the story had for the narrator? Here we come to Strauss' real discovery, a discovery which gives a positive reason and justification for assuming that the Gospels contain fictitious incidents or, as he calls them, myths.

It is not sufficient to consider a story in isolation and to examine its authenticity, as the rationalists do; one must see it in its context. The kernel of the event is the flocking of a great group of people out of the towns into the desert, where they are later miraculously fed. Previously all four Gospels tell, in different ways, how Jesus spoke to the people about the kingdom of God, and how he taught them and healed them:

> And great crowds came to him, bringing with them the lame, the maimed, the blind, the dumb, and many others, and they put them at his feet, and he healed them, so that the throng wondered, when they saw the dumb speaking, the maimed whole, the lame walking, and the blind seeing; and they glorified the God of Israel (Matt. 15.30f.).

It is a *messianic* scene that is being painted. Jesus appears as the one who fulfils Isaiah's ancient promise about the dawn of the messianic kingdom and the end of all human misery:

[1] *Ibid.*, pp. 199f.

Then the eyes of the blind shall be opened,
    and the ears of the deaf unstopped;
then shall the lame man leap like a hart,
    and the tongue of the dumb sing for joy. . . . (Isa. 35.5f.).

It is the signs whereby the Jews may recognize their long-expected Messiah which are being reported of Jesus in this passage. In answer to the question always present among the Jewish people: art thou he that should come? Jesus answers with a list of these same acts, which are also signs (Matt. 11.5f.). No other information appears to be necessary. The signs speak for themselves to those who can understand them.

The feeding of the multitude in the desert is also part of this messianic scene. Our conjecture that this miracle, too, is not simply to be interpreted as a spectacle but rather as a 'sign' is confirmed by the evangelists' pendant to the story: 'For they did not understand about the loaves, but their hearts were hardened,' says Mark about the disciples' lack of understanding. And Jesus asks them, 'Do not you yet perceive or understand? . . . Having eyes do you not see, and having ears do you not hear? . . . Do you not yet understand?' (Mark 6.52; 8.17–21)

What was there to understand, apart from the miracle itself? John, who was writing his Gospel for non-Jews and adds extensive commentaries to his miracle stories, gives a clue even to the reader who may be unfamiliar with the Scriptures. His version of the feeding of the five thousand closes with the remark: 'When the people saw the sign which he had done, they said, "This is indeed the prophet who is to come into the world." ' The expectation of a prophet was based on a classic verse from Deuteronomy, a verse quoted with equal frequency by both Jewish and Christian teachers. The dying Moses is addressing his people, at God's bidding: 'The Lord your God will raise up for you a prophet like me from among you, from your brethren – him you shall heed' (Deut. 18.15). Originally this passage probably only meant that after the death of Moses new prophetic leaders would continually arise for the guidance of the people. But, as Strauss convincingly demonstrates, it became the basis on which Jewish messianic expectation built up a whole system founded on the principle: 'As the first redeemer (Moses) . . . so shall be the second.'[1] The result was that all the signs and wonders performed by the first redeemer were also expected of the last. The leading of the people out of Egypt and the journey through the wilderness; this was the situation in which the first redeemer was active. The mountain

---

[1] Strauss, *Life of Jesus*, Introduction § 14, p. 83.

was the place where he was alone with God. These pointers indicate the religious background of the Jesus story. When features such as these recur in the story of his life we understand what they are supposed to tell us: Jesus is the promised prophet, the long-expected and final saviour of Israel.

Further, one particular miracle played an especially important role among the deeds of the first redeemer, Moses – the feeding of the hungry people with manna, the bread from heaven. 'What do you know about the first saviour?' asks a Rabbinic commentary, and goes on: 'He caused manna to descend, as it is said in Ex. 16.4: "Behold, I will rain bread from heaven on you. – So too will the last saviour cause manna to descend." And in the Gospel of John, the people really do come to Jesus full of this expectation. 'What sign do you do, that we may see, and believe you? What work do you perform? Our fathers ate the manna in the wilderness' (John 6.30f.).

An investigation of the religious-historical context[1] of the miraculous feeding therefore shows that there actually were reasons why miracle stories were told, or rather invented, about Jesus. Even a prophet established his credentials through mighty acts, signs and miracles. Not only Moses but other prophets, especially Elijah and Elisha, performed miracles, among which miraculous feedings played an important part.

'In famines, too, the prophets had proved their divine mission by sending miraculous relief. When, during the great drought under Ahab, Elijah lodged with the widow of Zarephath, Jehovah's miraculous operation . . . prevented the barrel of meal wasting or the oil failing in the widow's cruse, so long as the scarcity lasted (I Kings 17.7ff.).[2] A miracle of this kind said to have been performed by the prophet Elisha is the most closely related of all the miraculous feedings to Jesus' miracle. During a famine, Elisha fed a hundred men with barley loaves and some ground corn. 'How am I to set this before a hundred men?' asks his servant, as unbelieving as Jesus' disciples. Elisha answers: 'Give them to the men, that they may eat, for thus says the Lord, "They shall eat and have some left." And so it was' (II Kings 4.42–44).

It was naturally expected that the Messiah would surpass all earlier miracles. But the nature of the miracles through which the fullness of time was to be marked (healings, miracles connected with food and water, the soothing and binding of the elements, etc.) was laid down in advance

[1] An illuminating investigation of the theological motives for the miraculous feedings may be found in A. Heising, *Die Botschaft der Brotvermehrung* (Stuttgarter Bibelstudien 15, 1966).   [2] Strauss, *New Life of Jesus*, vol. II, pp. 252f.

by the messianic expectation of the Jews. Strauss in fact finds many suggestions in the texts that Jesus himself rejected miracles; and his formulation is no exaggeration:

> Meanwhile, however, Jesus might disclaim the performance of material miracles, it was supposed, according to the mode of thought of the period, and of his contemporaries, that miracles he must perform whether he would or not. As soon as he was considered a prophet . . . – and we cannot doubt that he might attain this character as well as the Baptist even without miracles – miraculous powers were attributed to him; and, when they were attributed to him they came of course into operation.[1]

It was primarily healings that actually took place in Jesus' circle – here Strauss agrees with all naturalistic interpreters from Reimarus onwards.

> From that time, wherever he showed himself, sufferers regularly crowded upon him in order only to touch his garments, because they expected to be cured by doing so. . . And it would have been strange indeed if there had been no cases among all these in which the force of excited imagination, impressions half spiritual half sensuous, produced either actual removal or temporary mitigation of their complaints; and this effect was ascribed to the miraculous power of Jesus.[2]

Here Strauss refers to cases known to medicine according to which some tremendous impression or a firm spiritual faith can lead to physical effects which may appear miraculous.

> And when in such cases Jesus dismissed the persons cured, as he did this man, with the words, 'Thy faith hath made thee whole', . . . he could not have expressed himself more truly, more modestly, more correctly, or more precisely.[3]

These 'natural' miracles put Jesus on a level with other 'wonder doctors' of the ancient and modern world rather than give him a unique position; but they have their limits in those cases where no historical parallel can be found, where every conceivable possibility comes to an end and where the impossible is asserted. But at this point, when a naturalistic explanation becomes impossible, Strauss' new and convincing *mythical* explanation proves itself. For it is obvious that it is as easy for the messianic faith to beget invented miracles as real ones – indeed much easier.

[1] *Ibid.*, vol. I, p. 365.   [2] *Ibid.*   [3] *Ibid.*

Does this mean that the first Christians deliberately spread false reports in order to commend their Messiah to the missionary churches? No, says Strauss; we are not dealing with conscious invention at all but with a process which came about through the popular transmission and elaboration of the Jesus tradition, independent of individual narrators. 'When men, I said, first a few persons, then a continually increasing number, had come to see the Messiah in Jesus, they supposed that everything must have coincided in him which, according to the Old Testament prophecies and types, and their current interpretations, was expected of the Messiah.'[1] 'Such and such things must have happened to the Messiah' – so much men knew, and they went on to conclude: 'Jesus was the Messiah; therefore such and such things happened to him.'[2] However certain it may be, on the basis of the earliert accounts, that Jesus came from Nazareth, 'as the Messiah, as the son of David, he must have been born in Bethlehem, for Micah had so prophesied. Jesus might have uttered words of severe reproach against the desire for miracles on the part of his countrymen, and those words might still be living in tradition; but Moses, the first deliverer of the people, had worked miracles, therefore the last Deliverer, the Messiah, and Jesus had of course been he, must likewise have worked miracles.'[3] This was, so to speak, an objective necessity compared with which the insignificant historical facts about the life of the carpenter's son from Nazareth had no weight. 'Can anything good come out of Nazareth?' asked the Jew familiar with the Scriptures.

Myth in its original form is therefore not the deliberate invention of an individual but the production of the folk-consciousness, or of a whole religious group. And even where, in later times, deliberate invention is intermingled, it can only become absorbed into the common stock of a community when the ground has been prepared for it in the general consciousness. There is no question of arbitrarily invented fictions.

Summing up, it may be said of the miraculous feedings that these stories are non-historical messianic stories through which the first Christians expressed in vivid terms, directly comprehensible to the Jews, their belief that Jesus was the promised Messiah. In the preaching of the Early Church the miracles served as the identifying mark of the Messiah.

This group of Gospel stories, then, centring on Jesus as Son of David and the second Moses, is unhistorical and has roots in the Old Testament and in myth: this discovery is the great achievement of Strauss' mythical

[1] *Ibid.*, vol. I, p. 191. [2] Strauss, *Life of Jesus*, Intro. § 14, p. 84.
[3] Strauss, *New Life of Jesus*, vol. I, p. 202.

interpretation. Strauss does not maintain that this is the only root of the miraculous feedings. In his later book he sees a second link, closer to the story of Jesus himself, namely a remembrance of common meals and the breaking of bread at the Last Supper, a connection most clearly brought out by John.

Strauss left one great remaining task for his successors in New Testament studies, as well as one remaining question. Since the discovery of the unhistorical elements in the Bible it has been the task of scholars to divide and distinguish between historical fact and the interpretative fiction of faith. The main question which thereby arises is: How did Jesus convince his contemporaries that he was the Messiah if it was not through messianic legitimation miracles – and indeed not through supernatural proofs of his divinity at all? The presupposition of all the messianic legitimation miracles is the thesis that Jesus actually was the Messiah; and his contemporaries would not have been convinced of this if he had not satisfied their expectations in some form or other. What extraordinary acts did Jesus perform to wake faith, if not miracles?

The question of miracle as such was, one would suppose, basically settled with Strauss' *Leben Jesu*. If a miracle story is no longer to be understood as a historical account but as a literary method of expressing faith, the next question can only be: What *meaning* did the story have for the narrator, and what made him choose this particular form in order to bring out the significance of Jesus?

A The Supernatural Interpretation

1 The event took place in reality.
2 It happened exactly as reported in the text.
3 With the miracle the text proclaims a divine act.
4 Since God performed the miracle, the search for a natural cause is irrelevant.

This means

The principle of causality is not maintained (the cause is God himself, not anything in the world).

The meaning of the text is maintained (the intention of the story has been correctly grasped).

B The Naturalistic Explanation

1 The event cannot have taken place in reality.
2 Hence it cannot have taken place in this way, but must have happened differently.
3 The text contains a natural event, not a miracle.
4 The natural cause must and can be given (the text must if necessary be supplemented or altered).

This means

The principle of causality is maintained (everything which happens in the world has a cause within that world).

The meaning of the text is not maintained (the intention of the story has been misread).

Dilemma

The explanation (A) which accords with the text is supernatural and conflicts with the principle of causality.

The naturalistic explanation (B) does not accord with the text and conflicts with its meaning.

In a convincing interpretation both the principle of causality and the meaning of the text must be maintained.

This is prevented in both A and B by their common premiss that the event is historical.

C The Mythical Point of View

1 The text undoubtedly aims to proclaim a miracle as a divine act (A is right).
2 Hence the search for a natural cause would be irrelevant (A is right).
3 But the event cannot have happened in reality as the text claims that it did (B is right).
4 Hence the alleged event is neither natural nor supernatural; it never happened at all. The text does not contain a historical but an invented miracle, not a fact but a 'myth'.

Definition

We distinguish by the name *evangelical mythus* a narrative relating directly or indirectly to Jesus, which may be considered not as the expression of a fact, but as the product of an idea of his earliest followers.[1]

Task

The 'idea' must be recognized, the meaning grasped and the intention understood.

What does the miracle story aim to show?

What ideas are being presupposed?

What is the origin of the mythical 'images'?

How are they to be interpreted in their original and their transferred form?

So perverted a view could arise only in a mind that refused to interpret the ancient records in the spirit of their age. . . . But they are the production of an infant and unscientific age; and treat, without reserve of divine interventions, in accordance with the conceptions and phraseology of that early period. So that, in point of fact, we have neither miracles to wonder at, on the one hand, nor deceptions to unmask on the other; but simply the language of a former age to translate into that of our own day.[2]

Qualification

The mythical interpretation (C) can only be systematically applied to miracles in the strictest sense of the term.

The naturalistic explanation (B) in part applies to miracle stories with a 'historical nucleus'.

[1] Strauss, *Life of Jesus*, Intro. § 15, p. 86. [2] *Ibid.*, Intro. § 6, p. 48.

8 Ludwig Feuerbach and the Psychology of Religion

Miracle is fantasy

Ludwig Feuerbach's theory is, for various reasons, of no small significance even today. Feuerbach (1804–1872) was the most important representative of an atheistic philosophy of religion in nineteenth-century Germany. Marx and Engels drew on him for their criticism of religion, only regretting subsequently that this criticism was itself too religious; they discovered that Feuerbach, with his exaggeratedly emotional and pathetic style, had replaced the old dogmatic religion by a new abstract religion of love, instead of drawing the radical, practical consequences for which the time was really ripe.[1] If his own disciples were dissatisfied with him, Feuerbach received an even worse report from Christian theologians. He was reproached with having 'dissolved' the Christian doctrine of God into a doctrine of man, and it was hardly thought necessary, at that time, to give his ideas serious consideration. Yet the great theological problem with which Feuerbach saw himself confronted at the end of the period of the Enlightenment has by no means been satisfactorily solved even in our contemporary Christian theology. This fact emerges from the newly kindled discussion over the meaning of the word 'God'. It is time that Feuerbach's attempt at a rendering was given serious consideration.

In order to understand Feuerbach's problem one must be familiar with the presuppositions of his thinking. These can be very simply described. Feuerbach takes for granted the scientific and historical Enlightenment. The assumption of a materially real, divine, super-

---

[1] See Karl Marx, *Thesen über Feuerbach* (1845), ET, *The German Ideology*, ed. by S. Ryazanskaya (Moscow 1964; London 1965); F. Engels, *Ludwig Feuerbach und der Ausgang der klassischen deutschen Philosophie* (1888); sections II and III are printed in Karl Marx, Friedrich Engels, *Über Religion*, ET, *On Religion* (Moscow, London, 1957). See also *Marx-Engels-Studienausgabe* in four vols. (Fischer Bücherei 746, 1966), vol. I.

natural world and its manifestations is no longer possible for him. The gods of the ancient religious records are not real in the way in which they were earlier thought to be. This applies to the Christian religion as well. But if God cannot be found in objective reality – in a physical heaven, for example – where is he? According to the witness of the early documents, God reached down from heaven to intervene miraculously in the history of men. If these miraculous acts were not real facts belonging to real history, what were they? One must abide by the given facts. The divine acts and miracles are not communicated to us directly in the objective world, but only indirectly through the stories of ancient peoples. Now such stories – whatever else may be said about them – are at all events products of the human mind, in which a certain kind of experience of reality is expressed; they are formations of the consciousness. They are not 'the expression of a fact' but 'the product of an idea', to quote David Friedrich Strauss' characterization[1] of the stories which deal with supernatural events, stories which (in common with the philologists of his time) he called 'myths'. 'The supernatural birth of Christ, his miracles, his resurrection and ascension, remain eternal truths, whatever doubts may be cast on their reality as historical facts.'[2]

Feuerbach was a contemporary of Strauss and was, like him, a student of Hegelian philosophy; but in contrast to the representatives of a purely idealistic point of view, he felt the urgent necessity of looking behind ideas to the origin and significance of these ideas in the real life of the real person. This is what is meant by Feuerbach's 'materialism'. How did people ever come to tell stories of this kind? What goes on in the mind of a person who believes in miracles? What is his motive? What importance do miracles have for him? Is there something in his personal world which forces him to believe in them? The figures of the gods demand further investigation all the more once they have ceased to be conceivable as genuinely existing supernatural persons. How do men come to 'imagine' such figures? What realities do the figures conceal?

Supernatural figures have some secret meaning. What is its key? A great guessing competition began in the nineteenth century, which only gradually acquired scholarly form and method. The process always began with a 'criticism of religion' and went on, as far as the enemies of Christianity were concerned, to an 'exposure', 'disclosure', 'process of disillusionment', etc.; the Christian theologians described it in more friendly terms as a 'rendering' or 'interpretation'.

[1] In his *Life of Jesus* (1835); see above ch. 6.
[2] *Ibid.*, Preface to first German ed., p. xxx.

Feuerbach took as his task the solving of the 'mystery of theology'. He read the familiar Bible stories and the classic witnesses of Christian interpretation like a man who goes on a journey of exploration in a new country. He wanted to discover what 'essence' lies behind the strange manifestations of religion. His most popular and most effective work is entitled *Das Wesen des Christentums* (1841) – *The Essence of Christianity*.[1]

For Feuerbach miracles are the most conspicuous feature of biblical faith in both the Old and New Testaments; they are not merely marginal. 'Faith is the belief in miracle; faith and miracle are absolutely inseparable.'[2] 'The apostle Paul illustrates the nature of Christian faith by the example of Abraham. Abraham could not, in a natural way, ever hope for posterity; Jehovah nevertheless promised it to him out of special favour; and Abraham believed in spite of Nature.'[3]

Feuerbach sees the fundamental connection between an individual miracle story of this kind and the whole concept of an almighty God, above Nature, who intervenes actively, as special 'providence', in the course of history. It is an essential characteristic of this God to perform miracles. He acts unpredictably, arbitrarily. Abraham is called away from the land of his fathers and receives the gift of progeny in a miraculous way; the people of Israel, favoured above all other nations on the grounds of an arbitrary election, are miraculously saved from various perils and are led towards a particular, historical goal; although they had, admittedly, also to bear special burdens and endure special suffering. Nothing happened normally in Israel. The normal course of events was cut through by the arbitrary decisions of the deity. Even the creation of the world was a pure miracle, for the world, being the work of an almighty will, is a creation out of nothing.

It is the first miracle, not only in time but in rank also; – the principle of which all further miracles are the spontaneous result. The proof of this is history itself; all miracles have been vindicated, explained and illustrated by appeal to the omnipotence which created the world out of nothing. Why should not he who made the world out of nothing, make wine out of water, bring human speech from the mouth of an ass, and charm water out of a rock?[4]

[1] New scholarly edition, Akademie-Verlag (Berlin, 1956); also Reclam Universal-Bibliothek Nr. 4571–75. (Leipzig, 1957). Like Strauss' *Life of Jesus*, Feuerbach's book was made available to English readers by 'George Eliot': *The Essence of Christianity*, trans. from 2nd German edition by Marion Evans (London, 1853; new ed., New York, 1957). The following page-references refer to the 1957 edition.   [2] *Ibid.*, p. 126.   [3] *Ibid.*, p. 129.   [4] *Ibid.*, p. 102.

How unusual such a view of God and the world is only becomes really clear when one takes a comparative glance at the neighbouring pagan religions. Feuerbach shows himself to be an expert, and obviously an admirer, of Greek religious philosophy. There it could be said that man was born 'for the contemplation of the sun, the moon and the heavens' (Anaxagoras) or *ad mundum contemplandum et imitandum*, 'for the contemplation and imitation of the world' (Cicero). Man is in harmony with the natural world; nature is for him the quintessence of order, of the cosmos, and of the divine itself.

> The author of the Book of Wisdom says truly of the heathens, that, 'for admiration of the beauty of the world they did not raise themselves to the idea of the Creator'. To him who feels that Nature is lovely, it appears an end in itself, it has the ground of existence in itself: in him the question 'Why does it exist?' does not arise.[1]

Characteristic of this human standpoint – Feuerbach calls it theoretical – is reserve in the sphere of subjectivity, a voluntary subjection to the general laws of nature. From this point of view the attitude of biblical faith appears utilitarian, self-interested, even egoistical.

At this point it becomes clear how Feuerbach jumps from a comparison of important phenomena in the history of religion to a kind of psychological interpretation which is highly characteristic of his method. He investigates the differing forms of man's attitude to his environment and thereby enquires into the subjective interest which is dominant in each case:

> Utilism is the essential theory of Judaism. The belief in a special Divine Providence is the characteristic belief of Judaism; belief in Providence is belief in miracle; but belief in miracle exists where Nature is regarded only as an object of arbitrariness, of egoism, which uses Nature only as an instrument of its own will and pleasure. Water divides or rolls itself together like a firm mass, dust is changed into lice, a staff into a serpent, rivers into blood, a rock into a fountain; in the same place it is both light and dark at once, the sun now stands still, now goes backward. And all these contradictions of Nature happen for the welfare of Israel, purely at the command of Jehovah, who troubles himself about nothing but Israel.[2]

In contrast to many Christian interpreters, who tried to save the biblical

[1] *Ibid.*, p. 112.   [2] *Ibid.*, p. 113.

miracles from the onslaught of reason either by attributing them to natural causes or by giving them as nearly natural an explanation as possible (the feeding of the five thousand is merely 'an accelerated natural process'), Feuerbach rightly stressed that all these manifestations are *contrary* to nature.

How does this anti-natural element enter into the biblical stories? Feuerbach and other materialist thinkers down to the present day have a number of answers to this interesting question, and these answers are worthy of serious consideration. Because, however, Feuerbach constantly has a counterpart before his eyes – the reason-dominated Greek view of the world – and because he glorifies its free and, as it were, disinterested and theoretical attitude (an attitude which has also become the basic principle of modern science), a hard, polemical tone often enters into his account of the 'utilitarian' standpoint of biblical faith. This tone is sharpened by the rationalist's aversion to everything irrational and by his distaste for the mental limitations of the Old Testament's thinking, still confined within national limits. The historical and human significance of the 'utilitarian' attitude is more clearly recognized and more justly depicted in the tradition which runs from Karl Marx to Ernst Bloch. But Feuerbach emphasized certain characteristic features correctly.

1. Man distinguishes himself from the natural order. A slavish dependence on the forces of nature expresses itself in the star-worship and fertility-cults of the paganism surrounding ancient Israel. Abraham's departure from the land of his fathers also meant a departure from the centre of an archaic nature-religion. Moses' zeal in putting down the cult of the golden calf, the later prophetic dispute with the priests of Baal, the constant warning against a reversion to the service of idols and its barbaric customs – all this reflects Israel's consciousness that it has been called to freedom from nature and is bound to a higher loyalty – loyalty to a power which is pursuing higher purposes with mankind. In this way Israel, and every individual within Israel, acquired a new position in relation to all merely natural being, with its never-changing progression through the alteration of the seasons; Israel becomes a peculiar people among all the nations; its peculiarity, however, consists primarily not in special qualities which it already possessed, but in its orientation and progression towards a predetermined goal in the historical future. Setting out, exodus, mobility – that is the core of Israel's history. The departure from natural forms of being and natural human attachments is a manifestation of liberty – a liberty which also contrasts with the rationally enlightened, theoretical and aesthetic nature religion of late

Greek philosophy, which Feuerbach has in mind as the counterpart to the Jewish-Christian faith.

The contrast between the Christian and pagan attitude to nature became particularly obvious at the moment when Christianity entered upon a mental struggle with the philosophy and piety of the late ancient world. Devout pagans regarded Christians as blasphemers and atheists because they refused to honour the sun, moon and stars.

> Why should I mention that the argument by which [the Stoics] infer that all the heavenly bodies are gods tends to the opposite conclusion? For if they imagine that they are gods on this account, because they have their courses fixed and in accordance with reason, they are in error. For it is evident from this that they are not gods, because it is not permitted them to deviate from their prescribed orbits. But if they were gods, they would be borne higher and thither in all directions without any necessity, as living creatures on the earth, who wander hither and thither as they please, because their wills are unrestrained, and each is borne wherever inclination may have led it.[1]

This was the way in which the Christian writer Lactantius contrasted the two attitudes at the beginning of the fourth century. His statements might be taken as confirming Feuerbach's supposition that the anti-natural and arbitrary elements in the Old Testament stories, as well as the notion of special election, point to a particular conception of man – man as he sees himself – and of his relationship to nature, a conception which is characterized by the idea of liberty.

2. Man disposes freely over the realities of nature. This characteristic is also invested with a negative accent in Feuerbach's account. Compared with the pagan belief in the eternal existence of matter or in the primal, creative power of nature, from which all things take their organic growth, the biblical doctrine of the creation of the world from nothing contains a clear depreciation of nature. And in favour of what? In favour of, as it were, personal interest, an 'absolutely subjective, unlimited will'.[2] Creation out of nothing is the dogmatic expression for the dominating will, superior to nature, of the God of the Bible; but it is also the expression for the will of man. The story of creation has a polemical meaning highly offensive to pagan ears: the eternal stars are only finite and created; the sun, greatest of gods, is a mere lamp hung in the

[1] Lactantius, *Institutiones divinae*, II, 5, trans. by W. Fletcher, in *Works*, 2 vols. (Ante-Nicene Christian Library, Edinburgh, 1867).
[2] Feuerbach, *op. cit.*, p. 102.

heavens by the supernatural creator for the benefit of man; the glorious and mighty beasts and the fruitful earth are given over to the lordship of man. The creation story also points, in a pictorial, mythical manner, to a genuine historical goal in the future for the human race; but Feuerbach misunderstands its universal and basic anthropological significance because, as Marx rightly points out, he admits only 'theoretical' behaviour as being truly human, and reduces the 'utilitarian' point of view to an 'impure Jewish manifestation', that is to say, to a rationally undeveloped form, marred by national egoism (see his 1. *These über Feuerbach*).[1]

3. The man who sets himself apart from nature and takes up a ruling position with regard to it becomes conscious of himself as *mind* or *subjectivity*. If the ordering into an existing cosmic framework and behaviour such as 'imitation' then no longer represents the meaning and purpose of human existence, man must find his own path in the world. He becomes conscious of himself as distinct from existing conditions; he sees himself forced by his practical position in reality to seek and desire alteration or improvement – an adaptation of these conditions to the demands of the goal before him; in other words, he faces reality as independent, demanding subjectivity. Human life is not to take the same course as all other created things, and need not do so; a particular opportunity is open to it. This opportunity is expressed in the Bible by a series of dispensations contrary to nature and through the promises of future salvation made by Almighty God.

Apart from instinct, the brute has no other guardian spirit, no other Providence, than its senses or its organs in general. A bird which loses its eyes has lost its guardian angel; it necessarily goes to destruction if no miracle happens. We read indeed that a raven brought food to the prophet Elijah, but not (at least to my knowledge) that an animal was supported by other than natural means. But if a man believes that he also has no other Providence than the powers of his race – his senses and understanding, – he is in the eyes of religion, and of all those who speak the language of religion, an irreligious man; because he believes only in a natural Providence, and a natural Providence is in the eyes of religion as good as none. Hence Providence has relation essentially to men, and even among men only to the religious. 'God is the Saviour of all men, but especially of them that believe.' It belongs, like religion, only to man; it is intended to express

[1] For a further criticism of Feuerbach see Ernst Bloch, *Das Prinzip Hoffnung* (Frankfurt am Main, 1959) Pt. II, ch. 19, pp. 288ff. Cf. especially p. 303.

the essential distinction of man from the brute, to rescue man from
the tyranny of the forces of Nature. Jonah in the whale, Daniel in the
den of lions, are examples of the manner in which Providence distinguishes religious men from brutes. If therefore the Providence
which manifests itself in the organs with which animals catch and
devour their prey, and which is so greatly admired by Christian
naturalists, is a truth, the Providence of the Bible, the Providence of
religion, is a falsehood; and *vice versa*. What pitiable and at the same
time ludicrous hypocrisy is the attempt to do homage to *both*, to
Nature and the Bible at once! How does Nature contradict the Bible!
How does the Bible contradict Nature! The God of Nature reveals
himself by giving to the lion strength and appropriate organs in order
that, for the preservation of his life, he may in case of necessity kill
and devour even a human being; the God of the Bible reveals himself
by interposing his own aid to rescue the human being from the jaws
of the lion![1]

Having thus expounded the meaning of the great miracle 'the mystery
of Providence and creation out of nothing',[2] and having thereby shed
light on the background of all the miraculous phenomena in the biblical
story of salvation, Feuerbach takes a closer look at individual miracle
stories, analysing the way in which they originated.

What is a miracle? Three points are particularly important:

1. The miracle serves to satisfy human wishes.

Miracle feeds the hungry, cures men born blind, deaf, and lame,
rescues from fatal diseases, and even raises the dead at the prayer
of relatives. Thus it satisfies human wishes, – and wishes which,
though not always intrinsically like the wish for the restoration of the
dead, yet in so far as they appeal to miraculous power, to miraculous
aid, are transcendental, supernaturalistic.[3]

Miraculous agency, is agency directed to an end.[4]

2. A miracle satisfies human wishes in a magical way.

Wishes own no restraint, no law, no time; they would be fulfilled
without delay on the instant. And behold! Miracle is as rapid as a
wish is impatient. Miraculous power realizes human wishes in a
moment, at one stroke, without any hindrance. That the sick should

---

[1] Feuerbach, *op. cit.*, pp. 104f.   [2] *Ibid.*, title of chapter X.
[3] *Ibid.*, p. 129.   [4] *Ibid.*, p. 130.

become well is no miracle; but that they should become so immediately, at a mere word of command, – that is the mystery of miracle.[1]

3. Where do miracles take place? In the sphere where reality cannot deny the wish or delay its realization – where there is in fact no reality at all apart from the desirous and willing subject: in the imagination.

> The power of miracle is therefore nothing else than the power of the imagination.[2]

Miracle is a thing of the imagination; and on that very account is it so agreeable: for the imagination is the faculty which alone corresponds to personal feeling, because it sets aside all limits, all laws which are painful to the feelings, and thus makes objective to man the immediate, absolutely unlimited satisfaction of his subjective wishes.[3]

Up to this point Feuerbach's view of biblical miracles is clear enough, whether one greets it with agreement, with indignation, or merely with a faint feeling of discomfort. But a further question now urgently arises: how can one explain the fact that the people in the Bible, who do not otherwise give the impression of being visionaries and dreamers, had such enormously productive imaginations? Why did they brush aside the bounds of their reality by means of their belief in supernatural miracles? The question demands a subtle analysis of religious psychology and religious sociology. Feuerbach only gives a few hints of a psychological nature. These seem at first quite beside the point because his notion of egoism again plays an excessive part; but they none the less contain a rational core:

> To the Jews Nature was a mere means towards achieving the end of egoism, a mere object of will. But the ideal, the idol of the egoistic will is that Will which has unlimited command. . . It pains the egoist that the satisfaction of his wishes and need is only to be attained immediately, that for him there is a chasm between the wish and its realization, between the object in the imagination and the object in reality. Hence, in order to relieve this pain, to make himself free from the limits of reality, he supposes as the true, the highest being, one who brings forth an object by the mere I WILL. For this reason, Nature, the world, was to the Hebrews the product of a dictatorial word, of a categorical imperative, of a magic fiat.[4]

[1] *Ibid.*, p. 129.   [2] *Ibid.*, p. 130.   [3] *Ibid.*, p. 131.   [4] *Ibid.*, p. 115.

In reading this passage it is impossible to avoid a particular association: is this not a description of childish behaviour? Helplessness, limitation – but extensive wishes and energetic demands; an incapacity to take a comprehensive view of the real situation, with all its possibilities, and to choose a reasonable path – 'But I want it! everything! now!'; the cry for help and a reverent looking-up to the great man, the father, who can apparently do everything. . . This is, more or less, what one could read if one replaced the 'egoist' by needy but childishly naïve man. Here, the Godhead who can do everything would be, according to Feuerbach's interpretation, an ideal figure into which are read all the characteristics and capacities which seem to the needy person perfect, desirable or necessary because he feels their lack in his own actual situation. This Godhead would be the imaginary counterpart to man's own actual reality. The gods do everything which man cannot – or cannot yet – do. The study of human cultures shows that in his development from lower to higher forms of civilization man ascribes progressively fewer things to the gods and increasingly more to himself and his own capabilities. This could be taken as confirmation that Feuerbach's thesis is not devoid of truth. According to this thesis the periods when belief in miracles flourish would be periods in which the human mind is still in its childish stage, in which man is still unable to comprehend the operations of his world and sees himself as delivered up in a thousand ways to the operations of incomprehensible forces; whereas through increased understanding and control of the world he himself acquires the means of fulfilling his wishes. The supernatural world pales in proportion to the degree in which the natural one becomes conscious of itself and its potentialities. There is less and less prayer and more and more work.

Such reasoning belongs to the common stock of all materialist philosophy and can be developed indefinitely. There is no doubt that it is of general application to the history of civilization and that its consequences affect the Christian religion, just as they affect other expressions of the human spirit in history. But at the same time the thesis has obviously failed to grasp the unique feature or, more precisely, the unique activity of the supernatural God of the Jewish-Christian faith. For, in the face of Feuerbach's theory, one must abide by the question already put: there is, in varying degrees, limitation, need and consequently desire wherever there are people; but why are these desires so unruly, so excessive and so productive at precisely this point, in association with this particular religious tradition?

Feuerbach's suggested solution has recourse to the explanation which he offered for the mystery of the great, or first, miracle of Hebrew faith. Israel, he says in effect, is distinguished from its heathen environment by a unique religious consciousness; only this was hampered by a particularist and nationalist interest. 'If we let fall the limits of nationality, we obtain – instead of the Israelite – *man*.'[1] 'Christianity has spiritualized the egoism of Judaism into subjectivity (though even within Christianity this subjectivity is again expressed as pure egoism), has changed the desire for earthly happiness, the goal of the Israelitish religion, into the longing for heavenly bliss, which is the goal of Christianity.'[2] In Feuerbach subjectivity is still understood in purely psychological and subjectivistic terms and is hence suspected of standing in inevitable contradiction to rational objectivity. Here it means emotion, warmth, feeling; the unlimited, unrestrained, exaggerated and supernatural certainty of the truth and reality (indeed the sole reality) of inner experience. Feuerbach would therefore answer our question by saying: the spiritual witnesses of the Jewish-Christian religion unquestionably reveal a subjectivity which, with an otherwise unknown strength and ruthlessness, leaps over the limitations of this earthly world in the interests of the desired salvation. This is an observation which can be made by everyone. As for the reason for the development of this type of subjectivity – Feuerbach would say that here he could offer no further solution; others might perhaps be able to discover more.

Feuerbach points out that passionate religious faith, from the Primitive Church to the time of Luther and again in the pietistic revival movements of modern times, believed in and longed for the imminent end of the world; and his explanation of this fact is impressive evidence for the correctness of his hypothesis:

> Faith does not limit itself by the idea of a world, a universe, a necessity. For faith there is nothing but God, i.e., limitless subjectivity. Where faith rises the world sinks, nay, has already sunk into nothing. Faith in the real annihilation of the world, – in an immediately approaching, a mentally present annihilation of this world, a world antagonistic to the wishes of the Christian, is therefore a phenomenon belonging to the inmost essence of Christianity.[3]

It is easier to admit the justification of Feuerbach's hypothesis when one detaches the concepts of faith and subjectivity, as well as the concepts of wish and imagination, from the capricious element which is constantly suggested by his polemical mode of expression. What, then,

---

[1] *Ibid.*, p. 120.   [2] *Ibid.*, p. 122.   [3] *Ibid.*, p. 128.

does faith believe, when it opposes the reality of the existing world so ruthlessly that the latter is reduced to nothingness? What does the fantasy or imagination think of when it supposes that powerful acts issuing from the supernatural world take place on the ground of real history? Feuerbach is undoubtedly sincere when he repeatedly assures his readers that his purpose is not to annihilate religion by declaring it a mere chimera. His aim is rather 'a faithful, correct translation of the Christian religion out of the oriental language of imagery into plain speech',[1] as he says in the preface to the second edition of his book. 'But I by no means say (that were an easy task!): God is nothing, the Trinity is nothing, the Word of God is nothing, etc.; I only show that they are not *that* which the illusions of theology make them, – not foreign, but native mysteries, the mysteries of human nature. . . .'[2]

What faith objects to in reality – a limited, incomplete, bad reality – and what it holds to be truer and more real than the supposedly fixed course of reality is what it recognizes as absolutely determining – the absolute criterion: what ought to be, can be and will be! 'That which is to man the self-existent, the highest being, to which he can conceive nothing higher – that is to him the Divine being.'[3] God is the name given in the history of religion to whatever is experienced by man at a given time as the absolutely determining thing. 'The kingdom of God', or heaven, or paradise, are conditions in which there has ceased to be any opposition to the will of God in the human sphere. The thing for which the name God stands in religion at a particular time can be discovered from the predicates or characteristics attributed to him. In the early stages of mankind the gods are the ruthless forces of nature; in early Greek civilization they are the personifications of human powers, virtues and capacities – one has only to think of Homer's pantheon. In the late, monotheistic phase of religion, the faith of the Bible, *one* God stands for the reality of such possibilities as righteousness, love, power, freedom and subjectivity. Whatever is of absolute and essential significance for man himself is embodied in the persons of the gods and their actions.

From observations of this kind Feuerbach arrives at his famous thesis, which is already indicated in the phrase about the 'native mysteries': the gods are not extraneous and objectively existing beings outside the world of men; they are objectifications of human nature.

> Consciousness of God is self-consciousness, knowledge of God is self-knowledge. By his God thou knowest the man, and by the man his God; the two are identical.[4]

[1] *Ibid.*, p. xxxiii.   [2] *Ibid.*, p. xxxviii.   [3] *Ibid.*, p. 17.   [4] *Ibid.*, p. 12.

God is the manifested inward nature, the expressed self of a man, – religion the solemn unveiling of a man's hidden treasures, the revelation of his intimate thoughts, the open confession of his love-secrets.[1]

Every advance in religion is therefore a deeper self-knowledge.[2]

Feuerbach's thesis has been simplified into the sentence 'Man created God in his own image' (a phrase which was already current among the French materialists and encyclopaedists and which meets us in similar form in the aphorisms of the German philosopher Lichtenberg: 'God created man in his own image. This presumably means that man created God in his.').[3] This sentence is written on Feuerbach's monument and it does in fact represent a milestone, if not a turning point, in the history of theological thought. But, like other for polemical reasons deliberately biased and provocative statements of Feuerbach's, it is in danger of being misunderstood and trivialized. What is man doing when he believes in God? Is he believing in himself? What is he doing when he prays? Is he praying to himself? It would seem so. But how does man arrive at this nonsensical doubling of his own self? And how can the circumstance be explained that in real religious consciousness the gods represent lofty figures, endlessly superior to the individual in power and might?

Whatever man conceives to be true, he immediately conceives to be real ... because, originally, only the real is true to him. ... Now God is the nature of man regarded as absolute truth. ...[4]

Man does not stand above this his necessary conception; on the contrary, it stands above him; it animates, determines, governs him.[5]

The essential, the criterion, whatever is determining – even if it is also 'imagined' by man through the power of his fantasy – always manifests itself to him as the superior, sovereign, confronting and demanding will; it is so far outside, above or before the empirically limited individual that in the mythical period it can take on the fixed material form of a hypostasis, that is to say, of an active supernatural person. As Feuerbach says, whatever a man conceives to be true, he also conceives to be real. In the Christian religion this hypostasis takes the form of the holiness that reveals to man a cleft in his own being:

If God is really a different being from myself, why should his perfection trouble me? Disunion exists only between beings who are at

---

[1] *Ibid.*, pp. 12f.   [2] *Ibid.*, p. 13.
[3] Lichtenberg, *Reflections*, trans. by N. Alliston (London, 1908).
[4] Feuerbach, *op. cit.*, p. 19.   [5] *Ibid.*, p. 19.

variance, but who ought to be one, who can be one, and who conse-quently in nature, in truth, are one.[1]

That which is absolutely opposed to my nature, to which I am united by no bond of sympathy, is not even conceivable or perceptible by me. The Holy is in opposition to me only as regards the modifica-tions of my personality, but as regards my fundamental nature it is in unity with me. The Holy is a reproach to my sinfulness; in it I recog-nize myself as a sinner; but in so doing, while I blame myself, I acknowledge what I am not, but ought to be, and what, for that very reason, I, according to my destination, can be; for an 'ought' which has no corresponding capability, does not affect me, is a ludicrous chimera without any true relation to my mental constitution. But when I acknowledge goodness as my destination, as my law, I ack-nowledge it, whether consciously or unconsciously, as my own nature. Another nature than my own, one different in quality, cannot touch me. I can perceive sin as sin, only when I perceive it to be a contradic-tion of myself with myself – that is, of my personality with my funda-mental nature. As a contradiction of the absolute, considered as another being, the feeling of sin is inexplicable, unmeaning.[2]

Such sentences throw light on the peculiar fact that for the religious person God is both the closest and the most unattainably remote being. He is eternally and without limitation that which man ought to be according to the purpose of his nature. So far Feuerbach, who here by asserting the reality of the Idea, completely adopts the point of view of Idealistic philosophy.

The true sense of theology is anthropology;[3] but it becomes clear to the reader who works his way through Feuerbach's by no means easy and not always clear exposition to this central theme of his whole life and thought that anthropology, on which he now takes his stand, is a no less mysterious affair. The Christian theologian who is willing to accept Feuerbach's method of proceeding has among other things to consider the question of whether the reality which is summed up in biblical faith under the name of God has its right place in the context of Feuerbach's anthropology.

To sum up: according to Feuerbach, God, his heaven and his miracles are, in the particular material and objective form which they have in the original faith of the Bible, figures conceived by the imagination, though not mere chimera. We must differentiate if miracles are to be justly

<hr>

[1] *Ibid.*, p. 33.   [2] *Ibid.*, p. 28.   [3] *Ibid.*, p. xxxvii.

evaluated. We must differentiate and distinguish in our modern theology between two fundamental elements which are still intertwined in the biblical belief in miracles: on the one hand there is a tendency which is so fundamental that it divides man from the animals and other purely natural forms of life and drives him to seek, in his historical progress, for new ways of shaping and re-shaping the world; on the other hand we have the sometimes fantastic forms which embody man's ideas of the dominance and the liberty to which he is called by the God who goes before him, as the Israelites believed that he once went before them in pillars of cloud and fire.

'Religion is the dream of the human mind.'[1] It is a dream which stops at nothing short of the complete mastery of the mind over nature, the final triumph of humanity in the reality of this world. When the fantastic coating has been stripped away, what is left is by no means a void. In altered form – with sharpened perceptions, so to speak, the story continues: 'When I became a man, I gave up childish ways' (I Cor. 13.11).

---

[1] *Ibid.*, p. xxxix.

9 The History of Religions Approach

Folk-tale and miracle in the Old Testament

With the beginning of modern times, men began to feel the gap that divides contemporary speech and the contemporary world-picture from the language and world of the Old and New Testaments. The Bible lost its familiar aspect. Strange and incomprehensible features were discovered in it which correspond to nothing in the present-day world. Among these features are the presence of angels and demons from a heaven or hell; and also the miracles which accompany the activities of many biblical figures.

The more people became conscious of this, the more difficult it was for them to make contact with the stories and message of the Bible. Faith was frequently felt to be an effort; it increasingly involved believing in things that were offensive, apparently meaningless and impossible. An alienation of the modern consciousness from the world of the Bible was the result – often even a conscious turning away and revolt. Theology's new task sprang from this situation: it had to mediate between the sacred records of the past and the changed interpretation of reality in the contemporary world.

From the eighteenth century onwards it was usual to view the Bible with scientific eyes, like all the other features of our environment. More and more branches of scholarship directed their attention to this subject; and since the second half of the nineteenth century the study of the languages, literature and civilization of the ancient world has been augmented by the study of comparative religion – a development which led to the evolution of a particular 'history of religions' school within Protestant theology.

This step did not come about unheralded. A lively interest in the cultural history of ancient peoples became general in the educated world of the nineteenth century and led to intensive research into the documents relating to early art, religion and philosophy. Classical scholars went back to the pre-Socratic writers before the familiar classical Greek literature, making them accessible through new editions of the texts. Oriental scholars made a great find with the discovery of the Assyrian king Ashurbanipal's library of clay-tablets in Ninevah and with the decipherment of cuneiform script; among other things this brought to light the ancient Babylonian story of the creation and a flood saga which went back to pre-biblical times and seemed to be related to the biblical accounts. The ancient world of Hellenism (the religious environment of the New Testament) also became known in outline. In this way the question of miracle, as well as other theological problems, appeared in a new light.

The books of the Old and New Testaments are not alone in telling miracle stories – this observation forms the starting point of the investigation based on the study of comparative religions. Myths and miracles of sometimes striking similarity are to be found in Indian, Persian, Babylonian and Egyptian sacred traditions, as well as in the late Hellenistic world. The unique or absolute character of Christianity can no longer simply be dogmatically asserted in comparison; it must be proved – if this is possible – by an unprejudiced examination of multifarious historical documents.

> For more than two thousand years man has attempted to comprehend Holy Scripture; yet who would dare to say that he has penetrated its depths! Every age has seen it in a different light. For our fathers it was a homogeneous unity, a direct utterance of God. We are aware of the variegated history to which it witnesses. Earlier readers entered ingenuously into these writings and constantly rediscovered what was best in themselves there. We strive, through the application of the finest historical distinctions, to discover the meaning which the ancient writers themselves had in mind; yet we would not have our forefathers surpass us in their reverent love of this majestic book ...

With these words Hermann Gunkel (1862–1932), one of the most prominent representatives of the 'history of religions' school, distinguished the new approach from the old. The words we have quoted are to be found in the great popular commentary, *Die Schriften des Alten Testaments, in Auswahl neu übersetzt und für die Gegenwart erklärt*,[1] which appeared in 1911 (Göttingen). The common aim of the editors is 'to open

[1] 'The Old Testament Writings, selected, newly translated and explained for the modern reader'.

the way for a vital and historical understanding of the oldest documents of Christianity'. The motto for the New Testament section ('The New Testament writings newly translated and explained for the modern reader') is a saying of Goethe's:

> I am convinced that the Bible will always appear more beautiful the more we understand it – that is to say, the more we observe and realize that every word which we accept in a general sense and apply specially to ourselves, bore, under certain temporal and local circumstances, a peculiar, special, direct, and individual reference.[1]

How was a historical understanding of the Bible achieved and what was the result? Hermann Gunkel (to take an example from his Old Testament investigations) starts from simple observations which every reader of the Old Testament has already made for himself; for example, the fact that in certain passages animals are made to talk.

In ancient times it was generally believed that animals could speak and that some of them were extremely wise. Thus the serpent knows the nature of the tree of knowledge and, malicious as he is, tries to stir man up against God (Gen. 3). But even Balaam's ass sees the angel who threatens his master with a drawn sword sooner than Balaam himself, man of God though he is. The ass, which turn asides from the path at the right moment, acts reasonably, whereas Balaam shows his foolishness by striking her. The ass then defends herself verbally and Balaam answers without any sign of surprise, entering quite innocently into conversation (Num. 22.23ff.); in the same way Adam and Eve in the Garden of Eden are not in the least startled when the snake speaks to them.

Where else are talking beasts to be found?

The acceptance of talking animals as a natural event is a marked characteristic of the folk-tale; Little Red Riding Hood is not at all surprised when the wolf speaks to her; nor is Achilles astonished when his horse Xanthus tells him of the nearness of his death; nor is the ancient Egyptian folk-tale hero Bata, when his cows warn him that his jealous brother is lying in wait for him with a knife behind the door. It is a common folk-tale motif for men to be warned by animals in this way.

Das Märchen im Alten Testament is the title of Hermann Gunkel's

---

[1] Goethe, *Maximen und Reflexionen* V; trans. by W. B. Rönnfeldt, in *Criticisms, Reflections, and Maxims of Goethe* (London, 1897), p. 211.

book on the subject. It appeared in 1917 in a series for the general reader called *Religionsgeschichtliche Volksbucher für die deutsche christliche Gegenwart*,[1] and is still interesting reading. It is worth following up Gunkel's examples of folk-tale motifs[2] in order to see what results emerge from the comparison of biblical and non-biblical material.

In ancient folk-literature animals seem more receptive to the promptings of the super-sensory world than man. It is an important theme in later hagiography that animals refuse to touch the body of a saint that is thrown to them. The same thing happens to Daniel in the lions' den (Dan. 6.16–28).

> In the same way Jonah's famous fish obeyed the divine command to swallow the prophet and spit him up again on land three days later (Jonah 2.1–11). . . . And the old saga of Elijah already contains the familiar feature that the prophet is fed by ravens who bring him bread and meat (I Kings 17.4–6). This too is a common folk-tale theme, the theme of the helpful beasts.[3]

> Folk-meditations have frequently centred on particularly noticeable animal characteristics, which they have tried to explain by some little story. There are stories to explain why the dove complains, why the cuckoo has its particular song, why the cock crows, why the magpie is so curious, and so on. The explanations are on the lines that the tortoise was carried up to the sky by the eagle and was dropped – hence its cracked back; that the raven was cursed because it chattered so much, hence its blackness; and so on.

Gunkel even finds an 'aetiological' folk-tale motif of this kind (that is, a motif which gives the *reason* for a thing – from the Greek *aitia*) in the story of the cursing of the snake in the Garden of Eden.

> Cursed are you above all cattle,
> and above all wild animals;
> upon your belly you shall go,
> and dust you shall eat
> all the days of your life.
> I will put enmity between you and the woman,
> and between your seed and her seed;
> he shall bruise your head,
> and you shall bruise his heel (Gen. 3.14f.).

---

[1] Series II, vol. 1, Nr. 23–26, 2nd ed. (Tübingen, 1921).
[2] Gunkel, *op. cit.*, p. 31.   [3] *Ibid.*, pp. 33f.

The considerations which led to this curse were more or less the following. People had noticed the uncanny characteristics which differentiate the snake from all the other beasts of the field. All others have feet – it is only the snake which creeps on its belly. And its wretched food is also unusual; for it was generally thought that the snake had to feed on dust. But the ponderings of ancient times were directed particularly to the cruel and never-ending struggle between snake and man. No other beast is so hated by man; wherever he comes across it he tries to crush it with his foot. The snake, however, revenges itself in its own way, striking out at man's heel whenever it has the opportunity. People in early times wondered about the reason for the snake's strange fate. And they arrived at the answer that God himself had cursed the snake in olden times. Therefore – it was the logical conclusion – the snake must once have committed a sin; and they lighted on this sin by setting the motif into the story of the Garden of Eden. Because the demonic beast once led man astray in the days of his innocence it was . . . cursed by God.[1]

Apart from the snake theme, the story of the Garden of Eden contains other motifs familiar from the folk-tales and sagas of various peoples – for example, the motifs of the tree of life, the proving of man by a divine being, and the disobeyed command. 'You may freely eat of every tree of the garden; but of the tree of the knowledge of good and evil you shall not eat, for in the day that you eat of it you shall die' (Gen. 2.16f.). Everything is permitted with one exception. This motif is also the basis of one of Grimm's well-known folk-tales, the story of Mary's child:

> 'Here are the keys to the thirteen doors of heaven,' says the queen of heaven to the child. 'You may open twelve of them and look at the splendour within; but you must not open the thirteenth door, to which this little key belongs. On no account unlock this last door, for if you do so it will bring you unhappiness.'

The idea of paradise is familiar enough to early literature:

> It was no doubt natural that a people forced to fight tooth and nail for its existence should indulge itself in imagination with fantasies of a life of purest happiness in which every wish is fulfilled – especially wishes of a material kind. Every civilization has had its stories of a primal period of bliss.[2]

[1] *Ibid.*, pp. 38f.   [2] *Ibid.*, p. 153.

The reader may now object that it is not surprising to find the imaginative and fictional elements typical of the folk-tale in a narrative like the story of the Garden of Eden; for this is in any case unhistorical and belongs by its very nature to the realm of myth. But what is the position with regard to the historical books of the Old Testament, which deal with the rise of the great prophets and kings, i.e., with historical personages?

The First Book of Samuel, ch. 17, tells the well-known story of the rise of the shepherd boy David to be page at the court of King Saul. By chance David arrives on the battlefield where Israel is at odds with the Philistines, and there experiences the challenge of the giant Goliath:

> He had a helmet of bronze on his head, and he was armed with a coat of mail, and the weight of the coat was five thousand shekels of bronze. And he had greaves of bronze upon his legs, and a javelin of bronze slung between his shoulders. And the shaft of his spear was like a weaver's beam, and his spear's head weighed six hundred shekels of iron; and his shield-bearer went before him. . . . The man who kills him, the king will enrich with great riches, and will give him his daughter . . .

David hears the bystanders say, and he immediately makes his decision. Without any arms except for his shepherd's sling, he fells the giant, cuts off his head with his own sword and triumphantly brings his trophy to the king. This story is rich in folk-tale elements, as Gunkel and Gressmann point out.

> His brothers sneer at him as a paltry creature, but while they are still sneering he has achieved his master stroke. He is led in triumph before the king but – here we must supplement – the king rues his promise and the hero who was so near to his highest goal sees his expectations disappointed. As soon as the names are removed from the story the folk-tale motifs shine out clear and unembellished. The ten-foot tall giant who is slain by an inexperienced youth, the youngest son who must stay at home and is despised by his brothers until he completely outdoes them through his bravery and good fortune, the shepherd boy who suddenly has the opportunity to become the king's son-in-law, the king who promises him his daughter and fails to keep his word – all these are typical elements in the folk-tale, especially the tale of success.[1]

[1] Hugo Gressmann, *Die Schriften des Alten Testaments* Pt. II, vol. 1 (Göttingen, 1910), p. 79.

In folk-tales, giants boast of their immense strength but a weak little creature, like Grimm's tailor, dispatches them by means of his nimble wits and good fortune.

The behaviour of the prophet is not free from folk-tale motifs and elements of the marvellous either. The analogue here is the tale of enchantment.

> According to ancient beliefs, magic power belonged particularly to the body of the enchanter himself. Thus we have the Israelite story of how Elijah stretched his body three times over the dead son of the widow of Zarephath, thereby bringing him back to life (I Kings 17.21). The magical element appears even more clearly in the related Elisha saga; on a similar occasion Elisha stretched himself seven times [see Gunkel's explanation in his book] over the boy, mouth to mouth, eyes to eyes, hands to hands (II Kings 4.34). Revivals of the dead are frequent in pagan enchantment stories. The fact that here the miracle had to take place in secret (the prophet first shut the door of the room) is particularly reminiscent of the pagan enchanter. Similarly the way in which the man of God lays himself on the body of the boy also occurs in a Babylonian story.[1]

The man of God's body retains its miraculous power even after death. 'When a dead man is laid in Elijah's grave and touches his skeleton, the man is restored to life (II Kings 13.21). Similar miracles, transferred to Christian saints, are extremely frequent.'[2]

The magic power can also transfer itself to *objects* connected with the man of God – for example, Elijah's mantle.

> When the prophet struck the River Jordan with this mantle, the water divided so that he could cross dry-shod (II Kings 2.8). He acquires his disciple Elisha by throwing his mantle over him without saying a word; and Elisha has to follow him immediately, willy-nilly (I Kings 19.19ff.). . . . Elijah left Elisha this mantle as his most precious legacy and it continued to prove its power in Elisha's hands (II Kings 2.13f.).[3]

Even today we cannot imagine a magician without his magic wand, and even the Egyptian magicians who competed in sorcery with Moses, and were defeated by him, already had wands and so did Moses himself.

> When the man of God throws this wand on the ground it changes into a crocodile (Ex. 7.8ff.). When he strikes the Nile with it the river

---

[1] Gunkel, *op. cit.*, p. 97.   [2] *Ibid.*, p. 99.   [3] *Ibid.*

turns to blood (Ex. 7.14ff.). When he stretches it over the water, frogs come up and cover the whole of Egypt [Ex. 8.1ff.]. He strikes the dust on the ground with it and the dust, whirling up, turns into mosquitoes [Ex. 8.6]. When Moses raises it at the Reed Sea the sea divides so that he can go through dry-shod (Ex. 14.16). When he strikes a rock with it the rock gushes forth water (Ex. 17.5ff.). When the 'rod of God' is raised it secures victory for the hosts of Israel; but as soon as the weary Moses lets it drop the Amalekites win the upper hand, until finally two companions support Moses' arms (Ex. 17.8ff.). Here, therefore, victory is magically linked with the raising of the staff. In the same way a contemporary Finnish folk-tale tells of a magic wand; when one end of it is waved the enemy falls; when the other is waved one's own soldiers are restored to life.[1]

All in all, the men of God in Israel have power over sun and moon, seas and rivers, sickness, life and death. At the same time – Gunkel stresses this in several places – the way in which the spirit of the Israelite religion grappled with such magical concepts and stories must not be overlooked.

> Only certain material was taken over; other things, which were held to be superstitious or absurd, were rejected . . . and even what was taken over was purified as far as possible. Thus the material was so shaped that the god is not compelled to act by the magic; rather, he himself gives his plenipotentiary the *command* to act in a certain way; when this is done God will perform the miracle. Or the magic act may be accompanied by a prayer: 'O Lord my God, I pray thee, let this child's soul come into him again' (I Kings 17.21 AV); what follows is the result of this prayer: And the Lord heard the voice of Elijah; and the soul of the child came into him again. . . . On other occasions the magical act has disappeared, being replaced entirely by a prayer.[2]

In spite of such 'spiritualizations' (which incidentally do not permeate the whole of the material), Gunkel concludes that the relationship of these stories to primitive enchantment tales is unmistakable.

In conclusion, mention may be made of a clear folk-tale motif from the story of the prophets Elijah and Elisha; they give the poor and needy magic objects which save them from dying of hunger. 'Once upon a time there was a poor but good girl who lived alone with her mother. They had nothing left to eat, so the girl went out into the forest, where she

---

[1] *Ibid.*, pp. 99f. [2] *Ibid.*, p. 102.

met an old woman. The old woman knew what was troubling the child and gave her a pot. When she said to the pot, "boil, pot", it cooked a good, sweet porridge . . .' – so the brothers Grimm tell. At the gates of the city of Zarephath, the prophet Elijah met a widow gathering wood, who had only a handful of flour in a jar and a little oil in a cruse for herself and her son: ' "And now, I am gathering a couple of sticks, that I may go in and prepare it for myself and my son, that we may eat it and die." ' On God's instructions, Elijah commands her to prepare a meal for him first of all, and to have no anxiety for herself. 'And she went and did as Elijah said; and she, and he, and her household ate for many days. The jar of meal was not spent, neither did the cruse of oil fail, according to the word of the Lord which he spoke by Elijah' (I Kings 17.8–16; see also II Kings 4.1–7).

It is true that folk-tales in an unalloyed form can hardly be found in the Old Testament – consequently the expositors only speak of the *motifs* which have been woven into different contexts. In the case of the stories of David and of Elijah, for example, what were originally folk-tale motifs are transferred from nameless and timeless folk-tale heroes to historical personages, so that in this case the stories might be more accurately described as sagas. The universal figures of the shepherd boy and the giant become David and the Philistine Goliath of Gath. Perhaps an Israelite really did once defeat a Philistine prince of giant strength called Goliath, as is suggested in II Sam. 21.19.

A saga frequently incorporates historical memory, in however obscure and distorted a form; or, rather, it links up with historical events. What connects it with the folk-tales and stories of the gods that we call myths is the poetic nature of the narrative. Exact history aims to present facts as they really are, unvarnished and without prejudice. A poetic narrative differs from it through its free mixture of fantasy and its less strict purpose. Gunkel says that its intention is not to give information about reality but to tell a story as one likes to hear it, to give pleasure, to touch the emotions, wake enthusiasm, or at least rouse sympathy with what is being related. 'Such invented stories have accompanied mankind from earliest times; they are, together with poetry, generally the oldest material that has descended to posterity from the spiritual culture of the peoples.'[1]

One inescapable question arises from the 'history of religions' approach: is it permissible to put the Bible on a level with the documents which witness to the civilizations of other peoples? Where is the unique

[1] *Ibid.*, p. 2.

character which in Christian eyes distinguishes the stories of the Bible from folk-tales and sagas of different origin and makes them 'the Word of God'? That the editors of the commentary have reckoned with this question is shown by the foreword to the New Testament exegesis:

> The contributors are assured that their work is free of any regard for theological schools and parties. Their aim was to put aside all preconceived ideas and to let the New Testament make its own impact on them; and in the same way they would wish to show the reader also the thing itself, as it really is. They wish to help him to read the New Testament with his own eyes, not through the spectacles of an acquired familiarity. If the view which is here expressed is not the traditional one, this is only because the Bible itself is different from the dogmatic theories about it with which we have grown up. Much that will have seemed to the reader a matter of course will therefore now become a matter of doubt; much that is dear to him will disappear; but instead he will gain much that he did not know before; above all, what is essential and eternal in these writings will become evident, when once we have recognized what is temporal and nonessential . . .

Does Gunkel's treatise really fulfil this promise? That is to say, does the objective and comparative study of a subject like folk-tale in the Old Testament show that the biblical treatment is special or unique? Gunkel has already given the answer in part, by speaking of a purification and spiritualization of the folk-tale material. He brings out, for example, that the biblical stories show a tendency to play down the magic, to dispense with magical acts and to replace them by the mighty word of Yahweh.

The very core of folk-tale has also to undergo severe change. In many passages it can be seen that the God Yahweh, who tolerates no association with any subordinate gods, drives out the spirits, witches and devils of the folk-tale or degrades them to the rank of his servants, so that one can speak of an almost complete elimination of the demonic polytheism of the folk-tale by the religion of Yahweh. Thus, considered against its background in the history of religion, the Old Testament becomes a document revealing the religious struggles of a nation's childhood. Where is God? Where is real power to be found? These questions had to be decided and they are answered in the texts.

A religious-historical process displays itself in these documents, deriving as they do from varying periods. It is a process in which Israel's conception of God itself has its part, since this was by no means fixed once and for all from the very beginning. Among the strongest impressions communicated by research into the history of religion is the sense of archaic strangeness which clings to the picture of God in the earliest texts – when the God Yahweh is described (even under other divine names) as a being who is to be met with on mountains, at springs and trees, who speaks through a thorn-bush, or through fire and wind; he is a God who mingles with men in disguise, alone or with companions; he can fall upon them atrociously and can equally show himself to be their friend; he sends floods and rains fire and personally shuts the door of the ark on Noah.

A long and bloody road had to be travelled from a Canaanite cult, when men sacrificed their own children to the gods, down to the God Yahweh, who enjoins the sacrifice of animals instead of sons (as is clear in the story of the sacrifice of Isaac); and it is a long road again from this God to the God of the prophets who proclaims, through the mouth of Hosea:

I desire steadfast love and not sacrifice,
the knowledge of God, rather than burnt offerings (Hos. 6.6).

The reader who does not close his eyes to the features of archaic and indeed barbaric strangeness in the oldest layers of the biblical tradition will recognize all the more clearly the unique character of the view of God and man towards which Israel advanced during the process of its history. A deliberately historical approach, therefore, does not result in a levelling of the Old Testament to the world of the heathen religions; on the contrary, a new understanding of its uniqueness emerges.

The question of miracle as such is not expressly raised in Gunkel's investigation, but indirectly it is pursued whenever the folk-tale and fantastic elements are under consideration. It is answered by the stress on the *poetic*, that is to say the *unhistorical* form of the stories in which miracles occur. It was also important to establish that miracles certainly do not represent a specifically biblical or Christian element, for they are to be found outside the Bible and, seen as literature, belong to a widespread type of ancient folk-tradition. Why they were taken over into the Jewish and Christian religion, and why, as Gunkel puts it, Jews and Christians crown their heroes with flowers plucked from the meads of folk-tale, is a question that has not yet received an answer.

10 The Form-critical Approach

Miracles in the world of the New Testament

The second-century writer Lucian of Samosata, the author of witty scenes of social satire in which he holds a mirror up to his time, introduces the reader to a discussion about miracles. One of the circle is a sceptic; in order to confute him, the others tell extraordinary stories of events which they have allegedly experienced personally.

'I will tell you of a strange thing that happened when I was a boy of fourteen or so,' says one of them. 'Some one came and told my father that Midas, his gardener, a study fellow and a good workman, had been bitten that morning by an adder, and was now lying prostrate, mortification having set in in the leg. He had been tying the vine-branches to the trellis-work, when the reptile crept up and bit him on the great toe, getting off to its hole before he could catch it; and he was now in a terrible way. Before our informant had finished speaking, we saw Midas being carried up by his fellow servants on a stretcher: his whole body was swollen, livid and mortifying, and life appeared to be almost extinct. My father was very much troubled about it; but a friend of his who was there assured him there was no cause for uneasiness. "I know of a Babylonian," he said, "what they call a Chaldaean; I will go and fetch him at once, and he will put the man right." To make a long story short, the Babylonian came, and by means of an incantation expelled the venom from the body, and restored Midas to health; besides the incantation, however, he used a splinter of stone chipped from the monument of a virgin; this he applied to Midas's foot. . . . (Midas, I may mention, actually picked up the stretcher on which he had been brought, and took it off with him into the vineyard! And it was all done by an incantation and a bit of stone.)'[1]

[1] Lucian, *Philopseudes* (*The Liar*), trans. by H. W. and F. G. Fowler in *Works of Lucian*, 4 vols. (Oxford, 1905).

Who would not immediately think, on reading this, of the story of the healing of the paralysed man in the Gospels – 'one sick of the palsy' as he is called in the Authorized Version? A paralytic is brought to Jesus (being let down through the roof of a house, because it was impossible to reach him any other way) and is healed with the words, 'Rise, take up your pallet and go home.' The passage goes on, 'And he rose, and immediately took up the pallet and went out before them all; so that they were all amazed and glorified God, saying, "We never saw anything like this!" ' (Mark 2.11f.). In both Lucian and the Gospel, the final sentence serves to cement the immense impression which the miraculous healing has made on the onlookers. Anyone who himself carries out the bed on which he was brought in has certainly been healed. But does this mean that there were also miraculous healings outside the New Testament, performed by pagan miracle-workers, such as the Babylonian in Lucian's story?

This would be a premature conclusion. In order to evaluate the matter correctly one must know that Lucian's little book, *Philopseudes* (The Liar), is a satire. We cannot be sure that he was thinking in particular of Christian miracle stories – he was writing a bare hundred years after the composition of the Gospels and at a period when the miracle-literature of the non-biblical apocryphal Gospels and Acts was at its height in the Christian churches. Lucian's mockery applies to miracle-literature in general, since this was evidently widespread throughout the late ancient world and appeared both reactionary and pernicious to a few enlightened spirits like himself. Lucian is a scoffer. So his little miracle story is meant, so to speak, as a warning, like many others which he tells. It is a parody, not a serious account.

But a parody is only effective where the form of the thing mocked is imitated as closely as possible – at most with a slight exaggeration of the salient features. Thus Lucian's stories, in spite of their critical intention, are an excellent source of information about the ancient world's belief in miracles and the forms in which this was expressed.

If one compares the act of healing in the two stories one is struck by the fact that the Babylonian miracle-worker needs a piece from a virgin's tombstone, as well as a magic formula, in order to achieve his effect; in the Gospel account the mere word of Jesus is enough. In other New Testament stories, however, curious manipulations are also described. Jesus takes the sick person's hand, or puts his finger in the ears of the deaf and dumb man, or even spits in the eyes of the blind man (Mark 7.33; 8.23). This last feature is further accentuated in the Gospel of

John: 'He spat on the ground and made clay of the spittle and anointed the man's eyes with the clay' (John 9.6). If we then look again at the Hellenistic miracle accounts – the accounts which are intended to be taken seriously, not the satirical ones – we discover that the moment of manipulation stands decisively and strikingly at the centre of the story. The Jewish historian Josephus reports the exorcism of a demon which was, so to speak, officially recorded because it took place in the presence of the Emperor Vespasian and his court. Eleazar – that was the name of the miracle-worker – freed a great number of Roman soldiers from evil spirits, using the established rules of an art which was supposed to be derived from the wise king Solomon.

> The manner of the cure was this: Eleazar put a ring that had a root of one of those sorts mentioned by Solomon to the nostrils of the demoniac, after which he drew out the demon through his nostrils; and when the man fell down immediately, he abjured him to return into him no more, making still mention of Solomon, and reciting the incantations which he composed. And when Eleazar would persuade and demonstrate to the spectators that he had such a power, he set a little way off a cup or basin full of water, and commanded the demon, as he went out of the man, to overturn it, and thereby to let the spectators know that he had left the man; and when this was done, the skill and wisdom of Solomon was shown very manifestly.[1]

Compared with this, the works of exorcism reported of Jesus are depicted with great reserve. The usual artifices of the ancient miracle-worker are very sparingly ascribed to Jesus.

It would seem to be a concession to the style of the non-Christian miracle story, however, when Mark makes Jesus speak the efficacious words in Aramaic, once when bringing someone back from the dead and once at the healing of a deaf and dumb person: *Talitha cumi* (little girl, I say to you, arise) and *Ephphatha* (be opened) (Mark 5.41; 7.34). It is true that Jesus spoke Aramaic, but everything else that he said is consistently translated into Greek (apart from the last saying on the cross, which is a quotation from one of the Psalms); it is only here that the original is preserved, which gives the phrases the character of some strange adjuration. This peculiarity of style derives unmistakably from the evangelist and is only found in Mark. In the actual scene – if it ever actually took place – this impression of a magic formula in a foreign tongue cannot have been

[1] Josephus, *Antiquities of the Jews*, VIII, 2.5, trans. by William Whiston (1737; reprinted Philadelphia, Toronto, 1957).

given, since Jesus spoke the Aramaic dialect familiar to all and did not suddenly change over to a different language.

The non-Christian miracle story occasionally influenced the New Testament account in another respect as well. In Josephus' story, the demon on its expulsion knocks over a vessel of water, put there for the purpose, as a proof to all those present that the exorcism has been successful. In other ancient miracle stories the demon also commits some deed of destruction on its expulsion; for example, in a story of Philostratus, who describes the activity of the miracle-worker Apollonius of Tyana, it overturns a statue. In at least one of the Jesus scenes (Luke 8.26ff.), this feature is clearly recognizable: after the expulsion of the demons at the Gerasene lake the homeless spirits enter a herd of swine and drive them into the water.

When a large number of ancient miracle stories are compared, it becomes clear that certain stylistic characteristics are common to the genre; true, they are not all to be found in every individual story, but as a whole they give the genre an unmistakable stamp.

The miracle story begins with an introduction or exposition, in which the situation of the sick person is described – the seriousness or length of the illness – how the doctors have tried in vain to cure it and how hopeless the case seems. A second section follows with the miraculous healing, which is often accompanied by particular manipulations and sayings. If we are dealing with the exorcism of a demon we are frequently told that the demon senses the presence of its master and begins to argue with him, or that it makes some request. This is the case in the genuine folk-tale of the exorcism at the Gerasene lake, where the demon cries out, 'What have you to do with me, Jesus, Son of the Most High God? I adjure you by God, do not torment me,' and begs the favour of being allowed to enter into the herd of swine (Mark 5). It is also characteristic that the miracle is not really visible even to the eye-witnesses; occasionally witnesses are not even allowed to be present during the actual action and are only allowed in when the miracle has been successfully performed. The third section and the close of the miracle story contains a demonstration of its success (the demon performs some work of destruction, the sick person gets up, the person who has been raised from the dead is given something to eat, etc.) and describes the reaction of the people: those present express their bewildered and joyful astonishment and praise the author of the marvellous deed.

Thus the ancient Hellenistic, Jewish and Christian miracle stories all show the same basic stylistic elements – the form is the same in all cases.

Have Jesus' miracles, then, nothing unique to show in substance either? It is frequently stated in theology that Jesus' miracles are to be accounted as the signs of divine power; in that case, were all these Hellenistic miracle-workers also men of God? Were they divinely commissioned, and do they have a claim to the same dignity as Jesus? The devout Christian would recoil from this conclusion – but he must then be able to say why he does not want Christ to be indistinguishable from the magicians of the ancient world.

Here a criterion is necessary which cannot be arrived at from a purely formal comparison. Has New Testament scholarship evolved methods of investigation which take one any further? The answer which has been given to this question since the 1920's is summed up in the words 'form criticism'; the 'history of religions' school, which flourished round about 1910, was followed by a 'form critical' school of New Testament studies. The school developed along the lines of an inner logic. From the nineteenth century onwards, researchers into the history of religion uncovered and published a mass of non-Christian material. When this is compared with the biblical texts, certain common linguistic or literary genres emerge which recur in the literature of all peoples: the song, the folk-tale, the saga, the legend, the myth, the *novelle*, to mention only some of the most important. These were first discovered in the course of research into the Old Testament, but they also play a part in the New.

Die Formgeschichte der Evangelien[1] is the title of the book which introduced this approach into New Testament scholarship in 1919. Its author was the New Testament scholar Martin Dibelius. In 1921 the book was joined by Rudolf Bultmann's *Geschichte der synoptischen Tradition*.[2] Today both books are classical text-books in the field of New Testament studies. The word 'history' (*Geschichte*) in the titles points to the fact that not only are the findings of linguistic forms enumerated (for example, sayings, speeches, credal formulae, parables, debates, legends and miracle stories) but that the aim is new insight into the history of the Primitive Church, in the midst of which, after long oral transmission, the Gospels received the written form in which we know them. The tradition did not come into being all at once; it grew, under the various influences of the surrounding Hellenistic world and determined by the situation of the primitive churches, to whom it

[1] ET by B. Lee-Woolf, *From Traditions to Gospel* (London, 1934).
[2] ET by John Marsh, *The History of the Synoptic Tradition* (Oxford and New York, 1963).

served as literature for their own and missionary use. The tradition itself has a history.

How does this affect the question of miracle? A comparison of the forms of miracle stories only goes a certain distance. The stories in the form in which we have them are clearly literary compositions, the work of the evangelists who, as we have seen, drew on the narrative method of the folk-literature of the time. But the stylistic treatment does not exclude the possibility that real events formed the basis of the stories. These events would then have been incorporated into an existing literary pattern – just as today, for example, the police report of a road accident conforms to a certain style. The fact is undoubtedly true, but its description is groomed for a certain purpose.

Can a form-critical analysis offer more than this? Can it go behind the completed structure and discover how a miracle story *originates*? This is possible in certain places. Luke's story of Peter's miraculous draught is an impressive example. Here the calling of the first disciples, Peter among them, is described in a brief scene. The fishermen have fished all night but have caught nothing. Jesus enters the ship and makes them let down their nets once more.

> And when they had done this, they enclosed a great shoal of fish; and as their nets were breaking, they beckoned to their partners in the other boat to come and help them. And they came and filled both the boats, so that they began to sink. But when Simon Peter saw it, he fell down at Jesus' knees, saying, 'Depart from me, for I am a sinful man, O Lord.' For he was astonished, and all that were with him, at the catch of fish which they had taken; and so also were James and John, sons of Zebedee, who were partners with Simon. And Jesus said to Simon, 'Do not be afraid; henceforth you will be catching men.' And when they had brought their boats to land, they left everything and followed him' (Luke 5.1–11).

If we compare the way in which the evangelists Matthew and Mark describe the calling of the first disciples (Matt. 4.18; Mark 1.16), we shall notice that the miraculous draught is not mentioned at all. But it is the same disciples who are called and, since they can only have been called once, the scene must have been identical.

Since we know that Matthew and Luke were using the earlier Gospel of Mark as source, it is clear that it is merely the literary imagination of Luke which has made a miracle take place here. There is no need to suppose any fraudulent intention; no writer can be forbidden to use his imagination. The process is also completely understandable; Luke was probably inspired to paint his vivid scene through a pictorial phrase which he found in his source: 'Follow me and I will make you fishers of men.' Since Luke wrote his Gospel towards the end of the first century, he already knew at the time of writing that Peter was to become the most important of all the disciples after Jesus' death; so his story of the calling takes the form of a particularly abundant catch of fish – a pictorial and proleptic description of Peter's marvellous missionary success. The story has a clear point – no-one needs to feel deceived; one must only have a correct approach to the evangelist's method of working. But of course the event he describes is not 'historical'. Anyone who clings to its historicity is in fact barring the way to the real meaning which it was Luke's intention to communicate. Luke's story is not a historical one but demands what we can perhaps best describe today as a symbolic or figurative interpretation.

A second example which shows the way in which a miracle story came into being is the scene of Jesus' arrest in the Garden of Gethsemane. Mark reports that one of Jesus' disciples drew his sword and cut off the ear of one of the high priest's servants. Matthew describes the event in exactly the same way, but adds some words of Jesus: 'Put your sword back into his place; for all who take the sword will perish by the sword' (Mark 14.47; Matt. 26.51ff.). In the Gospel of Luke the passage is as follows: 'And one of them struck the slave of the high priest and cut off his right ear. But Jesus said, "No more of this!" And he touched his ear and healed him' (Luke 22.50f.). The miracle is only related by Luke. Again, the relationship to the source shows quite clearly that he must have added it of his own accord. As Luke himself states in the prologue to his Gospel, he was not an eye-witness – not one of the evangelists was a disciple in the strictest sense of the word – and since he wrote later than Mark he had certainly no better sources of information than the earlier evangelist. Otherwise he would not have needed to follow Mark's account so closely in other passages. Also, if the miracle were a historical fact it is incomprehensible that the other evangelists did not transmit it; they would surely not have failed to take this opportunity to show Jesus' peaceable attitude. Matthew's additional words have exactly the same trend as Luke's miracle of healing, and the passage in the Sermon on the Mount about loving one's enemies shows that the episode in any case fits the content of Jesus' preaching. Here, too, therefore, Luke introduced the miracle on his own accord in order to show Jesus' peace-loving nature graphically or pictorially, not merely rhetorically.

The passage shows something else as well: the later accounts give an apparently more extensive and more exact account than the earlier ones. For example, Luke reports that it was the *right* ear which was cut off, a detail not mentioned in Mark. If we now look at the Gospel of John, which is still later, we notice that here even the names of the disciple and the servant who is attacked are given – Peter and Malchus. Since these details are not due to more precise information (John's distance from the event is far greater than that of the other evangelists) he can only have added it himself. The narrator's imagination paints in the individual details with increasing elaboration. Thus the reader is given the impression that the account is particularly exact and reliable.

There is nothing unusual about this. The same phenomenon can be noticed everywhere in the transmission of folk-narrative. Again and again relatively simple scenes, related almost in note form, are later elaborated in order to meet the increased desire for a vivid approach. The hearer or reader has become more demanding and wants to know more and more. One can get an impression of the process by comparing, for example, a scene from the Old Saxon Gospel adaptation, the *Heliand* (c. 830) with its New Testament original. In the *Heliand* outward features – clothing, weapons, etc. – are depicted in far more detail than they are in the biblical chain of transmission – to such an extent that the original significance has been lost in many places and is overlaid by the heroic tendency characteristic of Germanic legend. Here the very sword scene we have been considering is highly instructive; not only the outward appearance but also the faithful character of Peter, the hero of the sword, is strongly emphasized.

But one does not need to go so far into modern times. Within the early Christian tradition itself, in what are known as the New Testament apocryphas,[1] the most prolific growths of narrative material can be observed, particularly in miracle stories. These Gospels and Acts of the Apostles, which were composed in the course of the second century and were not admitted into the biblical canon, were in some cases also very popular with the churches. In what is known as the Protevangelium of James,[2] for example, Jesus' grandparents (of whom we are told nothing in the New Testament) are named: Saint Anne and the rich and pious Joachim. Mary's birth is foretold by an angel, her bringing up in the temple for a sacred purpose is described, and the proof of her virginity after Jesus' birth is offered.

[1] See E. Hennecke, *New Testament Apocrypha*, 2 vols., ed. by W. Schneemelcher, ET ed. by R. McL. Wilson (London, 1963–65).
[2] *Ibid.*, vol. I, pp. 370ff.

It is understandable that the later writers tried to fill in the gaps in the story. The Infancy Gospel of Thomas[1] fills up the time between Jesus' birth and his first appearance in the temple with all kinds of stories about Jesus the schoolboy, who is the terror of his masters and school-fellows because he immediately curses the people who annoy him, so that they fall dead (he restores them to life again, however!). Another gap is between the crucifixion and the resurrection. Here the Gospel of Nicodemus[2] introduces a series of scenes illustrating, with a wealth of imaginative detail, Christ's descent into hell. Christ seizes Satan by the hair and gives him to Hell to guard, then he wakes Adam and, raising the other dead, chases them all out of hell. Even the events which are described in the New Testament with a certain reserve are painted in bold colours in the apocryphal variants. Thus the great drama of the resurrection is unrolled in every detail before the Roman guard at the tomb. In the Gospel of Peter, for example, we are told that 'three men come out from the sepulchre, and two of them sustaining the other [*lit.* the one], and a cross following them, and the heads of the two reaching to heaven, but that of him who was led of them by the hand overpassing the heavens' (Gospel of Peter, 10.39–40).[3]

The imagination runs riot to an even greater degree in the apocryphal Acts of the Apostles,[4] which might almost be called a type of Christian novel, managing to combine edification and entertainment. Even in the New Testament Acts of the Apostles, the work of Luke, crudely popular effects are to be found among the miracles; for instance, the sick are carried out to the streets 'on beds and pallets, that as Peter came by at least his shadow might fall on some of them', and they were all healed (Acts 5.15). People took pieces of Paul's clothing and carried them to the sick, 'and diseases left them and the evil spirits came out of them' (Acts 19.12). In the apocryphal Acts, people are raised from the dead in such numbers that it becomes positively monotonous. One of Peter's healings of the blind comes about as follows: in answer to his prayer a bright gleam of light flashes through the room and a whole collection of aged and blind widows all receive their sight again.[5]

Animals who show respect to the apostles and martyrs play an important part. A huge watch dog 'acquired a human voice and said to Peter, "What do you bid me do, you servant of the ineffable living God?"' Whereupon Peter sent him into a certain house in order to carry a

---

[1] *Ibid.*, vol. I, pp. 388ff.
[2] *Ibid.*, vol. I, pp. 444ff.
[3] *Ibid.*, vol. I, p. 186.
[4] *Ibid.*, vol. II, pp. 167ff.
[5] *Ibid.*, vol. II, pp. 303f.

challenge to his opponent, the magician Simon Magus (Acts of Peter 9).[1]
Even the bed-bugs, which annoy the apostle John and his companion in a
lonely inn, obey his request and range themselves outside the door when
he says jokingly to them: 'I tell you, you bugs, to behave yourselves, one
and all; you must leave your home for tonight and be quiet in one place
and keep your distance from the servants of God' (Acts of John 60).[2]

The miracle of the talking dog actually makes some of the onlookers
believe, but as the others demand a further miracle from Peter, the
following occurs:

> But Peter turned round and saw a smoked tunny-fish hanging in a
> window; and he took it and said to the people, 'If you now see this
> swimming in the water like a fish, will you be able to believe in him
> whom I preach?' And they all said with one accord, 'Indeed we will
> believe you!' Now there was a fish-pond near by; so he said, 'In thy
> name, Jesus Christ, in which they still fail to believe' (he said to the
> tunny) 'in the presence of all these be alive and swim like a fish!' And
> he threw the tunny into the pond, and it came alive and began to swim.
> And the people saw the fish swimming; and he made it do so not
> merely for that hour, or it might have been called a delusion, but he
> made it go on swimming, so that it attracted crowds from all sides and
> showed that the tunny had become a (live) fish; so much so that some
> of the people threw in bread for it, and it ate it all up. And when they
> saw this, a great number followed him and believed in the Lord, and
> they assembled by day and by night in the house of Narcissus the
> presbyter. And Peter expounded to them writings of the prophets and
> what our Lord Jesus Christ had enacted both in word and in deeds
> (Acts of Peter 13).[3]

Peter reaches the height of his achievements when he defeats the magician Simon Magus in a trial of strength before a huge crowd in Rome.
Simon Magus, who called himself 'the Power of God', ascends into the
sky high above the city. 'And Peter, seeing the incredible sight, cried out
to the Lord Jesus Christ, "Let this man do what he undertook, and all
who have believed on thee shall now be overthrown, and the signs and
wonders which thou gavest them through me shall be disbelieved." '
The Lord sees Peter's point and Simon Magus falls from the sky, breaking his leg in three places. 'Then they stoned him and went to their own
homes; but from that time they all believed in Peter' (Acts of Peter 32).[4]

[1] *Ibid.*, vol. II, pp. 289f. [2] *Ibid.*, vol. II, pp. 243f.
[3] *Ibid.*, vol. II, pp. 297f. [4] *Ibid.*, vol. II, pp. 315f.

These examples are sufficient to show that in the earliest Christian churches, particularly those belonging to the Hellenistic world, the invention of miracles went to fantastic lengths and so did belief in them. In this respect Christians do not seem to have been any different from the pagan society described by Lucian. There was evidently an equally strong demand for this kind of literature among Christians and pagans alike.

The examples quoted also go to show that the miracle stories vary greatly in quality. But in what does the difference consist? Is it perhaps that the miracles reported of Jesus in the New Testament are *historically* more reliable or more probable – whereas the later miracles of Peter are quite obviously fantastic? To assume this would be premature; for the notion of quantities of fish streaming obediently into the fisherman's net at the Lord's command (as Luke tells us that they did) is in principle no less fantastic than the idea that all manner of beasts obeyed Jesus Christ's representatives, the apostles, or that wild beasts in the arena at the divine command refused to attack the bodies of the martyrs, as is several times reported in the *Acts of Paul*.[1]

But if the distinction does not lie in the historical possibility or truth of the miracles, where is it to be found? Why do Luke's miracles convince the reader that here something is being related in fictional form which deserves to be taken seriously, whereas he can only find the miracles of Peter for the most part childish spectacles?

If the miracle stories (in as far as they do not, like some of the healings, derive from real events which are now explicable) are to be understood as fiction or poetry, new standards must be developed in order to divide the wheat from the chaff. We shall return to this presently.

[1] *Ibid.*, vol. II, pp. 322ff.

11 Rudolf Bultmann's Existentialist Interpretation

The significance of miracles in the Gospel of John

If your right eye causes you to sin, pluck it out and throw it away; it is better that you lose one of your members than that your whole body be thrown into hell. And if your right hand causes you to sin, cut it off and throw it away; it is better that you lose one of your members than that your whole body go to hell (Matt. 5.29f.).

These commands of Jesus in the Sermon on the Mount are designed to explain the commandment: thou shalt not commit adultery. It does not occur to anyone who reads them in their context to follow them literally; nor will he take it that they are literally meant. What Jesus means is: you should ruthlessly eliminate any stumbling block which might make you act wrongly; and in doing so you should not shrink from a drastic measure of self-discipline or from 'mortifying the flesh'. This *meaning* is expressed in the *image* of the plucking out of the eye and the cutting off of the hand. Jesus makes use of language's capacity for speaking pictorially.

Another well-known pictorial expression is also found in the Sermon on the Mount: 'If any one strikes you on the right cheek, turn to him the other also' (Matt. 5.39). Again it would be a misunderstanding if one were to interpret this saying as a rule to be literally followed in dealing with the more aggressive of one's fellow men. There are certainly situations in which literal obedience could conceivably have a point; but the meaning of the saying goes much further. It is meant to be an illustration of the behaviour of the person who is not tied to revenge, retaliation or 'paying back', but who has the freedom to exchange his immediate reaction for one of neighbourly love and forgiveness. It is not an individual rule to be followed with pedantic accuracy, but serves to illustrate Christian liberty with regard to evil (a liberty which in a particular case might even decide in favour of a box on the ears if this were the best way to help the neighbour in his particular situation – which could conceivably be the case).

This example shows that it makes a considerable difference whether a sentence is interpreted literally or metaphorically. It is this which decides what meaning the reader gives to it and the conclusions he will draw. An essential difference, for instance, is that the literal meaning is narrowly related and confined to a particular case, whereas the meaning of an image – though superficially not definable – goes far deeper. The image points to something beyond the objects which it depicts.

The same can be true of a story. 'A man was going down from Jerusalem to Jericho, and he fell among robbers, who stripped him and beat him, and departed, leaving him half dead' (Luke 10.30–35). Jesus tells the story of the Good Samaritan as if he had a particular event in space and time before his eyes. Yet the whole story, with its theme of the blindness of the devout, learned though they were in the Law, and the attentive love of the religiously despised Samaritan, is an invented one. Jesus tells it to the learned Jew in order to give him an answer to the question: 'What shall I do to inherit eternal life?' That is to say, through a fictitious story Jesus makes something clear which is of general importance and is of interest even to those who are not journeying from Jerusalem to Jericho. The literal story serves as an image, and points beyond itself. Anyone who wishes to understand its meaning must not cling to its surface features.

The twofold level of image and meaning is particularly clear in the great parables of Jesus. When the father kills the fatted calf because the prodigal son has come home; or when the king invites guests to his great marriage feast and then calls in the poor from the highways and byways in place of the invited guests who have failed him, Jesus' listeners hear something more in the story: God invites men into his kingdom and happy is the man who accepts the invitation. The merchant who sells all that he has in order to acquire the costly pearl; the man who finds treasure in a field and sells all his worldly goods so that he can buy the field – these characters draw the listener's attention to the categorical question which faces him.

Like Jesus, the Old Testament prophets and wisdom teachers, as well as the psalmists, also spoke in images and parables. Indeed the pictorial style is common throughout the ancient east. But if this is true of Jesus' style, it may well be asked whether the same does not apply to his disciples and followers. The evangelists did not, admittedly, like

Jesus himself, speak directly of God's love and the coming of his king-dom; they talked about Jesus, through whose words and deeds they had found God. But we must at least reckon with the possibility that, when they depict Jesus' power and might in story form, their style differs from the language of our contemporary accounts.

The scholarly investigation of the language of the Bible, which has stood at the centre of Protestant biblical studies since the beginning of this century, has confirmed this supposition. It is true that in most of the writings of the Bible we have to do with stories that reflect historical events – the history of the people of Israel, the deeds and destinies of its prophets and kings, the story of Jesus of Nazareth and his apostles; but whereas in a history book, such as might perhaps be used in schools today, one expects simply exact figures and dates, with as objective and factual an account of events as possible, the historical books of the Old and New Testaments have a method of presentation which embodies a large number of poetic elements. In the Old Testament one comes across myths, sagas and folk-tale wonders; in the New, legends, artistically polished debates and stories with symbolic intent.

Should our knowledge of the pictorial nature of biblical language not be of significance for the interpretation of miracle stories? Those readers and interpreters who in these forms of narrative only gaze fixedly at the superficial details of what is related and either – according to their turn of mind – declare the contents to be literally true or reject them as simply false, are probably victims of a modern misunderstanding. They are behaving as if they were dealing with a historical account, the facts of which, as they are related, must be either definitely true or definitely false. A historical account is worthless and completely lacking in interest if what it reports is historically untrue. But have the miracle stories of the Bible perhaps a meaning, even if they are not accurate history?

Are these stories in fact finished and done with for us today? Every devout reader of the Bible is bound to ask this, as he sees with horror his supernatural Christ, the miracle-worker, fade away, eliminated by historical criticism. The same question faces the interpreters of the Gospels: what still remains to distinguish the stories of Jesus from all manner of lying pagan folk-tales, from fraud or harmless delusion and crazy superstition? What is the measuring rod for sense and nonsense if the criterion of historical truth is no longer to apply? The Christian miracles really happened, whereas the pagan ones were delusions and day dreams: this was the answer of earlier times, but it was apparently an over-simplification.

It is obvious that the importance and value of unhistorical stories can only be decided if it becomes apparent that they really have some inner meaning. But how can this be discovered? The historical *factualness* of a story can be examined and, in certain circumstances, *accepted*; its *meaning* can, possibly, be *comprehended*.

The same theologian whose form-critical studies made a decisive contribution to the discovery of the non-historical elements in the Gospels has now also pointed to the necessity of a new understanding of the mythical and miraculous texts and has himself worked out the guiding lines for a doctrine of interpretation, or hermeneutics. This theologian is Rudolf Bultmann (b. 1884),[1] professor of New Testament studies in the university of Marburg.

What are the points to be remembered when one is looking for the meaning of a text? A preliminary answer along the lines laid down by Bultmann can be arrived at from a familiar passage which has long been established as completely unhistorical: the story of the creation and the fall of man. If it is not historical reminiscence, what is expressed in these stories, which can be formally assigned to the myth group? This can only be briefly indicated.

The early narrators puzzled over how the supernatural God, whom the patriarchs of Israel had learnt to know in primitive times through the mouths of their prophets as guiding power, was related to the forces of this world – to the sun, moon and stars and the fruitful earth, the forces which were prayed to and worshipped by the other nations among whom

[1] The following books and essays by Bultmann on the theory and practice of interpretation may be particularly mentioned: 'Neues Testament und Mythologie. Das Problem der Entmythologisierung der neutestamentlichen Verkündigung', *Kerygma und Mythos*, ed. by H. W. Bartsch, vol. I, 5th ed. (Tübingen, 1967), ET, 'New Testament and Mythology, the Mythological Element in the Message of the New Testament and the Problem of its Re-interpretation', *Kerygma and Myth*, vol. I, trans. by R. H. Fuller (London, 1953); 'Zum Problem der Entmythologisierung', *Kerygma und Mythos*, vol. VI (Tübingen, 1963) and *Glauben und Verstehen*, vol. IV (Tübingen, 1965); 'Das Problem der Hermeneutik', *Glauben und Verstehen*, vol. II, 4th ed. (Tübingen, 1965), ET, 'The Problem of Hermeneutics', *Essays Philosophical and Theological*, trans. by J. C. G. Greig (London and New York, 1955); 'Zur Frage des Wunders', *Glauben und Verstehen*, vol. I, 5th ed. (Tübingen, 1964), ET, 'The Question of Wonder', *Faith and Understanding*, vol. I (London and New York, 1969); *Das Urchristentum im Rahmen der antiken Religionen*, 2nd ed. (Zurich, 1963; paperback ed. Rowohlt, 157–8, 1962), ET, *Primitive Christianity in its Contemporary Setting*, trans by R. H. Fuller (London, 1956; Fontana, 1960); *Marburger Predigten* (Tübingen, 1956), ET, *This World and the Beyond*, trans. by H. Knight (London, 1960), see particularly exposition of Luke 5.1–10 on pp. 155–166.

Israel lived. They knew that their God was Lord of the whole world and that neither constellation nor beast nor any other natural power deserved divine honours. They clothed their knowledge in a splendid story in which they depicted all these things as coming from God's creative hand. Man should not serve these things and depend on them; he should not make burnt offerings to them of the best that he has – his first-born son, his animals or the fruits of the field, as the heathen peoples did in their sometimes barbaric cults. Man is called to be lord over nature. They therefore told the story of how God gave all created things to man, telling him to find them names and rule over them.

The hard-won experience of everyday life as peasants and cattle breeders taught the Israelites – as the second account tells us – that the ground grows thorns and thistles, that man has to win his bread by the sweat of his brow, that a woman suffers in giving birth, that there is enmity and danger, sin and death among men. They believed that all this was not intended – that it was not so originally and was not to endure for ever... The early story-tellers knew or sensed this, having received a better promise from their God; and they passed it on to their descendants in vivid stories of a paradise on earth, of the disobedience of man and the wrath of God, of exclusion from paradise and the cursing of the earth because of the sin of man. They put their knowledge in the form of a simple pictorial story, not an abstract philosophical treatise – they were not capable of that. Like all early peoples, they related a myth in which they talked in childlike terms of God as of a person similar to other persons, who walks about on the earth, who formed man from clay like a potter, who speaks to man, tells him what to do, rebukes him when he fails to keep the commandments, punishes him, but is then kind again.

The mythical story therefore – and this is its intention – gives expression to the fundamental experience which the people of Israel had gained during the history of its exodus from Mesopotamia and Egypt; and it was written down and repeated in order to hold the people, in the events of their own day and in their disputes with other peoples, to the calling they had once experienced.

The details of the story are not particularly important – the particular concepts change with the times, as can already be seen from the two parallel but different stories of the creation. It is even conceivable that the same view of the position of man in the world and his responsibility to a non-worldly court of appeal, God, could find its expression in a story of quite a different kind. Today a story of this kind would certainly have a different colouring, if one were still to try to tell it at all. We do not even have to think of a creation story; one could express in abstract form the same understanding of man and the world that emerges here as the ideas of the early narrators are traced out for us.

The form of expression or framework of an idea can change, and indeed is bound to do so, since it is entirely dependent on a period's general outlook. Take, for example, the way in which man conceives of the seat of God and the nature of his activity on earth: it is clear that in a period in which space capsules circle the earth, the seat of God can no longer be thought of as being above the clouds or beyond the stars, or indeed as being in any one place in outer space, as children and myths so readily imagine. Thus today we no longer see angels ascending and descending and we can no longer imagine Jesus as disappearing into the sky at his ascension.

The example of the Old Testament therefore shows that what matters is not the outward form or the sensory objects which accompany a non-historical story; what is important, as Strauss and his adherents used to say, is the idea embodied in those sensory objects. Bultmann talks about 'significance' (*Bedeutsamkeit*) rather than 'idea'. The biblical texts must be examined for their significance, that is to say, for what they are trying to expound, for what they want us to understand. What is this significance which is open to the reader's understanding? The example of the creation myth shows that the story reveals a particular view of nature, history and God; but it does not reveal it in the form of a speculation divorced from the historical life of man; it is related back to men themselves. A view of man by man, and of his situation in the world, therefore stands at the centre. Bultmann calls this view which every man has of himself in some concrete form or other his self-understanding or – using an expression belonging to Existentialist philosophy, from which he draws useful terms – his understanding of existence.

The interpreter who, following the intention or aim of the text, tries to extract and comprehend the self-understanding which is crystallized in the story hence strives towards an *existentialist interpretation*, to use once more one of the central terms of Bultmann's hermeneutics. If in the course of this endeavour it should emerge that, if not the mythical form of expression, at least the basic meaning of the ancient story is still comprehensible and has something to say to us – because it points to possibilities still open to man today – than there is an encounter between interpreter and text, a gap of thousands of years notwithstanding. If this is impossible, if the meaning of a text stands or falls with the premiss of a world-view which has gone never to return and leaves no opening for man today – then it has no contemporary meaning and enjoys a purely historical interest. To which group do the miracles of Jesus belong?

Are we not dealing here with superstitious ideas which can be finally repudiated once they have been superseded by a scientific explanation of the world? This is not Bultmann's opinion. He is able to show that in the New Testament itself we can find the beginnings of criticism of belief in miracles as well as of the 'demythologizing' of Christ's message. Bultmann defines demythologizing as the procedure whereby a meaning in the text which is independent of the mythical form of expression is brought to light; it is the method we used in connection with the creation story. Paul and John, being apostles to the Gentiles, both had the task of transposing the message from Jewish forms of expression into terms which were also comprehensible to the Greek and Roman hearers of Asia Minor, and they treat Jewish laws and religious terminology with sovereign freedom when it is a question of expressing the substance of the Gospel anew in a changed mental environment. Whereas Paul is not interested at all in the miracles described in the Gospels and never mentions them – his understanding of Christ seems concentrated on the theological meaning of the cross and resurrection – in John we have the strange circumstance that on the one hand the miracles are intensified to the highest and most marvellous degree, yet on the other they are made almost irrelevant by the interpretation which John himself adds to them.

Let us look at some examples of this in more detail. The main question is: what meaning or what significance do Jesus' miracles have in the Gospel of John?

1. Matthew, Mark and Luke, who are known as 'the Synoptics' because of the 'comparable' viewpoint of their Gospels, tell the story of the *miraculous feeding* of the multitude in the wilderness without comment of their own. The only feature worthy of particular note is a somewhat later addition – the conversation of the disciples with Jesus about the leaven of the Pharisees (Mark 8.14–21) which ends with Jesus' reproach to the disciples that although they had gathered many fragments into their baskets, their hardness of heart had kept them from understanding the meaning of the feeding of the multitude. 'They did not understand about the loaves, but their hearts were hardened,' says Mark elsewhere (Mark 5.52). What was there to be seen, apart from or beyond the outward event which everyone saw? The miracle's secret *meaning* was the chief thing, as Strauss showed by pointing back to the religious tradition

of Israel. The feeding of the multitude was interpreted by the Jews as a sign of the presence of the second Moses, the Messiah. But the writers of the Synoptic Gospels do not find it necessary to discuss this point in detail.

John goes a step further. He is bound first to give his Gentile readers an explanation of the meaning which the story had for Jewish ears; but he has to do more: he has to offer these readers (for whom the Jewish messianic evidence had no particular cogency) a freer and more general intepretation of Jesus' miraculous action. He does this by appending to the 'Synoptic' story a long discussion in which Jesus examines the Jewish interpretation.

The Jews – so says John in the first place – understood Jesus' action as being an unequivocal manifestation of messianic status; the people come and want to seize him and make him king by force because they believe that 'This is indeed the prophet who is to come into the world!' (John 6.14). Is this opinion mistaken? Why does the story go on: 'Jesus withdrew again to the hills by himself'? When the people will not leave him alone, and even follow him in ships, Jesus attacks them with the words: 'Truly . . . I say to you, you seek me, not because you saw signs, but because you ate your fill of the loaves. Do not labour for the food which perishes, but for the food which endures to eternal life, which the Son of man will give to you . . .' (John 6.26f.). Jesus clearly dissociated himself from the Jewish understanding of the 'sign', according to which the Messiah is to bring about a worldly kingdom. Jesus even dissociates himself from the sacred traditions associated with the wanderings in the wilderness and from Moses himself: 'Truly . . . I say to you, it was not Moses who gave you the bread from heaven; my Father gives you the true bread from heaven (6.32). And: 'Your fathers ate the manna in the wilderness, and they died. This is the bread which comes down from heaven, that a man may eat of it and not die' (6.49f.).

What does Jesus himself put in the place of the manna in the wilderness? A puzzling and shocking sentence: '*I* am the bread of life; he who comes to me shall not hunger, and he who believes in me shall never thirst' (6.35).

One sees how in this phrase Jesus detaches the word 'bread' from the concrete, earthly meaning which it had in the miraculous feedings of the Old and even the New Testament. The earthly bread which satisfies bodily hunger becomes the sign or symbol of another kind of bread which satisfies another kind of hunger: 'I am the living bread which came down from heaven; if any one eats of this bread, he will live for ever' (6.51).

138

But what can Jesus mean by calling *himself* the bread of heaven or the bread of life? He himself, a human being? John the evangelist – or perhaps a later reviser of his Gospel, writing in the same spirit – loves an extreme and shocking turn of phrase; he paints a bold picture of the eating of a bread of life which is Jesus himself: 'The bread which I shall give for the life of the world is my flesh. . . He who eats my flesh and drinks my blood has eternal life . . . (6.51ff.). The meaning can only be a symbolic one. The believer attains eternal life by eating and drinking, that is to say, by absorbing the essence of the crucified Christ.

'Many of his disciples, when they heard it, said, "This is a hard saying; who can listen to it?" . . . [and] after this many of his disciples drew back and no longer went about with him' (6.60, 66). The Jews murmured as well and said, 'Is not this Jesus, the son of Joseph, whose father and mother we know? How does he now say, "I have come down from heaven?"' (6.42). The question is a justifiable one and must be addressed to the evangelist John by every reader; for his whole interpretation, his understanding of Jesus' meaning for himself and for those to whom he is speaking, is embodied in the sentence which he puts into Jesus' mouth: 'I am the bread of life.' And this is evidently not a historical saying of Jesus. What reality lies behind the image? What does Jesus give to men that possesses this nourishing power, the power of conferring eternal life?

'Will you also go away?', Jesus asks his disciples at the end of the chapter. But Peter answers, 'Lord, to whom shall we go? You have the words of eternal life . . .' (6.67f.). Are his *words* of such importance that they keep the disciples by his side? And what does John mean by saying that they give 'eternal life'? What words is he thinking of?

The Gospel of John does not give a satisfactory answer to this last question. The Johannine sayings of Jesus are all interpretative sayings of Johannine theology, which must remain incomprehensible to anyone who does not know what they interpret, namely Jesus himself, his own words and deeds. It is true that these are nowhere preserved in a completely pure form, untouched by interpretative ideas springing from the beliefs of the disciples; but in the earlier Gospels – one can think of the parables of the sayings in the Sermon on the Mount – they come to us with greater historical freshness and authenticity. Whoever thinks about these original words may perhaps understand the nature of the life which is called eternal in the Gospel of John as well as elsewhere in the New Testament. Jesus himself answered the question about eternal life, among other things, when he told the story of the Good Samaritan.

2. In the ninth chapter of his Gospel, John tells the story of *the healing of a man who had been born blind*.

As he passed by, he saw a man blind from his birth. And his disciples asked him, 'Rabbi, who sinned, this man or his parents, that he was born blind?' [For in Israel illness was thought to be the result of sin.] Jesus answered, 'It was not that this man sinned, or his parents, but that the works of God might be made manifest in him. We must work the works of him who sent me, while it is day; night comes, when no one can work' (John 9.1–4).

Even these sentences, which suggest an initiative on the part of Jesus, contain John's interpretation, which goes beyond the simple 'Synoptic' report of the healing of a blind person. The blind man is only sitting by the wayside – in fact the man is only blind at all – for one reason and one alone: in order to give Jesus the opportunity to reveal the works of God in his person. The miracle is, so to speak, an epiphany miracle; it manifests the glory of God.

After a few words which interpret the event in advance for the surrounding disciples, Jesus begins to act: 'He spat on the ground and made clay of the spittle and anointed the man's eyes with the clay, saying to him, "Go, wash in the pool of Siloam. . . ." So he went and washed and came back seeing' (John 9.6f.). In what way does the healing of a blind man reveal the world of God? Jesus says, 'As long as I am in the world, I am the light of the world' (John 9.5).

It is the characteristic of light to relieve darkness. Now the meaning of the story becomes clear: darkness for man means sitting without light; but the blind man sits in darkness for ever. Jesus could not demonstrate his divine power of acting as the light of the world more graphically than by lightening the darkness of a blind man. To be more precise – a narrator who wants to depict Jesus' power could not do so more clearly or spectacularly than through such a story. Blindness has a symbolic meaning. It is the dark background against which the light of revelation shines out in splendour.

But what meaning does the saying and the conception of light have in this context? Anyone familiar with the Old Testament knows that the word had a long history in Israel.

There are many who say, 'O that we might see some good!
    Lift up the light of thy countenance upon us, O Lord.'
Thou hast put more joy in my heart
    than they have when their grain and wine abound (Ps. 4.6f.).

Light shines where God inclines towards man, giving him what is more than bread and wine.

> The Lord is my light and my salvation;
>   whom shall I fear?,

says the psalmist (Ps. 27.1).

The *word* that proceeds from God is particularly full of light. 'For thy commandment is a lamp and the teaching a light,' says one of the Proverbs (6.23). For commandments and teaching show a man how he can live in the world, what he can hope for and what he can hold fast to; they shed light on his path:

> Thy word is a lamp to my feet
>   and a light to my path (Ps. 119.105).

These examples make it obvious that light here is not to be understood as external, physical brightness; indeed physical light is only an image to express what it means when a man emerges 'existentially' from the confusion and darkness of his situation into a clear knowledge of his path. Today one would say that this is a 'transferred' use of the word, although in poetry, language is no more confined to one level of meaning today than it was in the Old Testament. And enlightenment is still the word we sometimes use to express intellectual clarity.

Light streams constantly from God's revelations, yet the world of men remains dark. Then, with the prophets, the hope is expressed for the first time that in the history of Israel, experienced as darkness, a special light sent by God will dawn (Isa. 9.2). Israel itself is really destined as light-bearer, for on this people God has laid his spirit. Israel is the servant chosen by him to carry his truth to the nations.

> I have given you as a covenant to the people,
>   a light to the nations,
>   to open the eyes that are blind,
>   to bring out the prisoners from the dungeon
>   from the prison those who sit in darkness (Isa. 42.6f.).

God will abide by this election, in spite of all unfaithfulness on the part of the people (unfaithfulness which may again be pictorially described as blindness and deafness); this is the Old Testament hope.

Anyone who knows Israel's background of religious experience and hope will understand what it means when in the Gospel of John Jesus says of himself: '*I* am the light of the world; he who follows me will not walk in darkness, but will have the light of life' (8.12). And when Jesus appears as one who opens the eyes of the blind, he is performing a 'speaking' action, which visibly attests his messianic claim.

John's miracle story, too, is in all its characteristics a 'speaking' action which is designed to draw attention to what is beyond itself: as John says, it is a 'sign'. This is confirmed by the close of the chapter, where Jesus ends the dispute with the Pharisees which follows the miracle by some summarizing words of self-interpretation: 'For judgment I came into this world, that those who do not see may see, and that those who see may become blind' (John 9.39). The eyes of the blind are opened, not merely physically but also spiritually, since the blind man recognizes the divine act in what Jesus does and bows before him in faith; but the Pharisees are offended because the action is performed on the Sabbath (and is hence against the law of Moses) and will not recognize that this is a man sent by God. 'Some of the Pharisees near him heard this, and they said to him, "Are we also blind?" Jesus said to them, "If you were blind, you would have no guilt; but now that you say, 'We see,' your guilt remains"' (John 9.40f.). The scribes and Pharisees, who described themselves as seeing, are struck with blindness towards Jesus. Thus his appearance acts as judgment, as a dividing sword. Those who reject him open-eyed, because they fail to recognize him, remain in darkness; those who accept him, emerge from their blindness into sight and are illumined by the light of life.

What does 'to be in the light' really mean? The First Epistle of John gives an indication by naming a sign whereby one can recognize whether a man is in light or in darkness: 'He who says he is in the light and hates his brother is in the darkness still. He who loves his brother abides in the light' (I John 2.9f.). According to this it is not hard for the Gospel of John to answer the question put at the outset: what remains, or does anything remain at all, if the miracles are held to be unhistorical? In John nothing is lost at all, for all the outward circumstances which he describes have the characteristic of meaning something different from what they literally and at first sight imply. When God himself (in the Old Testament) and the man Jesus (in the New) are depicted as light, it is obvious that an image from the realm of the outward physical world is being used in order to express a fact in the human-historical sphere. 'To be in the light' is a possibility open to man; he can orientate himself in everyday life in this world in response to the proclamation of Jesus. What is left of the miracle, therefore, is, among other things, what Bultmann calls a particular existential self-understanding; and at the same time a non-miraculous understanding of the meaning of Jesus. What Jesus physically did to one single individual, according to John's story, was designed to make the world see that in his words and deeds a light has been kindled that lightens every man.

3. *The Raising of Lazarus* in John 11 is one of the most astonishing miracles of Jesus. The revivals of the dead in the Synoptic Gospels affect persons who have just died or have just been buried (and in Israel burials took place on the day of death, often only a few hours later). The 'Synoptic' raisings happened, that is to say, at a time when, according to popular belief, the soul of the dead person was still in the neighbourhood of his body. But according to John, Lazarus had aleady been in the grave for four days – his sister says that his body is already rotting – when Jesus wakes him with the words: 'Lazarus, come out.'

John therefore brutally intensifies what is in any case an improbable miracle. What the reader resents about his account is the fact that Jesus, who could have hastened earlier to the help of his friend, lets Lazarus die in order to proclaim his glory to the sorrowing sisters and the whole Jewish nation through a miracle which casts all the earlier ones into the shade.

'This illness is not unto death; it is for the glory of God, so that the Son of God may be glorified by means of it.' This is the answer which Jesus gives the sisters who send a message to him saying, 'Lord, he whom you love is ill': and he stays another two days in the place where he is, finally arriving at the tomb four days after he has learnt, through divine inspiration, of Lazarus' death. 'Lord, if you had been here, my brother would not have died,' says Martha to him. Jesus answers: 'Your brother will rise again.' Martha in her resignation believes that he is comforting her by a reference to the Last Judgment. But Jesus says: '*I* am the resurrection and the life; he who believes in me, though he die, yet shall he live, and whoever lives and believes in me shall never die. Do you believe this?' This interpretative sentence of Jesus gives the key to an understanding of the story. To John, who formulated and composed it in this particular way and whose view it reflects, the miracle simply means a tangible instance of Jesus' power to make earthly death meaningless.

Did these events really take place just as John relates? It is impossible to believe that they did. Whether John himself believed in them in a literal sense can no longer be determined. Many interpreters, Bultmann among them, think that it is improbable that he did, in view of the sovereign freedom with which he refashioned the narrative material as it came to him in order to bring out its theological content. In addition, Jesus' own interpretative statement suggests that the story has a different intention: he who believes in Jesus will live, even if he dies. That is to say, there is a kind of life which is untouched by the state of the body. And anyone who, through faith in Jesus, lives in this new and different life, will escape death eternally. He will not even die when he dies in the earthly sense. This is what the story is saying. It is a fundamental misunderstanding if one clings to the reality of a particular event. According to its own internal meaning the miracle points away from itself and cancels itself out by declaring in sovereign manner, as Jesus does with Lazarus, that the physical event is unimportant.

The question which the reader would now like to put to John, the evangelist and theologian, is: what kind of life is it that can be called eternal? What actually constitutes this life, if it is not the vital spark of physical existence? A familiar answer is: it is life after death, after the resurrection of the Last Day – Martha's answer in the story, in fact. But this generally accepted view is called in question by the story itself and by many other Johannine statements about eternal life. Two sentences in particular are worth considering:

> Truly . . . I say to you, he who hears my word and believes him who sent me, has eternal life; he does not come into judgment, but has passed from death to life (John 5.24).

> We know that we have passed out of death into life, because we love the brethren. He who does not love remains in death (I John 3.14).

The acts and words with which the historical Jesus opened up for his contemporaries a new understanding of the will of God and hence a new understanding of life, awoke in them the impression that he could only be the century-long awaited Messiah or – in the non-Jewish world – the son of God, the bringer of salvation, true man and true God. They therefore transferred to him in metaphor and story the highest titles and predicates they knew, calling him the Bread of Life, the Light of the World, the Resurrection and the Life, and proclaiming in miraculous stories his supreme power to overcome the world.

It is the task of our different period not to gaze with obtuse astonishment at these early witnesses, clinging with a well-meaning and forced piety to their literal or historical truth, but to take them seriously as documents written in what is for us a foreign language and to enquire into the spirit which they express. For 'it is the spirit that gives life,' says Jesus, according to John, after the feeding of the five thousand, 'the flesh is of no avail' (John 6.63).

12 From Feuerbach to Ernst Bloch

Miracle as pre-figuration of a new world

'The man who knows and says nothing about me except that I am an atheist, neither knows nor says anything about me at all.' Feuerbach has found an interpreter in our own time who is able to defend his position better than he could himself. This interpreter is Ernst Bloch (b. 1885). Bloch's chief philosophical work, *Das Prinzip Hoffnung*, 'The Principle of Hope',[1] includes among other things a development of Feuerbach's ideas and a new and highly individual theory of how Jesus' miracles are to be interpreted.

The explanation of miracles by feeling and imagination is regarded by many in the present day as superficial. But let any one transport himself to the time when living, present miracles were believed in; when the reality of things without us was as yet no sacred article of faith; when men were so void of any theoretical interest in the world, that they from day to day looked forward to its destruction; when they lived only in the rapturous prospect and hope of heaven, that is, in the imagination of it (for whatever heaven may be, for them, so long as they were on earth, it existed only in the imagination); when this imagination was not a fiction but a truth, nay, the eternal, alone abiding truth, not an inert, idle source of consolation, but a practical moral principle determining actions, a principle to which men joyfully sacrificed real life, the real world with all its glories; – let him transport

[1] Ernst Bloch, *Das Prinzip Hoffnung*, 2 vols. (Frankfurt-am-Main, 1959; special scholarly edition in 3 vols., 1967, with identical pagination). Of particular importance for our subject is ch. 53, 'Wachsender Menscheinsatz ins religiöse Geheimnis', which gives in compressed form a complete interpretation of biblical beliefs within the framework of the religions of the ancient world. For extracts, *see* E. Bloch, *Religion im Erbe* (selections ed. by J. Moltmann), 'Siebenstern Taschenbuch' (1967), pp. 134–219.

himself to those times and he must himself be very superficial to pronounce the psychological genesis of miracles superficial.[1]

This was Feuerbach's view. It is evident that from the very beginning he had to defend himself against the charge of superficiality; for it is an obvious inference that (since the outward, objective reality is denied to them) God and his miracles are now being explained as 'merely products' of human mental processes and hence – since we are here dealing with a product of unenlightened times – as what Engels calls 'higher nonsense'. Bloch recognizes, and not merely theoretically, the dangers of this inference and warns against an over-trivial secularization of Christianity. What, then, does this atheistic philosopher find so important in the Jewish-Christian faith that he is by no means prepared to support such superficiality? And how does he propose to save this element that he finds so important from critical annihilation?

'Feuerbach traces the content of religion from heaven back to men, so that man is not created in the image of God but rather God in the image of man – or, more precisely, in the image of man's own ideal figure at any given time.'[2] What Feuerbach believes to be conceived by the imagination and set up in contrast to the whole empirical world is not a random, arbitrary product of the fantasy, but a picture of *what ought to be*; Bloch calls it an interpretative projection of still-latent man and his world, with its still latent possibilities.[3] What is crystallized in these images or fantasies is therefore something over which man has no control; he is not, strictly speaking, its creator, although he gives the images a concrete form through his imaginative power and through language. According to the witness of the Old Testament, the imagination of the prophets takes the form of their being overtaken by a vision in the course of their everyday activities, a vision in which they hear words that challenge them with absolute authority to break away into an unknown future. Moses' experience while he was looking after the sheep belonging to his father-in-law, Jethro, is a case in point.

Where do these words and visions come from? Not from any place in the external world, although primitive man associated them with natural events such as thunder and lightning, storms and fire. (Traces of this can still be found in the Old Testament.) Today we can only say that such visions come from the human sphere, from unknown and still unplumbed depths of the human personality. Man is still concealed from

[1] Feuerbach, *op. cit.*, ch. XIII, pp. 133f.
[2] Bloch, *op. cit.*, p. 1517.
[3] *Ibid.*, p. 1522.

himself. The history of religion is a history of the growing clarification and unveiling of what is implied by the creature man:

> It is this still unknown future in men, not what is already at hand and present in them, which was essentially meant in all the changing hypostases of heaven. Thus the founders of religion have more and more put the human element into God, that is to say in this case, they have increasingly encircled the human incognito with ever-nearer figures from the beyond. Thus all the designations and names of God are giant images and attempts at an interpretation of the human mystery: a striving towards the hidden form of man, throughout and in spite of religious ideologies.[1]

Where does Christianity belong in the history of religion? This is of unexpected interest for the Christian theologian, accustomed, since the dialectical theology of the 1920's, to view the Christian proclamation purely for itself, as something in complete isolation. Jesus has rendered every previous idea of God obsolete. In the love of Christ God has finally arrived in man. For:

> In the ancient world love was Eros towards the beautiful and the radiant. Christian love turns instead not only to the oppressed and the lost, but in them to the insignificant. . . . Jesus himself is present among the helpless, as an element in their lowliness, standing in darkness, not in splendour: 'As you did it to one of the least of these my brethren, you did it to me' (Matt. 25.40). Christian love includes this stooping towards what is insignificant in the eyes of the world as encounter with him; and as visitation of this encounter it contains the pathos and mystery of littleness. This is the reason why the child in the manger is so important, together with all the lowliness of all the circumstances surrounding the cramped and remote stable. The unexpectedness of finding the Redeemer as a helpless child communicates itself constantly to Christian love.[2]

It is not a mythical and abstract Godhead, like the dying and reviving vegetation god of the calendar, which emerges from the Christian witness, but the real form of a historical person who can be imitated. This historical experience is striking because in it real man, who crouches in insignificance, at the mercy of his physical and spiritual needs, becomes the object of the highest interest and of a redeeming promise. The God who speaks in Jesus really has become man. Because he descends to the

[1] *Ibid.*, p. 1522.   [2] *Ibid.*, p. 1488.

ultimate ground of reality, he can also from that same point convert reality into saving reality.

For the point of Christian love is not to dissipate oneself in misery, to sacrifice oneself in suffering on the cross; the meaning of Christian love is revolutionary. The cross is merely the world's answer to Christian love. A real overthrow of the hierarchies of evil and a revolution in values are expected from God, and are longed for, in the messianic hymns:

He has shown strength with his arm;
he has scattered the proud in the imagination of their hearts,
he has put down the mighty from their thrones,
and exalted those of low degree;
he has filled the hungry with good things;
and the rich he has sent empty away (Luke 1.51f.).

The arrival of a new world situation, called the kingdom of God, is the central theme of Jesus' sayings and parables and even of his miracles. Indeed the miracles show particularly vividly that the nature of this world disappears in the face of the God who is now approaching and that a new creation is coming into existence. At first sight, indeed, the New Testament miracles can hardly be distinguished from all the other popular superstitions and magic:

Jesus certainly acts magically. He heals the lame, changes water into wine, feeds five thousand people from five loaves and two fishes, exorcizes the devils of sickness and raises the dead like Elijah. . . . Even evangelists like Luke the physician or the Hellenistically educated writer of the Gospel of John do not suppress the miracle stories; they merely give them an additional spiritual meaning, relating them to even higher miracles. The feeding of the five thousand is linked with the Last Supper (John 6.35), the healing of the blind man with Christ, the light of the world (John 9.30). Thus what is evanescent in these miracles, and pertains only to the particular occasion, evaporates; they are designed to benefit far more than the chance five thousand people of Jesus' time, and far more than the single blind individual. This very openness to re-interpretation is enough to show that what was spread by the peasants and fishermen of the New Testament did not belong to the sphere of primitive magic. It was also, and above all, completely new dogmas which stirred up the miraculous: Jesus as the Messiah, Jesus and the approaching kingdom of heaven. Both these are fundamental miracles which were the essential basis for the smaller ones which were expected of Jesus and which he himself thought of as 'signs'. The earlier magical significance of miracles was here replaced by a new, eschatological one. Miracles are *tokens* of the approaching end.[1]

Legends such as the changing of water into wine could, in the form in which they have come down to us, just as well have been told about the sorceress Medea as about the teacher of the Lord's Prayer and the Sermon on the Mount. In the Folk Book, Faust even made wine spurt out of wood. A mediaeval Jewish jest-book about 'Jesus the gallows bird' has hence very little more to say about these individual miracles than that Jesus learnt sorcery in Egypt and by this means led Israel astray.[2]

But in their context in the New Testament, Jesus' miracles, even his magical interventions, stand for a far greater transformation: 'for the transformation into the miraculous;' 'from the water comes the wine of miracle'. The contemporary observer has much to learn from these events.

1. Miracles have their place in the Gospel message as 'signs of the times'; they are signs that the new era brought into being by Jesus *genuinely transforms* the world. 'One single material line – a line not confined to the inner life – runs from the obligation to heal the man sick of the palsy to the proverbial faith which moves mountains: mountains, not psychologies.'[3]

2. The miracle is a *bursting apart* of the established state of affairs. With Jesus it always aims at being 'a new heaven and a new earth in miniature'. Miracle is the equivalent of *a disruption of the normal pattern of things*. Bloch points out that for human consciousness this normal pattern, with which the miracle is contrasted, acquires a different appearance with the passage of time. Knowledge of 'the pattern' was different at the time of Jesus from what it was in the Scholastic period and is different again in our modern post-Enlightenment period. Moreover the patterns which are broken in the 'explosive faith' (*Sprengglauben*) of miracle are determined by varying laws or forces. For example, the natural laws familiar to us, with which miracle collides according to our modern ideas, did not always determine the pattern of the world, subjectively speaking. Although natural laws and natural forces played a part in Hellenistic religious feeling at the time of Jesus, they did so not as

[1] *Ibid.*, pp. 1541f.   [2] *Ibid.*, pp. 1542f.   [3] *Ibid.*, p. 1544.

abstract physical regularities but as the demonic 'powers and forces' which fetter the body and soul of man. The world-pattern was religiously and ethically occupied territory, being ruled by the anti-divine, by evil. 'The world of Jesus . . . was the world of Mandaean-Persian dualism; Satan was the lord of this aeon, and the kingdom of light was the aeon of the immediate future. The disruption of the miracle came about *only in opposition to this world and its dark patterns.*'[1]

One is reminded of the words of Jesus: 'I saw Satan fall like lightning from heaven' (Luke 10.18); and 'If it is by the finger of God that I cast out demons, then the kingdom of God has come upon you. When a strong man, fully armed, guards his own palace, his goods are in peace; but when one stronger than he assails him and overcomes him, he takes away his armour in which he trusted, and divides his spoil' (Luke 11.20–22).

The marvellous disruption, however, also expresses itself as a breaking through of what we today understand as natural laws, – i.e., as miracle, even though the New Testament has no interest at all in this phenomenon as such. It is of the first importance when considering the activity of Jesus to realize where its centre of gravity lies, and what the essential aim of these 'breakings through' of the natural law is. We may proceed exegetically here, for example, by examining the question of which real 'powers' Jesus' proclamation was directed against; or we may ask what determines the particular people on whom Jesus confers liberty through his attitude of love.

The old era is now to come to an end. What does this look like? And what is the nature of the new one that Jesus brings? What is intended is a completely new order, and one of a miraculous nature.[2]

3. This miraculous character is not tied to physical miracles; it can also be conceived of in non-miraculous terms, and indeed must be so conceived today:

> Consequently the miraculous nature of Christ is united beyond the limits of his changing world-picture with what is conceivable today in two main respects: in the categorical form of the disruption and in the material form of its absolutely good content.[3]

From all this one fact becomes luminously clear: even though the character of a miracle has meanwhile been lowered to a trivial occultism, or has disclosed itself as such; even though it officially only lives on in the propaganda and commercialism of Catholicism, in hysterical

---

[1] *Ibid.*   [2] *Ibid.*   [3] *Ibid.*

virgins and paltry gates of heaven like Lourdes; yet apart from its transcendental superstition the concept of the miraculous contains the important and far from superstitious idea of *the leap*, an idea deriving from the concept of explosive faith.[1]

That is to say, even if the concrete idea of the miraculous which was once dominant is no longer generally acceptable as a possibility today, having been reduced to triviality through what Burke calls the march of the human mind, something still remains to be learnt or, as Bloch says, to be inherited.

To sum up: The form which disruption of the dark patterns or abrupt alterations of situations may take can be learnt from Jesus' miracles. Even today, happenings of this kind lead us to speak of a miracle; when we hear, for example, that someone's destiny has been altered because of an unexpected encounter; or that a man has discovered unsuspected possibilities in himself through some new task; or when some bold statement breaks down a taboo and shatters a paralysing silence which has held a community captive; or when a man enters public life and puts stereotyped thinking aside, bringing movement into the rigidity of the party lines and giving politics a new direction; and so we might go on. We come across situations in many spheres of public and private life which can be correctly described in Bloch's terms and which – though they are completely non-miraculous – are not unrelated to the happening of Jesus' miracles in which the world is 'made new'. As a Marxist philosopher, Bloch probably has in mind the series of basic and enduring disruptions of the dark patterns which occur in history on the level of society and which have the same goal of releasing from bondage and of fulfilling the possibilities of human existence. It is true that in a world of purely mechanical causality the concept of 'the leap' has no place, but it may still have one in a historical world which is procedurally open and not yet tied to a particular future.[2] In contradistinction to the mythical miracle, which is the breaking in of transcendental powers from outside, the new miracle, which can take place in the historical world in the sun of the spirit, is not a simple disruption of natural laws; it stands in relationship to the world of becoming and is fed from the 'fermenting' ground of what is objectively and really possible. 'And here above all, because of the obvious elimination of all transcendent factors, the 'exceptional situation' is lacking, into whose lawless vacuum the impossible could be inserted by a transcendent will.'[3]

[1] *Ibid.*, p. 1545.   [2] *Ibid.*   [3] *Ibid.*

What is left over from the content of Jesus' miracles is 'the miraculous'. Its name still means something even to the enlightened, and he takes it seriously in contrast to the gross nonsense of what is purely magical. It is the 'absolutely good content' which is constantly sought for in religious imagery and which gives to religion 'its remaining, demythologized truth, a truth deriving not from fear, need and uncertainty alone, but from a striving towards the light'.[1]

Bloch obviously shrinks from an extended description of the miraculous and its nature. Once a thing is pin-pointed, there is the danger that, a better state of affairs having been achieved, men will absolutize it as the best possible and bar their minds in narrow obstinacy to future opportunities and the continuing flow of historical tendencies – a proceeding which is a particular threat in the modern historical world. It is in accordance with the nature of the concept of salvation as something still to be sought for and hoped for that the religious images of paradise and heaven have always had the character of perpetual and infinite exaggeration and intensification – something which seems to surpass, once and for all, every earthly possibility of fulfilment: 'What no eye has seen, nor ear heard, nor the heart of man conceived, what God has prepared for those who love him' (I Cor. 2.9). With a caution similar to Bloch's, who finds in the present world merely suggestions, pre-vision, pre-experience, Paul speaks of an 'earnest', of the 'first fruits' of the Spirit, and of only partial knowledge: 'I consider that the sufferings of this present time are not worth comparing with the glory that is to be revealed to us' (Rom. 8.18). 'Not that I have already obtained this or am already perfect; but I press on to make it my own' (Phil. 3.12). This is the way in which Paul sees himself in relation to the goal he has before him – God's call to the resurrection of the dead.

Yet within the broad outline, or framework, of the constantly sought image of the 'miraculous', a real historical figure enters the stage in the New Testament as the final saviour-figure, as God becomes wholly man. 'Here a man acted with complete goodness, something which had never happened before.'[2] No other religion takes its life from the 'historical reality of its founder' as does the Christian faith; it is 'essentially the imitation of a life, not of a cultic image and its gnosis'.

This genuine remembrance still acts over the centuries. In spite of mysticism and spiritualization, the imitation of Christ was primarily a historical experience, and only thereby a metaphysical one. It was

---

[1] *Ibid.*, p. 1548.   [2] *Ibid.*, p. 1487.

Christ as an actual being who was important to those who believed in him; his factualness gave them, with stunning simplicity, what no religious image or picture of heaven could have given. It made even heaven empty and insipid. No initiate into the Attis mysteries, however practised he was in the realization of his God, could have said like Thomas à Kempis,[1] 'I choose rather to be a pilgrim with thee in earth than to have heaven without thee. Where thou art there is heaven: and where thou art not there is death and hell.'[2]

The miraculous – so much can be said about its nature – is present where it is really to be encountered, 'in itself unnoticeably, after so much seeming, pre-reflection, and even the pathos of indescribability';[3] for it is to be encountered in the insignificance of the lived moment, as the end of all alienation and the fulfilment of all desire, as man's arrival at his goal of being man.

This brief sketch of Bloch's interpretation of miracle and the miraculous must suffice; among the multifarious questions raised, one in particular must be mentioned because it touches on what is a central problem for Christian theologians.

'The atheist who has grasped that what is conceived of under the name of God is a pointer towards the latent content of man is no Antichrist.'[4] Feuerbach and Bloch are united in their concern that 'the treasures of transcendence' should not be squandered but should be consciously accepted as such once more. What these veritable treasures are, which neither moth nor rust have corrupted, is the question. But it is precisely this which is also the problem in the curiously isolated strivings of Protestant theology towards the 'demythologization' and 'secular interpretation' of the supernatural in the New Testament – strivings which run parallel to the materialist tradition. What could be more natural than that the two lines of development should take deliberate account of one another in the attempt to illuminate further the contentious question of 'what is conceived of under the name of God?' For in spite of a certain similarity of concern and method, one must not close one's eyes to the radical consequences which are drawn in the original, atheistical form of demythologization: that with the removal of transcendence as hypostatis and the tracing of it back to a 'human content', God as active subject ceases to exist in any form at all.

[1] Thomas à Kempis, *The Imitation of Christ*, III (1504; London, Everyman's Lib., 1943), ch. LXIV, p. 227.
[2] Bloch, *op. cit.*, p. 1486.   [3] *Ibid.*, p. 1550.   [4] *Ibid.*, p. 1527.

In Bultmann's theology, for instance, God appears after demythologizing as 'address' and 'word'; here the form of God's 'acting' is above all supposed to be preserved, this really being fundamental to the Bible, even after the whole magical element has been removed; and hence man – even the independent and active man of modern times – also remains a responding and responsible being. In Marxism in its original form, on the other hand (under the elemental impression made by liberation from religiously motivated tutelage, and with a view to the necessity of independent activity), the accent shifts completely from believing to achieving, from prayer to work, from hearing to doing.

> If instead of *believing* in a better life we *desire* it, and desire it not as single individuals but with our united strength, we will *achieve* a better life; we will at least remove the gross, infamous, heart-breaking injustices and evils from which men have hitherto suffered. But in order to desire this and to achieve it, we must replace the love of God by the love of man as the only true religion; we must replace faith in God by faith in man, faith in his strength, faith that the destiny of mankind is dependent on itself, not on a being beyond or above it, that man's only devil is man himself, rude, superstitious, self-seeking, wicked man; but that, equally, man's only God is also man himself.[1]

With these words Feuerbach closed his now famous lectures on the nature of religion, which he held in 1848, the year of revolutions, before students and workers in Heidelberg town hall; no room could be found for him in a university. As he says at the end, he had set as the goal of these lectures to turn 'friends of God into friends of man, believers into thinkers, those who pray into those who work, candidates for heaven into students of earth, Christians who, according to their own confession and creed, are "half angel, half beast", into men, in the fullest sense of the word'.

Karl Marx (1818–1883) tends in the same direction in his introduction to a criticism of the Hegelian philosophy of right (1844); but his observations are much more sober in tone and are already related to the new practical activity:

> For Germany the *criticism of religion* is in the main complete, and criticism of religion is the premiss of all criticism . . .
> *The task of history*, therefore, once the *world beyond the truth* has

---

[1] L. Feuerbach, *Gesammelte Werke*, ed. by W. Schuffenhauer, vol. 6 (Berlin, 1967).

disappeared, is to establish the *truth of this world*. The immediate *task of philosophy*, which is at the service of history, once the *saintly form* of human self-alienation has been unmasked, is to unmask self-alienation in its *unholy forms*. Thus the criticism of heaven turns into the criticism of earth, the *criticism of religion* into the *criticism of right* and the *criticism of theology* into the *criticism of politics*.[1]

For Marx the criticism of religion is not a purely intellectual occupation or a matter for a new and better 'interpretation'. For since religion had always also been the expression of real misery and a protest against that misery, it was impossible to take away its illusory hopes without at the same time laying bare real ones:

> The abolition of religion as the *illusory* happiness of the people is required for their *real* happiness. The demand to give up the illusions about its condition is the *demand to give up a condition which needs illusions*.[2]

If criticism of religion ends with the doctrine that man is for man the highest being, then it ends, as Marx says, with the categorical imperative, now, in reality, practically '*to overthrow all relations* in which man is a debased, enslaved, abandoned, despicable essence'.

With prodigious energy man addresses himself to the task of doing what the biblical hymns once lauded as the act of God: 'He has put down the mighty from their thrones, and exalted those of low degree; he has filled the hungry with good things, and the rich he has sent empty away.' What has the Christian to say in reply? Can he accept these conclusions as following inevitably from modern man's knowledge that no transcendent forces are coming to his help from beyond and that he is being challenged to govern the various aspects of historical life for himself? Will this knowledge, once it has really taken hold, revolutionize Christian convictions in the same way that it has revolutionized atheistical ones?

In this event the dispute about the question of God would shift on to a different plane of the human consciousness – the plane indicated by Feuerback and Bloch. God, having disappeared from the outward world, seems to sink into the depths, seems to lose himself in man's inner

[1] Karl Marx and Friedrich Engels, *Über Religion* (Berlin, 1958), pp. 30–44; *Marx-Engels-Studienausgabe*, 4 vols. (Fischer Bücherei, 1966), vol. 1, pp. 17–30; ET: K. Marx, *Contribution to the Critique of Hegel's Philosophy of Right* (On Religion), (Moscow, London, 1957), pp. 41f.
[2] *Ibid.*, p. 42.

nature or subjectivity. Yet Feuerbach's and Bloch's schemes show clearly (more clearly than the schemes of nineteenth-century Christian theologians like Schleiermacher) that what is thought of under the name of God acts out of the most highly subjective forms on world history, in that, as the determining aspect of subjectivity at any given time, it can also come to dominate the outward world formed by men. Whether there are contradictions here – perhaps absolute contradictions – between Christianity and atheism and where these lie has yet to be determined.

PART TWO

PRESENT PERSPECTIVES

1 The Problem of Miracles: A Scientific Discussion

Does physics allow the possibility of miracles?

In explaining the accounts of miracles in the New Testament, a scholarly method which proceeds purely along the lines of historical and literary criticism comes up against a clear borderline. Form criticism – how a miracle story began, its meaning and the purpose it serves – can only apply to this or that individual case. For example, it can be shown that Luke did not find the story of Peter's miraculous draught in the sources known to us, but inserted it himself. In addition, we can show that the story has a clearly symbolical meaning in the context of the calling of the disciples. Thus the historian has good reason for taking the story not as the reflection of a historical fact but as a symbolic fiction. But this judgment only applied to this particular example; it has no validity in principle for all miracle stories. Even if it can be shown that one individual miracle did not take place as reported, yet other miracles might still be possible – or so at least many readers of the Bible will continue to assert.

There is no convincing counter-argument to be urged against this assertion if one proceeds purely exegetically, that is to say, if one starts from the transmitted texts and takes these as the exclusive touchstone. One can only say: in the stories known to me no miracle can definitely be established; it is even highly questionable whether miracles can be proved at all and whether they should not be entirely excluded from the sphere of historical fact.

There are, for example, scholars who conscientiously apply the most modern methods of criticism in their investigation of the New Testament accounts of the resurrection and finally come to the conclusion that no absolute certainty about the historicity – the historical fact – of Jesus' resurrection can be arrived at from the accounts at our disposal. Since it is possible that there are important accounts – perhaps no longer extant –

which they do not know (a possibility with which the historian must always reckon) these scholars will not risk the dogmatic statement that the stories of the empty tomb are definitely unhistorical. (For the sake of simplicity we shall not consider the possibility that the tombs were confused or that Jesus' body was stolen.) The historians do not think that they can be responsible for a definite statement that the (actual) tomb of Jesus cannot have been empty. In their view, anything is historically *possible* – it is only that reliable accounts are missing in many cases.

There are also scholars who only declare that Luke's account of the ascension is unhistorical because the event is not mentioned in the oldest New Testament sources, i.e., in Paul and Mark; whereas the whole scheme of the Gospel of Luke clearly shows a particular theological tendency which makes the writer insert the story, both in order to give a conclusion to Jesus' post-Easter activity and also – through the sending forth of the disciples – to inaugurate the new period of church history.

The question now is whether the historian's modesty and reserve are really appropriate in questions of this kind. Of course a historian cannot deny a fact simply because it chances not to be mentioned in any document; far more actually happens than is ever passed down to later generations. To this extent it is sensible not to be too dogmatic in one's judgments about what really happened. But one must distinguish here between those events which – though not attested – are at least possible and conceivable and those which *cannot* have happened because they are inconceivable and transgress certain principles of our thinking and knowledge. Twice times two is always four and can never and in no place have been anything else. It would be absurd to say that this statement has always held good in the cases known to us, but that other cases may occur where this is not so. Here we have something like absolute certainty. This is of course a mathematical statement; but what is characteristic of it and all other mathematical statements – that they are universally and at all times true and are independent of individual experience – applies equally to certain basic truths on which we entirely depend in everyday life (usually without thinking about it) and which we cannot abolish even if we want to.

For example, everyone knows that in the course of time he will become older. It is an absolute certainty that the reverse process is not possible – however much we may wish that it were. It is only in the case of Dr Faustus (with the devil's help) or the portrait of Dorian Grey that a man is able, by mysterious means, to make himself younger or at least stay the same in spite of the passage of time; this does not happen in the real world. It is equally certain that a person can only be in one place at one time, not in several places simultaneously. It is obvious that here we do not need to ask the historians first. If they were to tell us that such unusual events have not up to now been historically established but that we cannot definitely exclude the possibility of their occurring, we should still know what to think and would at most be surprised at their pedantic caution.

Anything which deviates from certain principles or axioms cannot actually happen, either in the past, the present or – supposing similar conditions – the future. This is true in particular of the principle which determines the series of events in time, the principle of causality. This principle asserts that every happening and every alteration in the world is brought about by a cause.

Everything that happens has a cause. There can be no exceptions. Kant formulated the principle as follows: 'It is a universal law of the very possibility of experience, that everything which happens must have a cause, that consequently the causality of a cause, being itself something that has *happened*, must also have a cause. In this view of the case, the whole field of experience . . . contains nothing that is not subject to the laws of nature.'[1]

'It is a universal law of the very possibility of experience . . .' this phrase indicates that the principle cannot be accepted or rejected at will but that it is an essential part of our thinking and makes the claim to universality. (Whether it can be numbered among the categories, as Kant does, – as an *a priori* form of knowledge – is disputed nowadays; but that is not important here. It is enough to know that we cannot get along without it.)

The principle is also applicable to the future. We cannot plan or undertake anything if we cannot always reckon with the fact that one event follows another according to a certain law. In practical life the principle of causality is therefore invariably recognized; otherwise no regular mode of living would be possible – especially in a technically ordered world. But where this principle is presupposed in practice and recognized in theory, miracles – events outside the pattern of cause and effect – cannot be expected and cease to be conceivable.

It is true that the unexpected still happens in real life. Many events take an unexpected turn. But even the surprising was a possibility

[1] Kant, *Critique of Pure Reason*, trans. by J. M. D. Meiklejohn (London, Everyman's Lib., 1956), p. 317.

inherent in the natural circumstances; it only seems surprising because we had not considered the possibility earlier or were not in a position to anticipate it. The event can be explained retrospectively, and if the explanation is inadequate we look for another; for we are convinced as a matter of course that the event does have a cause. It does not occur to us to suppose that a 'miracle' has taken place.

In short, it may be said that there is no room for miracles in reality. Causality and miracles are mutually exclusive. This puts an end to the problem. But does it? Is reality perhaps more complicated than it seems?

This is the assertion of certain new theories which are calculated to shake our faith in a limitlessly applicable principle of causality. The germ of these theories lay in certain discoveries made by physicists in the 1920's. The essays of leading scientists began to contain disquieting sentences. In 1927 Werner Heisenberg (b. 1901) wrote in a paper, frequently quoted since, that 'quantum mechanics have definitively established the invalidity of the principle of causality'.[1] And the Danish physicist Niels Bohr (1885–1962) wrote an article the same year in which he said that in the case of atomic phenomena 'there can be no question of causality in the ordinary sense of the word'.[2]

These and other similar statements, sometimes intentionally formulated in extreme terms, acted as an irritant to certain theologians and other scientists. Without always taking account of what experimental observations had preceded the statements or noticing to which sphere remarks of the kind applied, these people isolated such remarks and concluded from them that causality had now been declared invalid. A long-standing fraud had now been exposed and abolished and one could again easily see miracles as acts of God that were conceivable in terms of physics. Scientific objections or reservations with regard to the miraculous were old-fashioned and done with. Appeals were made to the physicist and astronomer Arthur Stanley Eddington (1882–1944), for example, who had somewhat ironically suggested that religion had become possible for a reasonable scientist only after 1927. And today statements like the following may be read: 'The deeper insight into natural law which we have today forbids us to exclude the miraculous on scientific grounds'; or 'Scientifically speaking, a miracle is a highly improbable, statistically rare, but not impossible event.' In certain circumstances sentences of

[1] W. Heisenberg, 'Über den anschaulichen Inhalt der quantentheoretischen Kinematik und Mechanik', *Zeitschrift für Physik*, vol. 43 (1927), p. 197.
[2] N. Bohr, *Atomtheorie und Naturbeschreibung* (Berlin, 1931); ET: *Atomic Theory and the Description of Nature* (Cambridge, 1934; reprinted 1961), p. 54; this particular article appeared originally in *Nature* in English (1927).

this kind are accompanied by a personal confession of faith in the miracles of the Bible; '*Even as a scientist, or rather, because I am one, I can believe that they happened as they are reported as doing.*'[1] What has happened? Anyone who has up to now argued against supernatural theories on the basis of the unbreakable chain of natural events, feels taken at a disadvantage. The representatives of supernaturalism have apparently gained allies whose motives and scientific methods cannot be called in question. Who is more competent in this question than the physicist, and who has more claim to recognition in matters touching on the study of nature? In addition, one feels disquieted because these scientists have such an impressively complicated apparatus at their disposal – electronic microscopes and cloud chambers, reflecting telescopes and spectographs – how can one compete? Are we not simply bound to accept what they tell us are the results of research and be thankful when we can more or less understand what they are talking about at all?

But we do not need to be deterred. Research physics, especially in the field of these important specialist investigations, are certainly outside the intellectual range of the average person. But it is still quite possible, with the help of the physicists, to gain from examples an idea of the main point at issue. Let us look more closely.

Max Planck (1858–1947) gave a clear picture of the new situation in 1932 in a lecture called *Die Kausalität in der Natur* ('causality in nature'):

The so-called Uncertainty Principle, discovered and formulated by Heisenberg, constitutes a characteristic feature of quantum mechanics; it asserts that for any two canonically conjugate magnitudes, such as position and momentum or time and energy, only one can be measured to any desired degree of accuracy, so that an increase in the precision of the measurement of one magnitude is accompanied by a proportional decrease in the precision of measurement of the other. Consequently, when one magnitude is ascertained with absolute accuracy, the other one remains absolutely indefinite.

It is evident that this principle fundamentally precludes the possibility of translating into the sense world, with an arbitrary degree of accuracy, the simultaneous values of the co-ordinates and momenta of material points, as these are conceived in the world-picture of classical physics; this circumstance constitutes a difficulty with respect to the recognition of a universal validity of the principle of strict causality,

[1] H. Rohrbach, 'Biblische Wunder und moderne Naturwissenschaft', *Naturwissenschaft und Gotteserkenntnis* (Mannheim, 1965), pp. 26, 24.

and it has even caused some indeterminists to regard the law of causality in physics as decisively refuted. However, upon closer scrutiny, this conclusion – founded on a confusion of the world picture with the sense world – proves a rash one, to say the very least. For there is another, more logical way out of the difficulty, a way which has often rendered excellent service on previous occasions – namely, the assumption that the attempt to determine simultaneously both the co-ordinates and the momentum of a material point is physically completely meaningless. However, the impossibility of giving an answer to a meaningless question must, of course, not be charged up against the law of causality, but solely against the premises which produced that particular question; in other words, in this particular instance, against the assumed structure of the world-picture of physics. And since the classical world-picture has failed, another must take its place.

This is what actually has happened. The new world-picture of quantum mechanics is a product of the need to find a way of reconciling the quantum of action with the principle of strict determinism. For this purpose, the traditional primary constituent of the world-picture, the material point, had to be deprived of its basic, elementary character; it was resolved into a system of material waves. These material waves constitute the primary elements of the new world-picture.[1]

It is obvious that Planck is arguing very much more cautiously than the theologians who would like to declare that causality is non-existent. All that has happened up to now is that the physicists have found themselves forced by certain experimental observations to re-examine the basic concepts and ideas by which they have up to now tried to order and explain natural events. Earlier ideas have proved to be insufficient to explain certain phenomena – even misleading. Anyone who, for example, wanted to cling to the principle of causality found himself involved in inextricable confusion in the interpretation of what he had observed about electrons. Since for a physicist, reality always takes priority over the principles of interpretation, the law of causality had tentatively to be suspended in this field. If causality were eliminated, would it then be perhaps easier to form a convincing picture of the unexpected processes which had been observed?

The physicists had long been accustomed to this notion. For example,

[1] M. Planck, *Wege zur physikalischen Erkenntnis*, vol. 1, 3rd ed. (Leipzig, 1943); trans. by F. Gaynor, 'The Concept of Causality in Physics' in M. Planck, *Scientific Autobiography and Other Papers* (New York, 1949), pp. 133–135.

if one knows the precise position of an object – say, a billiard ball – as well as its mass (which is dependent on the material and size of the ball) plus other relevant conditions (e.g., the extent of gravitational force) then one can calculate exactly the point to which the billiard ball will move if it is struck by a precisely calculated impact or impulse. One can therefore predict precisely the behaviour of an object if one knows the co-ordinates of its position, its mass and the forces which act upon it.

This had ceased to be possible in the case of the primary nuclear particles of the atom. The act of observation altered the object which was to be observed, 'disturbed' it, so to speak, so that it was already in another state from that which one had been about to observe. The ball on the billiard table does not move when one subjects it to sharp observation – the nuclear particle jumps violently aside. It is obvious that in this case one cannot say how the nuclear particle will behave when subjected to outside influence; for it is fundamentally impossible to ascertain precisely and simultaneously the prerequisite 'position' and 'impulse'.

Must the principle of causality therefore really be abandoned? That depends on how one defines it. The physicists have reformulated it, trimming it to their own needs; in the essay quoted above, Planck puts it as follows: '*An occurrence is causally determined if it can be predicted with certainty.*'[1]

From what has been said it is easy to see, however, that this statement is bound to prove inapplicable in the sphere of microphysics. So formulated, there is no disputing Heisenberg's statement that the non-validity of the law of causality has been 'definitively established' through quantum mechanics. The matter becomes clearer when one reads what Heisenberg writes immediately before: '. . . in the strictest definition of the law of causality – that "if we know the present exactly, we can calculate the future" – the flaw lies in the premiss, not in the conclusion; for it is fundamentally impossible for us to know the present in all its determining factors'. But if one looks more closely into the matter, this does mean that causality as such has no validity, but that the conditions of its application do not exist. It is really unusable in this sphere. But is this not merely due to the experimental results?

Here it is important to realize that the principle of causality appears to be qualified and modified in its physical formulation. It may be useful to go back to an earlier definition. Planck writes at the beginning of his essay: 'It is agreed *a priori* that whenever a reference is made to a "causal

---

[1] *Ibid.*, p. 122.

relationship" between two successive events or occurrences, this term is understood to designate a certain regular connection between them, calling the earlier one the *cause*, and the latter one the *effect*'.[1] This is clear and unequivocal. Planck develops his statement into the definition given above because a physicist is particularly interested in predictability and strives for definitions which can be verified though experience in the form of experiment. What, then, of Planck's definition that 'an occurrence is causally determined if it can be predicted with certainty'? This sentence is by no means so unequivocal. One must examine the word 'if'. If it means 'only if' then the statement would be false. But if it means 'at least if', then all is well. The statement sets up a relationship between the causal conditionality and the predictability of an event. It will be clear to every unprejudiced observer that predictability must depend on the causal conditionality. The causal conditionality has to do with the *objective* connection with the preceding and following events; predictions can only be made when an observing subject has recognized this connection and deduced from it what will presently occur on its basis. Hence it would be better to formulate the definition as follows: 'An event can (in principle) be predicted with certainty when it is causally conditioned.'

The causal connection guarantees the possibility of predicting what will happen when a certain cause is present.[2] This by no means implies that the connection can necessarily be subsequently observed or, so to speak, seen in action.

The person who puts sixpence into a slot-machine and sees peppermints fall out cannot know the details of this astonishing metamorphosis either, unless he takes the machine to pieces. But he is in no doubt at all *that* there is a link or connection between the two events. And he would consider any attempt misguided which asked him only to recognize causal dependence where he can predict the course of events with certainty. It is true that *if* he can do this, causal dependence certainly exists; but it also undoubtedly exists in many cases where he would hesitate to commit himself to a precise prediction; for example, if the lettering on the slot machine has been painted out or is illegible, no one will be able to say what will drop out when the coin is put in.

We can see from this that Planck's statement about causality only brings out one aspect – the one in which the physicist is particularly interested (predictability), and is in turn dependent on the more com-

[1] *Ibid.*, p. 121.
[2] cf. H. Korch, *Das Problem der Kausalität* (Berlin, 1965), especially pp. 47f.

prehensive proposition which defines the objective linking of cause and effect as the primary reality. The more comprehensive proposition, the old complete principle of causality, applies, however, whether or not one attempts to use it for purposes of prediction. Luckily one can normally do so, but not invariably. And the new discoveries of the physicists compel us to the conclusion that it can basically no longer be used as an instrument for precise prediction in the processes of microphysics. But for deducing one event or state from a previous one, that is to say, for *explaining* a phenomenon by ascertaining what gave rise to it, what cause was operative, it is as indispensable as ever – even in microphysics.

For one point is particularly worth noting in the discussion about the new physics: the observations and thought-processes which allegedly do away with the principle of causality come into being on the basis of a strict recognition of that very principle. No-one knows this better than the physicists involved, Niels Bohr writes: 'The applicability of this way of looking at things and of the law of causality is the pre-condition of all scientific experience, even in modern physics. For we cannot communicate the progress and result of a test except by describing the necessary manipulations and readings as objective events taking place in space and time as we perceive them; and we could not use the results of the test to deduce anything about the characteristics of the observed object if the law of causality did not guarantee a definite connection between the two.'[1] Similar remarks may also be found in Heisenberg.

We can therefore say with certainty that the new theories do not mean the surrender of the principle of causality; they merely restrict its application. But there is no need to throw a fork away because it proves unsuitable for eating soup.

Up to this point the matter is relatively simple, and some measure of agreement with the defenders of miracles could probably be achieved. Admittedly, two reproaches might be levied against us. In the first place, in the interests of lucidity we have greatly oversimplified and have given too rough a sketch of the pro-miracle position. Today hardly any supporter of miracles would argue in quite so direct or simple-minded a way as has been suggested above. Secondly, we have not up to now discussed a very important concept which has become indispensable in modern physics for the explanation of natural processes: the concept of statistical law; and this also affects the possibility of a more sophisticated argument by the apologists.

[1] Quoted in O. Spülbeck, *Der Christ und das Weltbild*, 4th ed. (Berlin, 1957), p. 80.

It is highly instructive to notice the way in which this concept was formulated by the physicists themselves immediately after the discovery of incalculabilities. In spite of a recognition of the contradiction of the earlier world-picture, the cosmic structure did not collapse in 1927; and indeed there were no recognizable changes except in the minds of the scientists. There must be a reason for this; and it would appear that the human mind is apparently incapable of doing without a concept of something like law or natural law. Bernard Bavink spoke in this connection of a human 'need for causality' which absolutely demands to be met. It might be said without exaggeration that 'statistical law' was an attempt to satisfy this need for causality when the earlier view of a mechanically fixed natural law fell apart, at least partially, and proved to be no longer adequate. This attempt was successful because it made it possible to explain uncontrollable processes rationally and at least as convincingly as the earlier methods of explanation in mechanics had done. What is the point at issue?

Experimental observations had shown that the behaviour of minute particles in the atomic sphere is not clearly discernible for a particular moment and hence cannot be predicted for the moments that follow. The particles seem to behave more or less irregularly and arbitrarily. Even so, laws can be determined when these particles are observed in great numbers in the system as a whole, instead of singly. The laws already known then apparently continue to apply.

A similar case has long been known to physicists and has already found an explanation in the gas laws. The behaviour of gas molecules in an enclosed space cannot be observed individually but only as a whole. If one blows up a balloon, one only knows that molecules are introduced into it which become violently agitated and continually collide with the walls. In this way pressure is produced which causes the rubber to stretch. It would be useless to try to discover which molecules strike the rubber walls and with what degree of force. It is only known that the pressure depends on the number of molecules (each having a particular mass) and on the temperature. When the temperature rises, the pressure increases and the molecules move more quickly. There is so clear a relation between the temperature of the gas and the pressure exerted that this can be formulated in a law. Although the behaviour of the individual molecules is quite incalculable, when a great number of molecules is involved, the total effect can be calculated with precision. Through 'statistical addition' a surprisingly exact result may be achieved from the imprecise average of the behaviour of the molecules (in which the chances appear in the order of their probability). But this has nothing to do with atomic physics.

If, now, in the atomic sphere, the behaviour of the particles appears to be equally incalculable – as the physicists' experimental results taught – then the fact that the behaviour of larger objects is still regular and calculable can be explained similarly. However cautiously one may apply the analogy, in principle behaviour here will be as in the case of gas. Provided that the average emerges from the chaotic welter of individual processes, everything remains in its regular course. But if this should not be the case? According to our new ideas, can there not also be exceptions to the rule? This is the most interesting point in the new physics for the modern apologist for miracles. Here, if anywhere, must lie the point where miracles can take place as exceptional phenomena with the approval of physics. According to this view natural laws would no longer be fixed and unalterable principles; they would be the formulations of average behaviour.

> What is known as the statistical natural law gives the most probable course of an event, but certainly permits the possibility of different behaviour, even though this is highly unlikely. Earlier, science said ... miracles are . . . impossible because if they happened they would throw the whole mechanism of the world into disorder. Today physics has ceased to say this. . . . The miracle performed by divine agency, the event which supersedes the forces of nature, does not destroy the universal pattern. On the contrary, it is through miracles that God's mode of activity becomes particularly visible, since not merely one 'improbability' but a combination of 'improbabilities' are fused together into a meaningful and striking act through the sovereign will of God. . . .[1]

Is this a valid argument? Before we can answer this question we must examine the implications which the statistical approach may usefully have for the evaluation of reality. Since they are here trying to think correctly in terms of physics, the theologians cannot be intending to dissolve the standards of the possible and the impossible through sleight of hand and to set up a world picture in which every absurdity is fundamentally conceivable. We must look more closely.

Our best plan will be to adhere to the statements made by competent physicists. In one of his essays Heisenberg points to some everyday examples which show both the way of thinking which belongs to atomic

[1] *Ibid.,* p. 68.

physics and also the special character of our everyday dealings with these things. Heisenberg points out:

> Even in the ancient atomic theory . . . it was assumed that large-scale processes were the results of many irregular processes on a small scale. That this is basically the case is illustrated by innumerable examples in everyday life. Thus, a farmer need only know that a cloud has condensed and watered his fields. He does not bother about the path of each individual drop of rain. To give another example, we know precisely what is meant by the word 'granite', even when we are ignorant of the form, colour, and chemical composition of each small constituent crystal. Thus we always use concepts which describe behaviour on the large scale without in the least bothering about the individual processes that take place on the small scale.[1]

It is true that our knowledge of the structure of the smallest material particles influence the formulation of natural laws in general: 'If the processes which we can observe with our senses are thought to arise out of the interactions of many small individual processes, we must needs conclude that all natural laws may be considered to be only statistical laws.'[2] But granite goes on being the strong material we can use for building, even when we know that it is made up of an endless throng of microsystems and in the last resort consists entirely of non-material energy. Consequently Heisenberg can go on to say: 'In large-scale processes this statistical aspect of atomic physics does not arise, generally because statistical laws for large-scale processes lead to such high probabilities that to all intents and purposes we can speak of the processes as determined.'[3] Statistical laws 'can lead to statements with so high a degree of probability that they are almost certain, but there can always be exceptions in principle'.[4] Cases must therefore be investigated individually. But at least the individual results do not suggest a general weakening of the laws which have up to now applied to large-scale processes. What is the position as regards exceptional cases? 'Frequently, however, there arise cases in which a large-scale process depends on the behaviour of one or of a few atoms alone. In that case, the large-scale process also can only be predicted statistically.'[5] Thus the force of an atomic explosion cannot be precisely predicted because it depends on the behaviour of only a few atoms at the moment of firing. In the mutation

---

[1] W. Heisenberg, *Das Naturbild der heutigen Physik* (Hamburg, 1955); trans. by A. J. Pomerans, *The Physicist's Conception of Nature* (London, 1958), p. 35.
[2] *Ibid.*, pp. 35f.   [3] *Ibid.*, pp. 41f.   [4] *Ibid.*, p. 36.   [5] *Ibid.*, p. 42.

of genes during hereditary processes it also seems to be the case that large-scale events are set off by processes in individual atoms.

The nature of these particular examples shows how little one can generalize. But such discoveries have led non-experts (particularly those who are interested in the possibility of miracles) to form the firm opinion that it is now basically possible everywhere for microscopic effects to work through to the macrocosmic surface – that the freedom of atomic particles can cause revolutions, so to speak.

A particular miraculous event, one which it is relatively easy to formulate in terms of physics, may suggest how we are to react to this assumption: is it possible for a body to escape subjection to the law of gravity, as is presupposed in the idea that Jesus walked on the water? One would willingly find out how much probability statistics would assign to this miracle.

The French physicist and Nobel prize winner Jean Perrin once worked this out on the basis of a simple example. Bernhard Bavink tells us:

> He calculated how long a bricklayer working on the third storey would have to wait until, as the result of a chance irregularity in the distribution of the molecular blows, a brick would jump up 'by itself' from the ground into his hand. He found that the bricklayer would have to wait on the average $10^{10^{10}}$ years. This is 10 with 10 milliard noughts after it. . . . So minute a probability it is practically identical with absolute impossibility, and every builder will therefore arrange for bricks to be transported in the usual manner, rather than rely upon such a possibility.[1]

Since the theologians will find this example extremely trivial, Bavink has altered it so that a tile falling off a roof could be diverted from the head of a passer-by, which it would otherwise have struck, through 'chance unevenness in the distribution of nuclear pressure'. Would this be a genuine miracle? He goes on:

> But if the argument is put forward in theological quarters that the possibility is thus proved the result would only be to damage theology's own case. For in the first place as we have seen, the probability is so small that it may be regarded as practically identical with impossibility. If one such tile had fallen every second since the beginning of the history of humanity, no noticeable fraction of the time would have passed which, according to Perrin, would be necessary for the case

[1] B. Bavink, *Die Naturwissenschaft auf dem Wege zur Religion*, 3rd ed. (Frankfurt am Main, 1934); ET, *Science and God* (London, 1933), p. 51.

to occur. And secondly, even if such an immeasurably small possibility should actually once be realized, there would again be a second, almost equally great, improbability that it should happen just at the very moment when the passer-by, who was to be 'providentially' protected, was under that particular roof.[1]

In view of all this, is it still necessary to calculate when, according to the law of addition of probabilities, a person's force of gravity could be abolished, so allowing him to walk on the surface of water – quite apart from the possibility of ascension into heaven? An intrepid physicist could try to work out the statistical chances, but it is certain that the probability would turn out to be much less than in the case of the falling tile and that it is really inconceivable to the human mind.

Anything of this kind is for our thinking and concepts so absurd that it is hardly exceeded by the assumption that miracles of this kind, and others even more complicated, should only have happened in the one or two years of Jesus' activity. We can see that if the explanations offered by physics and mathematical statistics are taken literally, the result is a complete fiasco. Nothing has changed except that the impossibility of such events *in principle* has been replaced by their impossibility *in practice*.

Every clear-headed reader will have to admit that the nature-miracles in the Bible are not affected in the least by quantum physics; and there can be no question of the rehabilitation through physics of the biblical miracles in general, or of miracles as a whole (as would be the logical conclusion). It still remains true that miracles in the strict sense, such as Jesus' nature-miracles, are events which contradict experience as well as natural law, both in its classical and its statistical formulation. (Most of the miracles of healing may form an exception, since these are open to psychosomatic explanation.) This conclusion is certainly not due to an *a priori* principle or a philosophical premiss; it does not depend on an obstinate clinging to causality, for example; it is simply the result of mathematico-physical calculations. As early as 1933, Bavink uttered a warning which is still worthy of notice:

> The theological world cannot be too strongly warned against attempting to make capital in this way out of the new discoveries. Regarded as rules governing events in macroscopic dimension, the laws of nature are not less invariable in practice for us, because they have been recognized theoretically as based upon statistics, a statistics

[1] *Ibid.*, pp. 131f.

which in sub-microscopic dimensions depends either upon pure chance or free decision.

Nevertheless, our new knowledge does not by any means appear to have no bearing on the theological problem of miracles. For it teaches us, quite without possibility of misunderstanding, a fact that wise investigators of this question have always stressed, namely that the whole question is not in any way *quaestio juris*, but rather *quaestio facti*. For those who hold to strict causality in physics also recognize quite clearly that an omnipotent God can perform miracles. Why should not a God who settles the laws of nature not be able, if he so desires, to put them out of force? The question whether God can perform miracles is meaningless in itself, it contradicts its subject, namely the omnipotence of God. The only question is whether God has actually performed them, or whether we have reason for supposing that he will, and not can, perform them. But this question is one concerning only history, or biblical criticism. I have no intention of raising it here. . . . I can only beg all those who seriously think about such problems to examine the question entirely without prejudice from the historical point of view, which, of course, must not begin by saying that miracles have not occurred because they are impossible. But doubts concerning the credibility, or at least the correct interpretation of the miracle stories of the Bible will perhaps also occur to anyone who simply considers, quite soberly, the question as to what really happened.[1]

But let us not stop here. The arguments based on physics are always coming up and troubling people's minds, as far as one can see. Let us follow them up with a few concluding reflections.

Let us for a moment assume that the argument in favour of miracles which we have indicated had been found to hold water. Let us suppose, for the sake of argument, that the physicists had been less critical and that the attempt at a solution *via* the quantum theory had been generally accepted and welcomed. What would have been gained? Would anything which could be proved possible on the basis of statistical probability be a miracle at all? As far as the traditional concepts of the Church go, a miracle is the breaking through of the normal pattern of nature by a

[1] *Ibid.*, pp. 132f. For a further discussion along these lines see two introductory paperbacks: Ernst Zimmer, *Umsturz im Weltbild der Physik* (dtv 1964) and Arthur March, *Das neue Denken der modernen Physik* (Hamburg, 1957; rde 1967). See also A. March and I. M. Freeman, *The New World of Physics* (New York, 1962) based on the above.

direct divine intervention. What the scientific defence would like to offer us instead is really nothing other than a grandiose attempt at a natural explanation such as has been undertaken again and again since the Enlightenment. A miracle which is supposed to be possible according to natural law, in the face of all previous assumptions, is no longer a miracle at all; it is merely an – admittedly rare – natural phenomenon. Belief in miracle in the strictest sense could hardly welcome aid of this kind. Science would not have opened the way for miracles by these means; it would simply have explained them away altogether.

And what would one have in exchange? Are uncontrollable and fortuitously cumulative processes in the atomic sphere supposed to have seen to it that Jesus was able to walk on the Lake of Gennesaret (and Peter, too, for a moment, until his faith deserted him), an event in which Christians earlier saw the divinely supernatural power of faith?

Or, however unbelievable this may seem, did millions of simultaneous changes see to it that at least thirty gallons of water in six different pitchers were changed into wine at the marriage at Cana – and excellent wine at that? In this case how could the miracle serve to reveal Christ's glory – its sole point, according to the Gospel of John?

It must be clear without any further examples that ideas of this kind are untenable, both physically and theologically. There is no through way here to an understanding of the New Testament miracle stories; it is a *cul-de-sac*. One is merely substituting questionable atomic accidents for the old supernaturalism and with these one cannot cope theologically. The physicist theologians are not even consistent.

If one looks into their arguments more closely it appears that they themselves are not satisfied with the atomic accidents which physics offer them; for they are not interested in blind chance but in *God's activity in nature*. The findings of physics, which one might describe as a huge field of oscillation, must be supplemented by an extra power or force which sets into significant motion the elemental processes in the direction of calculated miraculous effects. The notion of 'God' as a physically active force must be added if miracles are to be possible through physics. In the words of Hans Rohrbach, a supporter of the physical explanation, this is a personal decision of faith, an 'unprecedentedly bold conclusion', far beyond the limits of what is open to scientific investigation. 'God speaks, his word comes to pass and manifests itself in the physical world as oscillation, as atomic particles, as matter.' The way in which God can act through his word, so interpreted, is described by Rohrbach as follows:

And now let me ask: is it not obvious that God can perform miracles? If it is God's will that the oil in the widow's cruse should never grow less, it only costs him a word – a word that creates the atoms which form oil and never let it come to an end. The same is true of the feeding of the five thousand. As long as Jesus breaks the bread and gives thanks, the bread increases in his hands because God wills that it should be so – increases so that at the end twelve baskets more of 'matter' are left over than was there at the beginning. . . . As regards the changing of water into wine at the marriage at Cana, one may perhaps think in the following way: that in one moment, through his life-giving and life-ending word, God calls in the atoms which make up the water molecules and creates those which form wine. For he calls us as well, when he no longer wills us to be there. Thus we read in the Scriptures: 'Thou turnest man to destruction; and sayest, Return, ye children of men' (Ps. 90.3); or: 'Thou takest away their breath, they die, and return to their dust' (Ps. 104.29). Scientifically speaking, this expresses the fact that through his word God dissolves the structural cohesion of the ultimate particles which he had once – again through his word – created in order to make our human organism a living one (Gen. 2.7). He called Lazarus to die. Why should he not also, on Jesus' plea, be able to rebuild into new life the atoms which made up Lazarus' body?[1]

One sees the natural explanation (which is supposed to make miracles once again conceivable) being quietly supplemented and completed by purely supernatural assumptions. An 'invisible kingdom of God' stands beyond or behind the field of oscillation; one might say that for faith our cosmos is not a closed system; it is open to divine influence; at any time 'new energy can flow into it' from God's word and energy can even be called in.[2] With the help of this assumption of faith, the literal sense of the biblical stories can indeed be preserved; but the supplementary assumptions which are necessary make the whole carefully constructed argument, which aimed to show the possibility of miracle purely from the point of view of physics, fall to the ground. A supplementary source of energy, 'God', who has now suddenly become responsible for certain (or all?) events within physical reality, is an impossibility physically speaking. Miracles are as inconceivable as ever.

When the naturalistic explanation is extended or strained in this way, it changes back into a supernatural one – otherwise the biblical miracles

[1] H. Rohrbach, *op. cit.*, p. 29.   [2] *Ibid.*

cannot be retained. Quantum jumps are apparently not enough. The enrolment of the most modern arguments from the sphere of physics ends in the same old supernaturalism, though admittedly in a more sophisticated form. Earlier, everything was crudely stated and described in concrete terms: heavenly or demonic forces, conceived in personified terms, intervene in the natural cosmos, manipulating things as they like and hence performing 'miracles' which do not occur naturally. A new supernaturalism deriving from physics says the same thing, but with a sovereign vagueness. It is now the atoms, not the angels, which carry God's commands to the world. Anyone who, like Rohrbach himself, is concerned to find an interpretation of miracles which can be reconciled with rational thought and does not condemn the believer to spiritual schizophrenia is not helped by this attempt. If the miracle stories of the Bible are to have a meaning today it must be sought for on a different plane of reality. For miracles cannot be retained on the level of historical fact.

A theological postscript

Anyone who has followed the discussion up to this point may well ask: why this display of acrimony on both sides? Must the question of whether miracles really happen be decided at all? Can it not be left open? Does what we think about it really matter anyway?

There are many people today, even among professing Christians, who would maintain that the question should finally be dropped. We know today, they say, pointing to one of the results of literary and textual study, that the texts are not proposing to relate 'miracles' to astonish the reader; they are witnessing to the glory of Christ and are a call to faith. Their purpose is kerygma, proclamation. It is high time that we took this seriously and buried the old, fruitless controversy about the historicity of miracles – a controversy which means putting a 'rationalis-tic' question to the texts which is entirely alien to the biblical point of view. In short, the question of whether the miracles really happened should simply cease to engage our interest. But this would be a suppres-sion of the problem, not a solution to it; and the dilemma cannot be resolved quite so easily.

In the first place, it is a matter of experience that the question of whether everything really happened as we are told that it did is one that is put by every child and by every even faintly interested contemporary; it is a question about which everyone has his own private opinion. In the second place, it is highly questionable whether an honest question of this kind can be eliminated by a reference to the kerygma. For the kerygma cannot be set up *a priori* as unquestionable authority to the man who wants information about the meaning of a text. It is itself involved in the historical cleft between the text and the modern reader and is as much a question as miracles themselves. Finally, we cannot reject a question because it is alien to the text itself. Anyone who follows this method is being blind to historical distinctions, is overlooking the fact of a constantly changing consciousness and is denying to modern times their right to raise their own questions.

What, then, depends on the answer to the question, theologically speaking? What is it that feeds the acrimony? Why do some Christians even resort to doubtful scientific arguments in order to preserve God's miraculous activity in nature? And why do others – also Christians – deny nature miracles, simply *because* of their faith in God? Is it enough to say: the former belong to the group of child-like spirits on whom a proclamation can only make an impact when it is accompanied by a powerful outward impression; their longing for miracles is so ineradicable that, as Heinrich Heine ironically remarked, they even cause God himself to make concessions to their capacity for understanding in his mode of revelation. And is it being just to the latter group when one says that they are incurably rationalistic and contentious, people who always know best and are even able to tell God himself the way in which he is to act, instead of listening humbly to his word. What difference does it make what group one decides for?

For one thing – if one looks at the New Testament first of all – it makes a difference to the way one thinks of Jesus. Is he a mighty being of superhuman power, who can manipulate the elements as he wills, stilling the storm and the waves, conjuring fish into the fisherman's net, abolishing the force of gravity, and altering his own material substance so that at one moment he is a man who can be touched and can eat and drink, and at the next a spirit who can pass through closed doors? Or is he an ordinary man who did nothing like this at all, and never wanted to; a man whose enormous significance expressed itself not in any physical abnormality but merely in his behaviour and in his destiny?

Nor is it Jesus' person alone which presents a different aspect according to the way one looks at it; his importance for those who make him their lodestone is also different. For faith itself bears a different stamp according to the object towards which it is directed.

The expectation and the hope of the believer is different – a difference which shows most clearly in his idea of prayer. Is God a God who can be found in the clouds and the winds, one who can be asked to send rain in time of drought? Can one attribute to him all kinds of direct interventions in nature and history and make him responsible for natural catastrophes as well as for 'special providences'? Is he a God of whom one can justly and reproachfully ask, after appalling wars: how can God allow these things?

What, in fact, is at issue in the question about miracles? It is apparently a number of antiquated habits of thought and belief which depend on the view that God is the direct and immediate ruler and guide, not only of human affairs but also of natural events. He can punish human sin through natural catastrophes, for instance, as the God of the Bible does in the primeval stories of the flood, and the fire which is rained down on sinful mankind. He can also save men through marvellous and exceptional dispensations in the sphere of nature when they call upon him in their need; for instance, he lets all kinds of plagues, drought, poor harvests, locusts, etc., descend upon the enemies of his chosen people and divides the sea for Israel, while letting Israel's pursuers drown.

Is this understanding of God, and the view of the world that goes with it, a Christian one? Is it part of the substance and unrelinquishable centre of the Christian faith that one should believe that God can, in principle and practice, perform miracles like this? Research into the history of religion has answered the question, showing that this picture of God and the world is not specifically Christian at all but is in fact, to varying degrees, the common stock of all the ancient religions down to the primitive stages of polytheism and polydemonism. Prayer, the magical invocation belonging to all the early stages of religion, presupposes that in natural events or behind them supernatural forces dwell and are effective and that these forces have to some extent a personal character which makes it possible for them to understand a human appeal and to react to it.

Today this religious picture of the world is largely faded and forgotten, even though traces of it still remain in the subconscious and its desires, sometimes rising to the surface in superstitions and day-dreams, in childish and poetically symbolic language, as well as in the primal spring of prayer, rising from some moment of need. Traces such as these have still not finally been absorbed into or reconciled with a new consciousness, and are still unconquered by a new interpretation of reality. In everyday life people do not come into contact with gods and demons any more, and even the God whom Christian faith visualizes as reigning above the world is no longer to be found in the space where the space capsules whirl. His sphere of influence – if we can still speak of it at all – has shifted in the minds of men; or should one rather say, has become concentrated in another place?

The sphere in which we can nowadays usefully speak of God's activity, his will, his rule, his promise, etc., is the 'heart' and 'conscience' of man; this has been so since Luther and Pascal, in whose thinking the consciousness of modern times first became theologically articulate. Man is responsible to God. God's 'word' is a word which is to bring man to knowledge of himself. . . . God is, for example, 'competent' for the question of the position man is to take up in the decisions which determine his existence, the way in which he is to interpret his life in the world, the opportunities he has and the goals he sets himself. Some present-day theologians support a well-founded thesis that this is the way in which God was always understood at the core of the biblical tradition – in the prophets, Jesus and Paul; indeed that God's command to men in the creation account – subdue the earth and have dominion over it – points clearly to the fact that according to biblical experience the historical process of the de-divinization and human domination of the world (i.e., the autonomy of man) had been marked out from the beginning and is not at all something to be lamented. Rather, what the biblical knowledge of God really means for the world has only now emerged, worked out, so to speak, through the process of history. It is only now being realized how radically the God of the Bible differs from the nature gods of the heathen and how different Jesus' claim on men is from the claim of the founders of the religions of the ancient world.

Where do we encounter God? This is the question one puts to the proclamation of Jesus. The parable of the Last Judgment gives the answer. As you did it to the least of these my brethren, you did it to me. God meets us in the history in which men live with one another; he is interested in *how* they live together – for instance, in righteousness and love. Jesus' prayer is therefore that God's kingdom may come on earth, in history. This is also the hope which drives Paul to proclaim God's revelation in Christ to the whole world. Even according to this view of the biblical proclamation, there is a point in speaking of God as the Creator and Lord of the world. In this view, too, God is the Lord of history. But the way he rules is conceived of in different terms – no longer directly or through nature but through the mediation of man and history. God acts by claiming men. What other point could the Christian doctrine of the incarnation have?

Two different views of Jesus Christ, God and the world therefore really come up against one another in the dispute about the interpretation of miracles or, more precisely, the historical factualness of Jesus' miracles. The person who is convinced on both rational and theological grounds of the rightness of the second view must, however, be prepared for some pressing questions from the opposing side. By declaring the miracles to be unhistorical, one is left without any explanation for the stories. How did they get into the text? Are they perhaps only fossils, survivals from the store of tradition, or concessions to the thought of the time? Are they merely confusing and should they simply be abandoned?

Or have they an enduring meaning, if not as historical records, yet as 'poetry'? Had Jesus' activity, even though non-miraculous, qualities which can be appropriately described through the concepts and concrete images offered by the miracle?

What was 'marvellous' about Jesus' work?

2 Belief in Miracles: A Theological Question

Does Christian faith contradict reason?

It is well known that since its beginnings, Protestant biblical criticism has found little favour with the institution which its varied attempts were ultimately designed to serve, that is to say the Church itself. Even today there is still in certain quarters a strained relationship between theological scholarship and the churches. The criticism of miracles in particular came up against violent opposition, even when this criticism was intended to be positive – that is to say, where it continued to give a positive meaning to the New Testament miracle stories.

It is important to remember that the conflict came, and comes, not only from basically conservative theologians and Christians or from those living with an out-dated world-view; it springs up again and again, seemingly from the very centre of the Christian faith. Why are there such obstinate objections in the Church to giving free rein to criticism of miracles?

One theological and apparently ultra-Christian argument hovers over every discussion on this theme. Is man not here making his reason the universal touchstone? Is he not, with the aid of science, prescribing the way in which God may and may not deal with the world? Is it not colossal arrogance when man says about the miracle stories of the Bible: I am going to decide what is a fact and what is not?[1] The subjective reasons which move the critics – love of truth, faithfulness to the facts and a sense of scientific responsibility – may be praiseworthy. But do not these motives conceal the less praiseworthy longing of the old Adam to prove oneself in the face of God right in all circumstances? Entrenched behind his up-to-date laboratories and libraries sits man as he has always been, not willing to recognize the sovereignty of God and anxious to put himself

[1] See, for example, A. Görres, 'Psychologie des Wunderglaubens', *Kontexte* I (Stuttgart and Berlin, 1965), p. 83.

in God's place.[1] Natural laws are an attempt to shield himself from God's intervention. The critic of all religious dogmas is dogmatic enough in his own views about miracles; he holds a dogmatic belief in science and reason. He is proud. He is unwilling to accept the 'humiliation' (Görres' word is *Demütigung*) which lies in the idea that he could be dependent on certain unique facts of history communicated by a witness whose reliability he is unable to test.

It is more seemly for a Christian to abandon all arrogant ideas and to accept the biblical proclamation in simple faith and without reservations. 'Am I, with my petty reason, to venture to judge the mighty acts of God?' This is the answer of piety in its most ingenuous form. The glorification of simple faith is matched by a depreciation of the possibilities open to human reason. This argument has accompanied the history of modern thought since the beginnings of the Enlightenment. It is old, but is it really Christian? Has it the support of the New Testament?

If we are going to consider this question seriously, it may be useful to look back to the beginnings of that movement of mind which first challenged the opposition of the Church. Two hundred years ago Reimarus, one of the originators of Protestant biblical criticism, wrote a little treatise with the title 'Of the Decrying of Reason from the Pulpit'[2]. It was published by Lessing in his Wolfenbüttel writings and contains a list of the opposing party's most important theological arguments together with Reimarus' answer.

> To these [the congregation] reason is painted as a weak, blind, corrupt and seductive guide; so that hearers who do not even properly know the meaning of reason or the reasonable become afraid to use their reason at all in seeking knowledge of divine matters, because they might perhaps thus be easily led into dangerous errors.

What do the preachers really say?

> It is there said that nothing that man knows of God through his own powers is an aid to salvation, for everything which does not spring from faith is sin. The natural man cannot grasp the things which are of God; they are to him foolishness and he cannot know them because they must be judged spiritually.

It is obvious that the argument derives from the New Testament and especially from Paul's epistles: 'They therefore admonish us, as with the

[1] *Ibid.*, pp. 81ff.
[2] *Von Verschreyung der Vernunft auf den Kanzeln* in G. E. Lessing, *Sämtliche Schriften*, ed. by K. Lachmann, vol. 12 (1897), pp. 304–316.

words of the Apostle Paul, that we should make our reasons captive to the obedience of faith.' Before Reimarus proceeds to a theological discussion, he considers the psychological and sociological effects of such precepts. Here we will only reproduce one of his highly remarkable observations – his indication that the behaviour of the believer shows a certain schizophrenia: 'This notion can in the mind of the devout believer only have the effect that, however he may apply his reason to the affairs of the world, he will take care as regards knowledge of God not to think rationally but will rather study to believe with meek obedience.'[1] In the inmost sphere of his life, where he is concerned with the knowledge of God and an interpretation of the meaning of his existence, man voluntarily renounces all his own means of judgment and submits himself blindly to a religious tradition. Here Reimarus puts a theological question: 'Are our revered theologians right in using faith to repress and smother reason and rational religion through faith?' Many arguments may be brought against this.

1. 'The example of their great teacher Jesus is not on their side. For he preached nought but a reasonable and practical religion.' This point, that Jesus himself has nothing to do with an anti-rational faith, is as clear as day to Reimarus and his successors and seems to them to need no further discussion.

2. 'Paul, however, whose words they constantly cite, did by no means intend to say what our revered theologians would like to extort from his writings. In part the words are wrongly translated, in part the purpose and context is contradicted by the interpretation.' This assertion must be proved from the text. 'The [natural] man does not receive the gifts of the Spirit of God, for they are folly to him and he is not able to understand them, because they are spiritually discerned' (I Cor. 2.14). This is the first of the Pauline sayings on which the preachers take their stand. What does Paul mean by the 'natural' man? 'The theologians interpret this as if the apostle is speaking of a man who is given over to his natural powers, particularly his innate reason, in contrast to a man whose mind has been illuminated by supernatural revelation. . . .' If one passage is not completely clear by itself, one puts all the passages together in which the word in question occurs and compares its meaning in the different contexts. It is also important to look at the wider context as well, in order to find out whether other related meanings for the word occur. Reimarus discovers that in the Letter to the Corinthians Paul sees in the envy and bickerings of different groups in the church a proof that the Corinthians

[1] *Ibid.*, pp. 305f.

are still *psychikós*, 'earthly', or, as it can also be translated, 'fleshly'; they do not yet possess the true spirit of Christ. He arrives at the following conclusion:

> If, then, the question is not concerned with the natural powers of understanding and with what they can and cannot grasp, but with a perverted, sensual will . . . which hinders the living knowledge or fear of the spirit: then it is apparent that our theologians commit an impropriety in applying these words to the incapacity and blindness of natural reason in spiritual things.[1]

Reimarus' conclusion is well founded, even if he has over-simplified. According to what he says, a misunderstanding of Pauline language would be responsible for the decrying of reason from the pulpit. Reimarus finds his thesis confirmed by a second passage: 'Yet another passage is busily held up to us, in which Paul also apparently gives Christians the precept that we must make our reasons captive to the obedience of faith. The passage I mean (II Cor. 10.3ff.) certainly contains no such thing, but rather the contrary.' In his Second Epistle to the Corinthians Paul writes:

> For though we live in the world we are not carrying on a worldly war, for the weapons of our warfare are not worldly but have divine power to destroy strongholds. We destroy arguments and every proud obstacle to the knowledge of God, and take every thought captive to obey Christ (AV: bringing into captivity every thought to the obedience of Christ) (II Cor. 10.3ff.).

Does Paul mean that reason itself must be overthrown? First of all, Reimarus explains Paul's pictorial method of expression very neatly:

> He pictures himself under the guise of a warrior who goes into battle in order to take a stronghold, destroys all the mighty fortresses which stand against him, and takes the now defenceless inhabitants prisoner. This makes everything plain. The campaign is his work of conversion; the spiritual weapons are his arguments; the strongholds, high walls and towers . . . which he overturned were the reasonings and objections . . . which the Corinthians had brought against him at the beginning; the clearing away of these bulwarks means the thorough answering of all doubts pertaining to the knowledge of God; the taking prisoner points to the complete conviction of the Corinthians as to the

---

[1] *Ibid.*, pp. 307ff.

truth of the Gospel, once that all their ways of escape had been taken from them; and the final result is the gaining of the obedience of those that are overcome, by which is meant obedience to Christ. I hope that here everything is as clear as anyone can desire.[1]

The point of Reimarus' answer is that what Paul says is the precise opposite of what his opponents would like to make him say: Paul does not overcome his opponents through the complete suppression and dismissal of reason but through the use of his *own* reason. Only certain deductions made by reason are overthrown, not reason itself. The end is an inner conviction of the truth of the Gospel and it is only in this way that true, and not slavish, obedience can be arrived at.

> Therefore obedience to Christ is an effect and achievement of Paul's persuasive preaching. The Corinthians are finally brought to their decision to obey Christ through irrefutable reasoning and through the complete removal of all their doubts. But to bring reason into captivity to the obedience of faith sounds as if faith, or the intention to obey the dictates of faith, was there from the first and must be a cause for the assent of reason: I believe and hence it must be true, let reason say what it will. But this is certainly the wrong order.

This last observation of Reimarus' about the wrong order finds confirmation even today, when many Christians view faith as a kind of payment in advance which must be made before they are prepared to enter into a discussion about individual points. First one must 'simply believe' (as they call it) a number of dogmatic statements – for example, that the Bible is the word of God, that Jesus is the Son of God and that he died for us; faith is not to grow from experience – what Reimarus calls inner conviction or persuasion – as is the normal and only honest method of forming a judgment in 'secular' matters. 'Reason cannot be subjected to obedience, its assent is not arbitrary, its satisfaction must be guaranteed before one can believe that a doctrine is true, that a witness is divine, before one can decide freely and willingly to obey what the doctrine demands.'[2]

Those who call themselves Protestants, at least, can have nothing to say against statements like these; for here, couched in the language of the Enlightenment, is the continuation of the Reformation, in which the liberty of a Christian struck out against an illiberal and legalistic ecclesiastical faith. An arbitrary faith, faith as payment in advance, fell under

---

[1] *Ibid.*, pp. 309ff.   [2] *Ibid.*, p. 312.

Luther's condemnation in the same way as mediaeval good works, the works of the law, the works of men. Nor will one easily be able to reproach reason with arrogance and imperviousness to divine influence as long as it strives after inner conviction and assent before it decides.

In this question, at least, Reimarus is right. Whether he has not finished with his Pauline text too soon and too lightly is another matter. For the theologians and preachers could now reproach him with having deliberately passed over a word which Paul thought very important: the word folly or foolishness. 'They are folly to him, and he is not able to understand them' stands clearly in the text in reference to the natural man's helplessness as regards spiritual things. Reimarus is doubtless right when he says that in Paul the natural man is largely characterized by his evil will or worldly attitude. But it cannot be seriously maintained that there is no reference to the natural man's *reason*. The 'inner conviction of faith' of Reimarus' naturalistic and rational religion cannot be read quite so smoothly into Paul's exposition. 'Where is the wise man?' Paul demands challengingly of the Corinthians with their pride in their wisdom. 'Where is the scribe? Where is the debater of this age? Has not God made foolish the wisdom of the world? For since, in the wisdom of God, the world did not know God through wisdom, it pleased God through the folly of what we preach to save those who believe' (I Cor. 1.20).

Paul can appeal to the fact that even in the Old Testament, in Isaiah, wisdom fell under divine condemnation: 'For it is written,

"I will destroy the wisdom of the wise,
  and the cleverness of the clever I will thwart" ' (I Cor. 1.19).

The matter seems to be clear: here is the root of the traditional Christian rejection of reason and for the recommendation of a simple faith in an apparently foolish message. This is the invasion point for the *credo quia absurdum*, 'I believe because it is absurd', and for that abandonment of the criteria of reason which is summed up in a sentence of Duns Scotus, one of the last of the scholastics: if God had so willed it, he could have been incarnate in a donkey. Here man places himself wholly, with all that he has, at the disposal of the absolute power of God, even when this appears arbitrary.

Naturally enough, Christians who willingly believe in the biblical miracles and cling determinedly to the whole supernatural structure, even if it is irreconcilable with the discoveries of science, appeal to sentences like these. They do so because they see their faith in what is humanly speaking impossible as an act of holy folly, pleasing to God. Are they right? It would seem like it. The preaching of Paul is not without offence, without what he calls folly. Reimarus overlooked this. Paul stresses firmly to the Corinthians that he has not come to them 'with eloquent wisdom' – as one might think after reading what Reimarus has to say. His preaching was thought by the Gentiles to be simply silly and by the Jews was even viewed as provocation: 'a stumbling block to the Jews and folly to the Gentiles'.

The 'stumbling block' of faith is an expression which is also, in discussion, frequently held up to the supporters of a rational interpretation of the miracle stories. Are they not through their criticism destroying the stumbling block of faith? Are they not tailoring faith much too neatly to the requirements of 'modern man'? But what in actual point of fact is the stumbling block, the *skandalon*, the offence? What did Paul have to say to his hearers in Corinth that it so antagonized the intellectuals in the congregation? Was it the miracles which the Gospel accounts tell us Jesus performed, walking on the lake like a spirit, turning water into wine and raising the dead? Or was it the miracles connected with his own person: that he was conceived from heaven, without the aid of any earthly father; that he was born of a virgin; that he rose from the grave and ascended into heaven? It was nothing like this. Paul does indeed report the appearances of the risen Christ, but apart from that there is not a word in the epistles about Jesus' miracles. It is important to be clear on that point. And Paul was not even writing at a much later period, when perhaps details of the kind had been forgotten. His letters are the earliest documents we have telling of the Christ of the New Testament. Although, therefore, Jesus' miracles play no part at all in Paul's letters, he still speaks of faith in Jesus Christ and this faith has some inherent stumbling block for Greek and Jewish thinking. In Paul, therefore, reason's stumbling block must be looked for in another direction; it is not the much discussed stumbling block behind the modern question of whether one must believe in miracles.

'For Jews demand signs and Greeks seek wisdom, but we preach Christ crucified, a stumbling block to Jews and folly to Gentiles' (I Cor. 1.22f.). The stumbling block for Paul is the cross. Why? The concept of a stumbling block or offence can be found elsewhere in the Bible. In Isaiah God himself becomes for the house of Israel 'a stone of offence, and a rock of stumbling. . . . And many shall stumble thereon; they shall fall and be broken . . .' (Isa. 8.14). Here the ways are to part, for good or evil. It is in recollection of this saying that the prophetic word can be spoken over the child Jesus at his presentation in the temple: 'Behold, this child is set for the fall and rising of many in Israel, and for a sign that is spoken against' (Luke 2.34). And if one follows the Gospel accounts of Jesus' words and actions, he himself gave continual offence – to his family, to the scribes and Pharisees, and in the end even to his disciples. 'You will all fall away (AV 'be offended') because of me this night,' says Jesus on the road to Gethsemane, 'for it is written, "I will strike the shepherd, and the sheep of the flock will be scattered"' (Matt. 26.31). The imprisonment of Jesus, his humiliation and crucifixion were the stumbling block *per se* for all who had hoped that he would redeem Israel (Luke 24.21). Rejected by the world and abandoned by God – such a son of God was bound to be an offence to Jews and Gentiles alike, all of whom expected visible power and glory from their gods.

Despised, persecuted for religious reasons, shamefully executed by the political authorities – this man was now proclaimed by Christians as the revealer of God and saviour of the world. It was a scandalous reversal of values. And the same reversal of values was visible in the lives of those who believed the message. Paul points this out to the Corinthians:

> For consider your call, brethren; not many of you were wise according to worldly standards, not many were powerful, not many were of noble birth; but God chose what is foolish in the world to shame the wise, God chose what is weak in the world to shame the strong, God chose what is low and despised in the world, even things that are not, to bring to nothing things that are, so that no human being might boast in the presence of God (I Cor. 1.26–29).

The reversal of values has its root in the will of God himself. What kind of God is this, and why does he deal with the world in this way? Why does he reject the wisdom of the wise? Is it out of pure capriciousness? The saying of Isaiah which Paul quotes in this context shows the reasons which lie behind this belief about God:

> And the Lord said:
>   'Because this people draw near with their mouth
>   and honour me with their lips,
>   while their hearts are far from me,
>   and their fear of me is a commandment of men learned by rote;
>   therefore, behold, I will again
>   do marvellous things with this people,

wonderful and marvellous;
and the wisdom of their wise men shall perish,
and the discernment of their discerning men shall be hid' (Isa.
29.13f.).

God rejects worship and obedience which does not come from the heart,
from inner conviction. Wisdom which dissociates itself from his commands has no validity. 'Behold, the fear of the Lord, that is wisdom,'
says Job, 'and to depart from evil is understanding' (Job 28.28).

Anyone familiar with the Old Testament knows how highly knowledge,
insight, wisdom and understanding are regarded there. But not everyone
is wise, and insight can be lost, and the understanding can be darkened.
Paul testifies that his Jewish brethren are zealous for God, but this zeal
is not bound up with true knowledge (Rom. 10.2). 'Woe to you lawyers!
for you have taken away the key of knowledge,' says Jesus to the scribes,
'you did not enter yourselves and you hindered those who were entering'
(Luke 11.52).

In his words and deeds Jesus revealed a new knowledge of God and
proclaimed a new message of salvation to men – one has only to think of
the Beatitudes in the Sermon on the Mount, which nearly all speak of the
salvation of which all partake who suffer under the injustices of the
world and still remain steadfast in love.

The crucifixion is the answer which the world gave to the man who
preached these things. But death cannot touch the truth of his preaching. On the contrary, to the faith which overcomes the offence of the
cross, Jesus becomes Lord of the world. Paul can even say that God
made the crucified Christ, who is an offence in the eyes of the world, 'our
wisdom'. A higher wisdom grows out of the folly of the cross: 'Let no
one deceive himself. If any one among you thinks that he is wise in this
age, let him become a fool that he may become wise' (I Cor. 3.18).

Anyone who has followed Paul's train of thought is now in a position
to answer the question put at the beginning about the rights and wrongs
of 'the decrying of wisdom from the pulpit'.

The teachers of ancient Israel did not demand the abandonment of all
wisdom but rather the renewal of that wisdom in the fear of the Lord.
Not abandonment, but rather a *metánoia*, a rethinking of reason, is also
demanded of his hearers by Jesus: not a blind acceptance of his message but attention to it and a conscious decision based on knowledge.
The world of the cross is not nonsense but new sense to the man that
understands it; not folly but the power and wisdom of God.

Christian faith therefore does not mean that reason should be abandoned, but that it should be correctly orientated. And the offence with which reason is confronted is not an intellectual hindrance, something inconceivable, like some of the miracles; it is the difficulty of believing, practically and existentially, that love overcomes death. The overcoming of the offence is not achieved, according to the New Testament, by deciding through an effort of will – or even cheerfully! – to believe an absurdity; it comes about, as the Whitsun story shows, through the spirit, or the illumination of the understanding; or, one can say with Reimarus: through an inner conviction of the truth of the proclamation.

Reimarus is therefore right in the main point under discussion: Paul is talking about something different from what the theologians and preachers suppose when they appeal to him in their attempts to suppress and smother reason through faith. When Paul holds up the cross to worldly wisdom as a touchstone, he is calling in question, for both Jews and Gentiles, a total spiritual and religious interpretation of reality which had always offered a particular answer to the question of God and the true path of man. He is not thinking of discrediting human capacity for reason as such. On the contrary, he presupposes this, and to a demandingly high standard, in every sentence that he writes to his congregation. He appeals to wisdom as the prophets and teachers of Israel had always done and as Jesus himself also did. The cross of Christ becomes a decisive new argument in Paul's dispute with Greek and Jewish thought, but it certainly does not mean the beating down of all arguments or the annulment of all argumentation. In other words, the discussion is carried on within the confines of reason, not outside them.

It is hence only open to us to conclude that a disastrous misunderstanding, with the resulting false application, of Paul's theology of the cross has led the Church for centuries to extol a Christianity of holy simplicity and broken spiritual backbone, and to confuse humility with the subjection of reason. With all his reservations as regards the wisdom of this world (today one might perhaps speak of the ruling ideologies), Paul would probably have had no objection to the fundamental endeavours of Protestant biblical criticism. He was in any case not interested in physical miracles; they do not fit into the picture which he gives of the earthly Jesus and they are meaningless for the Christology that he preaches. As for those Christians and theologians who find it necessary, in the name of the sovereignty of God, to admonish the critical reason as to the need for humility, – they are zealous for God, but is it possibly zeal without understanding? Perhaps it is not this particular sacrifice that God is asking, although they are willing to make it. Perhaps he wants something different. And perhaps in this particular case their diffidence is inappropriate.

Is their doctrine of humility safe from the danger of itself becoming a mechanical law which may today prevent men, in Isaiah's phrase, from drawing near to God with their hearts?

3 A Counter-question: Is Criticism of Miracles Justified?

C. S. Lewis: *We must ask the right preliminary questions!*

> And when you turn from the New Testament to modern scholars, remember that you go among them as a sheep among wolves. Naturalistic assumptions, beggings of the question . . . will meet you on every side – even from the pens of clergymen . . .[1]

In 1947 C. S. Lewis, literary scholar and author of popular books on Christianity, published a book about miracles in which he defended the ancient supernatural standpoint in the face of all modern objections. Lewis works philosophically, not exegetically, for he is convinced of the essential pre-eminence of the philosophical question: 'Those who wish to succeed must ask the right preliminary questions.'[2] 'It is no use going to the texts until we have some idea about the possibility or probability of the miraculous. Those who assume that miracles cannot happen are merely wasting their time by looking into the texts; we know in advance what results they will find for they have begun by begging the question.'[3] 'What we learn from experience depends on the kind of philosophy we bring to experience.'[4]

Lewis, that is to say, points out that the presuppositions with which an exegete approaches a text have an important, even a decisive, influence on the result of his investigations. The correctness of this observation is obvious. For example, a scholar's view of the life of Jesus will take its colouring from whether he accepts the unusual events before and after Jesus' birth, the later miracles and the final resurrection and ascension as simple matters of fact or not. Even his view of external

---

[1] C. S. Lewis, *Miracles* (1947; Fontana, 1960), p. 168; the page references are taken from the Fontana edition.

[2] Aristotle, *Metaphysics*, II, (III), i, quoted by Lewis as chapter sub-heading to *Miracles*, ch. 1.

[3] Lewis, *op. cit.*, p. 8.   [4] *Ibid.*, p. 7

facts, such as the date when the Gospels were written and their author-
ship, will depend largely on how far he accepts the supernatural as fact
or not. An example will make this clear. The answer to the question of
whether the Gospel of Luke was written before or after the Jewish War
of AD 70 will depend in part on one's attitude to one of Jesus' prophecies, which refers directly to the destruction of Jerusalem (Luke
19.43ff.; Luke 21.20ff.). It is the general practice in such cases for
scholars to assume a later formulation, *ex eventu*, after the event had
taken place – a formulation which the evangelist puts into Jesus' mouth
at a suitable opportunity for a particular theological reason. This viewpoint is particularly acceptable here because this definite prophecy is
not found in the earlier Marcan text, which is the basis of Luke. But if
Jesus' words are accepted as genuine prophecy, it is possible under
certain circumstances to arrive at an earlier date of composition.

It is therefore important to establish the presuppositions on which the
standards of historical criticism which are applied in any given case
depend. This is undoubtedly true – even though one could argue that
Lewis' statement is reversible: the presuppositions with which we approach experience depend in their turn mainly on what we have learnt
from experience in the past. The history of liberal critical exegesis can
show examples enough of how scholars, under the influence of unexpected results achieved through research, abandon the presuppositions to
which they had clung earlier.

The presuppositions with which Lewis himself approaches miracles
can best be gathered from his polemic against the attitude of mind which
he is combating and against whose representatives he finds it necessary
to warn his readers in urgent terms at the end of his 'preliminary study'.
He gives the name of 'naturalism' or 'monism' to the attitude he
means.

> In using the books of such people you must therefore be continually
> on guard. You must develop a nose like a bloodhound for those steps
> in the argument which depend not on historical and linguistic know-
> ledge but on the concealed assumption that miracles are impossible,
> improbable, or improper. And this means that you must really re-
> educate yourself: must work hard and consistently to eradicate from
> your mind the whole type of thought in which we have all been brought
> up.[1]

We all have Naturalism in our bones and even conversion does not

---

[1] *Ibid.*, p. 169.

at once work the infection out of our system. Its assumptions rush back upon the mind the moment vigilance is relaxed.[1]

Lewis gives the name of naturalism to the philosophy which includes, roughly speaking, the following features: the world (the totality of being) is largely characterized as nature. Nature is an ultimate existence, complete in itself, neither set in motion by nor dependent on any 'supernatural' power. Within nature there are evolutions from lower to higher forms of life; man, too, as a physical and spiritual being, is viewed in the flux of evolution as natural existence. The mind is largely determined in terms of nature; it is not a separate entity and has no bonds with anything outside nature; for there *is* nothing at all outside nature. Hence naturalism (because it knows no opposition of different principles within the system of nature and recognizes no confronting reality outside that system) is in its very nature 'monism'.

What Lewis thus describes as monism is a particular variety of what can be generally observed since the European Enlightenment as a concentration of methods of knowledge on the *one reality*; as a forcing back of the supernatural to the same extent to which man gains a general picture of, and control over, his world (this was the first phase of the Enlightenment); and as an interpretative tracing back of the supernatural (on the basis of human reality) to a projection of man's own consciousness (the second phase of the Enlightenment). Like the Scottish novelist Bruce Marshall, who shares his attitude, Lewis resists this development vigorously. He swims consciously against the stream. And we cannot ignore the element of truth in the point of view of the two writers. Both are completely convinced that in its mental and spiritual manifestations hitherto, the monistic system has no room for what they would comprehend under the headings of spirit, reason and truth. Consequently both are determined to cling to the old supernaturalism, even at the cost of appearing hopelessly old-fashioned.

The two clergymen who stand talking outside the doors of their churches in Bruce Marshall's novel *Father Malachy's Miracle* symbolize the problem inherent in their mental situation. One of them, a fine, well-dressed, upstanding gentleman with 'semi-Grecian features' (a Protestant latitudinarian of course) thinks that miracles are 'really so very unnecessary and so very impossible',[2] because they contradict natural law. 'Surely we must bring religion into line with modern

---

[1] *Ibid.*, p. 168.
[2] Marshall, *op. cit.*, p. 31.

thought, must we not?'[1] An advertising slogan is pinned up on the door of his church:

> COME TO EVENSONG.
> IT'S CHEAPER
> THAN
> THE PICTURES.
> GOD DOESN'T MIND IF YOU HOLD HER HAND.[2]

The other, Father Malachy, is a small shrivelled figure in shabby clothes. He represents another way of thinking.

> For monks think, funnily enough, that the Christian religion was true when it was delivered by the apostles and that therefore it cannot be improved or made more true, since truth, like God, is eternal.[3]

> I am just as entitled to believe that two and two make five as I am to believe that Our Lord could let the world be deceived in essential matters for nearly sixteen hundred years.[4]

So here we have on the one side 'the normal healthy English mind'[5] which moves with the times: with no real point of view, relativist and stupid; and on the other 'the obstinate obscurantism of the monkish mind'[6] for which history simply does not exist, taking its stand on absolute truth but 'a little *vieux jeu*'.[7] What is the purpose of this anti-thesis?

The more superficial and relativistic a view of the meaning and happi-ness of life is, the more inappropriate it would seem that the Christian Church should deliver over the treasure of its divine marvels and truths to this way of thought – a way of thought which is not even capable of developing ethical norms. As long as the Christian spirit sees no chance of incorporating itself anew in modern reality, it persists outside that reality in its old form – sacramental, undeveloped and mystical. Yet the reader has the distinct feeling that things cannot go on as they are; this is a situation which must be overcome; it is a transitional stage. Neither of the points of view which confront one another in a fruitless alterna-tive are really genuine. They are caricatures.

The arguments of both authors sound confusing, although they are clearly formulated. Justifiable criticism of the contemporary scene is mixed with old-fashioned apologetics. If one examines the arguments

[1] *Ibid.*, p. 26.   [2] *Ibid.*, p. 24.   [3] *Ibid.*, p. 26.   [4] *Ibid.*, p. 27.
[5] *Ibid.*, p. 30.   [6] *Ibid.*, p. 26.   [7] *Ibid.*, p. 28.

more carefully one discovers an occasional direct reversal of such concepts as mind, reason and understanding; for these concepts are intended to support belief in a supernatural world as counter-move to naturalism. For Lewis, reason is itself supernatural! Rational thinking must hold fast to, and even re-justify, the old supernatural standpoint, unshaken by the eddies of merely natural and emotional convictions. This is Lewis' intention in his book when, with strained reasoning, he tries to show an irrational belief in miracles to be a rational possibility; and his readers are to learn to do the same.

And yet . . . and yet . . . It is that *and yet* which I fear more than any positive argument against miracles: that soft, tidal return of your habitual outlook as you close the book and the familiar noises from the street re-assert themselves. Perhaps (if I dare suppose so much) you have been led on at times while you were reading, have felt ancient hopes and fears astir in your heart, have perhaps come almost to the threshold of belief – but now? No. It just won't do. Here is the ordinary, here is the 'real' world, round you again. The dream is ending . . .[1]

Your rational thinking has no foothold in your merely natural consciousness except what it wins and maintains by conquest. The moment rational thought ceases, imagination, mental habit, temperament, and the 'spirit of the age' take charge of you again. New thoughts, until they have themselves become habitual, will affect your consciousness as a whole only while you are actually thinking them. Reason has but to nod at his post, and instantly Nature's patrols are infiltrating. . . .[2]

Now all reasonable people and all reasonable Christians have always known that it is not a mark of the spirit to be conformed to this world at all costs, as the apostle Paul puts it. A critical reserve in the face of the spirit of the age (such as Father Malachy embodies through his whole attitude of mind and such as Lewis tries to justify intellectually in his book) is for Paul the sign of the liberty for which Christ has set men free. A deep-lying distrust of natural indolence, a strict mental control of immediate feelings and habits of thought are an indispensable part of the believing person's self-reflection. In so far Lewis is right. The only question is whether such herculean efforts (leaving the theoretical impeachableness of the results on one side) really serve the cause to which

[1] Lewis, *op. cit.*, p. 170.   [2] *Ibid.*

they are dedicated and whether this is the right way to make the things of faith effective in the world.

Does not the thorough 're-education' of one's thinking which Lewis demands, and the total 'eradication' of the kind of thinking customary in modern times mean that Christian faith no longer has any immediate reality or any direct power of conviction? Does it not mean that the sacred story, like a novel of former times shut away between the covers of a book, can find no continuation in the everyday environment of the contemporary reader? That it needs an enormous, forced and artificial mental *tour de force* of the kind that Lewis' book represents if even the shadow of a right to existence is to be secured in the real world of today for a supernatural world order and a providential ordering of history?

This is no more than a question as to the practical results or fruits of a theory; but it is clearly a not illegitimate one from the Christian's point of view. Lewis puts a scholarly question about the presuppositions which permit us to make a basic decision for or against miracles. Bruce Marshall, in a witty theological satire, points to the Achilles heel of a theology which, through the uncritical assimilation of a still immature 'modern' thinking, is in danger of losing the substance of what it stands for. Both writers justly demand that modern theology should re-consider the presuppositions of its thinking. But, though one may recognize the good intention, it is impossible to avoid reproaching the writers, as well as a whole school of pious and purely conservative literature, for making matters too easy for themselves by merely caricaturing the ideas of their opponents instead of taking their genuine problems seriously and helping to clear up difficulties for which historical factors may be made responsible. Lewis and like-minded writers take their stand on the ground of a spiritual absolutism which is in fact also merely a historical point of view. They think it is enough to leave things as they were. But by so doing they are probably doing poor service both to God and to modern thought.

But the question of presuppositions is worthy of serious consideration and we shall turn to it in our next chapter.

4 The Presuppositions of the Historical-critical Method

Ernst Troeltsch: Everything is made relative

What standards does the historian adopt when he makes the stories of the Bible the subject of his research? One can only suppose that his standards are the same as those he believes to be right and appropriate in other contexts. Or ought he to have two different standards? If, therefore, he views with extreme scepticism the story of an ancient writer which tells that a god's arrow, aimed at the vulnerable heel of a god-like hero, gave a decisive turn to the battle of Troy, he will not ascribe any more probability to the story in Exodus of how the Lord God divided the waters for the children of Israel, while allowing their enemies to drown. And how are we to react to the account in the Book of Joshua of how at the battle of Gibeon God told the sun and moon to stand still until Israel had taken complete revenge on its enemies? Why should the historian, when using a historian's normal standards, make an exception for the God of Israel? He will certainly not simply dismiss such stories as the purest nonsense or fantasy; but neither will he seriously take them as adequately reported facts. They are primarily no more than documents of a (to us) alien and antique method of grasping the events of reality and expressing them in words. The real event which was the original basis is therefore not directly derivable from the texts, but can only be indirectly deduced, if at all, from them. With this aim the historian can try to distinguish what the real occasion of the story might have been and what interpretative, formative elements have penetrated from the subjective world of the story-teller into the language of the report. The historian can try to solve the first question (the real occasion of the story) by examining the general reliability of his source and – if the event is related several times, as is the case with the story of Moses – by comparing the various accounts and weighing one against another. He will also look for extra-biblical sources, drawing on archaeological finds, taking account of geographical factors, and so on. He can try to solve the question of the subjective elements by investigating the linguistic characteristics of the text. Here he may observe, for example, that natural events which are of an unusual kind but which those familiar with the country would not find at all extraordinary (such as the drying up of water, or its ebb and flow, under the influence of strong winds; or the unexpected appearance of manna and quails in the desert) were interpreted by Israel during its exodus from Egypt as special dispensations of Yahweh. Indeed it is in general a feature of the style of the Old Testament historical accounts to lay all events, even normal and natural ones, at the door of divine providence – a point to which Spinoza and Reimarus drew attention at the beginning of the Enlightenment.

It is therefore characteristic of the historian's method of approach that (irrespective of the period from which the material derives) he does not simply 'believe' a historical account, but views it on principle with, so to speak, professional scepticism. Scepticism here means only that he does not accord the material immediate acceptance, but reserves judgment. For it is now his function to preside over the case for truth, to hear the witnesses for both sides, to listen to expert opinions, to form a judgment as to what degree of probability can be ascribed to the various witnesses and finally to form a picture of the course which events probably took 'in reality'.

This procedure is known simply as historical criticism. In sketching the stages of the procedure, the analogy of the trial, the legal method of arriving at truth, inevitably presents itself; the historian shares some of the judge's characteristics, but also some of the detective's, for he looks behind the façade of outward appearances and tries to discover what these really conceal. Historical criticism is in fact not only a matter for scholars; it plays an important role everywhere in life where we want to discover the exact circumstances of some happening or other. 'We think historically, in other words, when as parents we try to determine which one of the children is telling the truth about the crayon marks on the bedroom walls, or when, as friends, we try to discover the root of a mis-understanding, or when, as citizens, we try to make out the real meaning of a public pronouncement on a civic crisis. Historical thinking is an ingredient in all of our thinking.[1]

[1] Van A. Harvey, *The Historian and the Believer* (New York, 1966; London, 1967), p. 78. Harvey's book offers an acute and suggestive investigation of the nature of historical criticism and the problems of its application to the Bible, together with a consideration of the different perspectives of 'historian' and 'believer'.

One would now like to know more precisely from where the historian gets the standards according to which he forms his judgments. And what presuppositions does he hold about the events of the past, including the biblical narratives, when he submits them in this way to the process of historical investigation?

1. The historian decides, after careful consideration, on the degree of probability which the report of an alleged fact can justly claim for itself; but he cannot do this without drawing, as a criterion, on the whole store of knowledge which has been won from experience up to date – or at least not without having this in the background. To return to an example we took at the beginning: a historian will treat reports about a miraculous intervention by the gods in the wars of the nations as highly improbable, because he knows of no analogy in the whole sphere of contemporary knowledge. Today no gods hasten to the help of those in danger, even in cases of the most flagrant injustice. And the historian will prefer the natural explanation of manna and quails to the story of miraculous provender, because it has long been known from travellers' tales (and meanwhile from the encyclopaedias) that these manifestations are unique neither in nature nor occasion; they are normal events which may be described as follows:

> Manna is tamarisk manna which is produced by scale-insects (*Trabutina mannipara* and more especially *Najacoccus serpentinus*) in the course of the metamorphosis of the nutritious content of tamarisk leaves. The insects excrete whitish or yellowish syrupy drops which crystallize in the dry air and reach the size of peas. They fall to the ground towards morning and are gathered early in the day by the Bedouins and later by the ants. Their season is May to July.
>
> Similarly, the appearance of great flocks of quails in the desert between Egypt and Palestine is nothing extraordinary. They come from the African interior in the spring and fly north over Egypt, returning by the same route in the autumn. The tired birds can easily be caught with the hand.[1]

If the criteria used in forming judgments derive in each case from the particular stage reached by contemporary knowledge, then they are in a certain sense themselves historically relative: they develop and are modified to the degree to which knowledge develops and is modified in the individual fields of empirical research. Consequently they may quite

[1] See A. Heising, *Die Botschaft der Brotvermehrung*, Stuttgarter Bibelstudien 15 (1966), p. 23; quoted from *Lexikon für Theologie und Kirche*[2], VI, 1361.

possibly be advanced and thoroughly established in certain areas of knowledge and still be uncertain and incomplete elsewhere. In his investigation of the way in which a historian arrives at a judgment, Harvey draws attention to this fact in order to explain a phenomenon which leaps to the eye in connection with the contemporary critical evaluation of miracle stories: the fact that we declare without any hesitation some stories to be absolutely impossible, whereas we allow an element of doubt to remain about others which are no less remarkable:

Very few historians, for example, would hesitate to apply the category 'legend' to the story of the saint who, after being beheaded, walked a few hundred yards to a cathedral with his head under his arm, entered the sanctuary and there sang the *Te Deum*. The historian calls it a legend because it is 'impossible'; i.e., knowing what we now know about vocal chords, their relationship to the brain and to the lungs, he can bring forward the strongest warrants in rebuttal of any such conclusion. The warrants are tight, and it is inconceivable how they could be loosened. There are countless other judgments relatively new in the history of thought that one cannot conceive of being altered or relative to the time – the spherical shape of the earth, the circulation of the blood, the necessity of oxygen for the brain, etc. On the other hand, a good historian may be less skeptical of a report of a miraculous cure, not because he believes in miracles, but because psychosomatic medicine is still in its infancy and no tight warrants are forthcoming. This being so, there is considerable room for rebuttal arguments.

The varying degree of tightness of our warrants casts some light on why some alleged miracles are harder to believe than others, a phenomenon that is, on the face of it, quite odd, since in the realm of miracles, no one miracle should be any more difficult to believe than another. Why, for example, does the modern mind have more difficulty believing that Jesus could calm a storm or walk on water than that he could heal the sick? The answer, I think, lies in the fact that we know enough about the causes of weather to believe it to be highly unlikely for it to be altered by fiat. So, too, we know enough about weight, specific gravity, and the like to make it difficult to believe that a man could, by exercise of will power, walk on water. On the other hand, we are aware that sickness often has a relationship to the mind, and we are acquainted with stories of strange cures even in the present. To be sure, we make a kind of distinction between the cures of broken bones and the cures of hysterical blindness, but we neverthe-less do not think ourselves justified in ruling out a healing miracle. The warrants, in short, are less tight in the latter area than in the former. Not all of our warrants stand on the same level. Some of our modern knowledge is virtually certain; a great deal of it is less so and subject to change.[1]

Are the standards of contemporary knowledge therefore valueless or nearly so? This would be a purely abstract conclusion. In real life no-body seriously interested in discovering the truth – in whatever sphere – would fail to make use of all the means at his command. He is bound to the limitations of his own time. Certain tools are at his disposal. How-ever conscientiously and cautiously he may go to work, he is none the less bound to make use of them. What point would there be in waiting?

The non-historian may occasionally be surprised by a habit which might be ascribed to the historian's conscientiousness and caution: he avoids on principle using the terms possible or impossible in his evalua-tions, but weighs up the degree of probability of every type of trans-mitted material. According to distinguished historians, this field (unlike the fields of mathematics or logic) only allows judgments as to proba-bility. This is perhaps understandable in view of the fact that the events of past history are no longer open to inspection. This does not make a great deal of difference to the question of miracle. Practically speaking, the least degree of probability is enough to exclude miracle as the expla-nation of an event. It makes as little difference as it does to the physicist's view of miracles, although in recent times he also only speaks, in the strictest sense, of statistical or probability judgments.

The present scientific criteria, as well as those of religious and cultural history, are sufficient to explain most religious miracle stories, including the biblical ones; this has been demonstrated in the previous chapters from the varying perspectives of the different disciplines. Apart from the healings mentioned by Harvey, there are related cases – 'expulsion of demons', healings from a distance, 'appearances' of all kinds – which belong to the realm of psychology and parapsychology. We shall perhaps discover that more things are possible in this sphere than the enlightened mind generally accepts. But these manifestations are not, according to the scientific view, actually miracles; that is to say, they are not empiri-cally absolutely inexplicable events which force us to believe in the inter-vention of a supernatural world; they remain still unexplained *earthly*

---

[1] Harvey, *op. cit.*, pp. 116f.

phenomena. Significantly, one speaks of still obscure depths of reality, not of manifestations of a supernatural world. Even Christians who would not agree with this classification of miracles, respond with great reserve to the question of whether it is possible or profitable to rest faith in the supernatural ultimately on occult phenomena. For numerous other Christians the critical and historical attitude to miracles has at least a positive result in that it has led Christian faith away from the occult angle, presenting it as a thing which can be a meaningful possibility even for people without any particular religious aptitude in the unmysterious everyday life of the modern workaday world. But this outcome is a result of the historical method – the application of present knowledge as standard for the evidences of the past. Anything that meets these standards is something which can stand up to contemporary scrutiny and which can at least lay claim to be taken seriously by the contemporary mind.

2. In this procedure, however, one presupposition must not be overlooked – one where there is a fundamental division of opinion in the dispute about the application of historical methods to the Bible. When the historian forms a judgment, on the basis of present-day knowledge, about the probability or improbability of events as they have been handed down to us, and further, when he makes the attempt to reconstruct the course of those past events, he presupposes a certain homogeneity of all historical happenings, at least in broad outline. Instead of homogeneity one might perhaps speak of *analogy*. The observation of homogeneity in the happenings of the world surrounding us – that summer follows spring and age follows youth, that fire burns, bread satisfies hunger, etc. – is the presupposition which makes it possible for men to know or learn anything at all; it is only on this basis that they can acquire a store of knowledge derived from experience beyond the succession of fleeting momentary impressions. But while the homogeneity of natural events is obvious to everyone, it is an open question, and a highly controversial one, how far one can speak of a homogeneity of phenomena in human and historical life (in spite of proverbial wisdom like 'clogs to clogs in three generations' and 'too many cooks spoil the broth'). We need not here enter into the difficult philosophical and anthropological problems which are involved in a thorough discussion of this question, but we shall see that in the context of the historical method, the concept of homogeneity can only be used in a very wide, general and formal sense which leaves plenty of room for all possible differentiation of content in individual historical phenomena.

At the beginning of this century – at the end of the epoch of Protestant liberalism and in the heyday of historical research – the important historian and religious philosopher Ernst Troeltsch (1865–1923) indulged in some reflections on the historical method which are still a matter of dispute in modern theological thinking.[1] His exposition of the principle of analogy and two further principles of the historical viewpoint – the interplay or correlation of all happening and a universal historical coherence – show with extreme clarity the main difficulties which arise from the intrusion of the historical attitude into dogmatic Christianity.

> The only method which makes criticism even possible is the application of analogy. The analogy of what we actually see happen before our eyes and what goes on within ourselves is the key to criticism. The deceptions, shifts, creation of myths, frauds and factions which we see before us are the means whereby we recognize the same things in the material that has come down to us. Agreement with the normal, usual or at least frequently attested manner of events or conditions which are familiar to us is the hallmark of probability for events which criticism can accept or allow really to have happened. The observation of analogies between similar events of the past makes it possible to ascribe probability to them and to interpret the unknown from the known. But the almighty power of analogy involves the homogeneity which is certainly not *identity* in kind, leaving endless room for variation; but beyond these variations it presupposes a core of similarity which is the starting point for an understanding and appreciation of the differences.[2]

The homogeneity of historical events is more precisely defined for Troeltsch as 'the community and homogeneity of the human spirit and its historical manifestations'.[3] It is far from Troeltsch's intention to maintain that there are only similarities and no essential differences. But differences (one has only to think of the multifarious types of human religion, art, morals, ways of life and economic structures which have accompanied the development from cave men to the men of a sophisticated civilization) can only be grasped and described as such when they are observed comparatively; that is to say, against the background of the

---

[1] See in particular his essay, 'Historische und dogmatische Methode in der Theologie', *Gesammelte Schriften*, vol. 2, 2nd ed. (Tübingen, 1922), pp. 729–753. There is a discussion of Troeltsch's theories in Harvey's book.
[2] *Ibid.*, p. 732.   [3] *Ibid.*, p. 733.

most general basic features which characterize man as distinct from nature. 'At every point something individual and original emerges which our capacity for sympathetic appreciation tells us belongs to the common stock of mankind. . . .'[1]

Even Christianity, when it is considered and investigated on the principle of the historical method, does not count as something withdrawn from the universal web of happening. It is constantly viewed in one context or another: the political, social and intellectual history of the ancient world, the history of the religion and civilization of mankind, as one system of values among other systems of values, as one affirmation of truth among other affirmations of truth. Before the historian is in a position to grasp its special character he must investigate the manifold threads which bind it to all these different spheres; and this means quite simply that Christianity must be relativized.

> This is the crassly obvious effect of the historical method. It relativizes everything, not in the sense that every standard of values must be excluded and that a nihilistic scepticism is bound to be the final result; but in the sense that every factor and every historical structure can only be thought of in association with others and ultimately in connection with the whole; and that the setting up of any system of values can therefore proceed only from a survey of the whole, not in isolation.[2]

A judgment about Christianity cannot therefore be derived from the Church's own isolated judgment and claim, 'as so many theologians would like to persuade us', just as a judgment about the cultural contribution of the Greeks and Romans cannot be solely based on these peoples' evaluation of themselves. The historian sees the facts of the past *in their context*, not only when he tries to establish what these facts are, but even more when he tries to understand them, interpret them and evaluate their importance for the present and the future.

But is it in fact possible to relativize the stories of the Bible, to place them parallel to other expressions of the human spirit as essentially the same in kind and to order them into the overriding context of human history in general? Do not these stories tell of an absolutely unique event, namely a *divine* action – indeed the actual appearance of the Son of God on the stage of world history? Do not these unique events reveal an absolute truth and authority which bursts apart all human standards? This is undoubtedly the case according to the assertions of faith, both old

[1] *Ibid.*   [2] *Ibid.*, p. 737.

and new. 'Is God to be thought incapable of performing real miracles?'
With this argument convinced Christians have always tried to shut away
historical-critical methods into their earthly and human compartments,
declaring them not competent for the sphere of divine revelation. Are
they right?

The term 'context', which, in association with the concept of 'homogeneity', may be said roughly to characterize the historical method, first
arose in the Enlightenment period in a crasser scientific and philosophical form; the aim then was to defend the new explanations, derived from
reason and experience, of certain aspects of reality (such as thunder and
lightning, hail, poor harvests and sickness of all kinds) against the rival
interpretations of supernatural faith. 'No just idea of the true nature of
history is possible, without a perception of the inviolability of the chain
of finite causes, and of the impossibility of miracles.' These were the
simple terms in which David Friedrich Strauss later summed up the
consequences of the Enlightenment for historical thinking, noting by
the way that this was a recognition which was 'wanting in so many minds
of our own day'.[1]

> In the ancient world, that is, in the east, the religious tendency was
> so preponderating, and the knowledge of nature so limited, that the
> law of connection between earthly finite beings was very loosely re-
> garded. At every link there was a disposition to spring into the Infinite,
> and to see God as the immediate cause of every change in nature or
> the human mind. In this mental condition the biblical history was
> written. Not that God is here represented as doing all and everything
> himself . . .: but there prevails in the biblical writers a ready disposi-
> tion to derive all things down to the minutest details, as soon as they
> appear particularly important, immediately from God. He it is who
> gives rain and sunshine; he sends the east wind and the storm; he
> dispenses war, famine, pestilence; he hardens hearts and softens them,
> suggests thoughts and resolutions. And this is particularly the case
> with regard to his chosen instruments and beloved people. In the
> history of the Israelites we find traces of his immediate agency at
> every step: through Moses, Elias, Jesus, he performs things which
> never would have happened in the ordinary course of nature.
>
> Our modern world, on the contrary, after many centuries of tedious
> research, has attained a conviction, that all things are linked together
> by a chain of causes and effects, which suffers no interruption. It is

[1] Strauss, *Life of Jesus*, vol. 1, Intro. § 13, pp. 74f.

true that single facts and groups of facts, with their conditions and processes of change, are not so circumscribed as to be unsusceptible of external influence; for the action of one existence or kingdom in nature intrenches on that of another: human freedom controls natural development, and material laws react on human freedom. Nevertheless the totality of finite things forms a vast circle, which, except that it owes its existence and laws to a superior power, suffers no intrusion from without. This conviction is so much a habit of thought with the modern world, that in actual life, the belief in a supernatural manifestation, an immediate divine agency, is at once attributed to ignorance or imposture. . . From this point of view, at which nature and history appear as a compact tissue of finite causes and effects, it was impossible to regard the narratives of the Bible, in which this tissue is broken by innumerable instances of divine interference, as historical.[1]

This classic formulation of the new historical consciousness, dating from 1840, forms the basis of all later reflections, including Troeltsch's. It makes clear what must be thought of when the historian speaks of the homogeneity in principle of the objects of history, and of their place in a total context. The meaning of these concepts can be gathered from the viewpoints against which they are directed: they maintain, in a simple physical sense, the firm outline and homogeneous structure of a single reality, in opposition to the old naïve notion, conceived of in simple, material terms, of the physical intervention of supernatural forces in a world of unfixed structure; and in opposition to the consequent parallelism and opposition of two different natures and causalities in the world of history. Such basic premisses of a scientific world outlook are not applied arbitrarily to historical events; they proceed from the inescapable evidence of contemporary man's conscious experience.

3. On the other hand, from the point of view of Christian faith a number of questions arise. The main one has already been touched on: how can a mode of approach in which everything is relativized be just to the essential distinctions in historical events which are important for faith – the distinction between divine and human history, acts of redemption and evil acts, the wonders of a divine power above the world and the drab sameness of everyday life in the 'wicked' world, in which nothing new ever happens and no-one can exceed his own capacities? Is the historical method a new non-Christian or even anti-Christian philosophy which simply stops the mouth of the Christian creed? Is it

---

[1] *Ibid.*, vol. I, Intro. § 14, p. 78.

inevitably bound up with a 'mechanistic world-picture', with 'historical relativism' or with a 'purely materialistic view of history' – that is to say, with all those wholesale atheistical diagnoses about the meaning of the world and life which stray nightmare-wise through theological literature?

This last question is not difficult to answer. The historical method is not a ready-made philosophy, but merely a tool capable of further development. The philosophical premises involved are of so general a nature that they are shared by all modern fields of knowledge. One must not identify them with any particular historically conditioned nine-teenth- or twentieth-century philosophy. But as regards the essential differences which are of absolute importance to the Christian faith, it must be noted that two things have radically changed: differences can no longer be dogmatically asserted *a priori*; they must be substantiated anew, comparatively, by the production of evidence. And secondly, differen-ces – even if they are as fundamental and essential as the difference between heaven and earth, God and man, or God and the devil – can no longer be linguistically expressed by designating the places and powers of a heaven and hell outside this world; they must be so formulated that we may differentiate and decide for ourselves, in the face of the number and multifariousness of the proclamations and acts of mankind, through which voices the voice of God is speaking to us *within our one, single reality*. 'I choose rather to be a pilgrim with thee in earth than to have heaven without thee. Where thou art there is heaven: and where thou art not there is death and hell,' says Thomas à Kempis in the *Imitation of Christ*, a popular late mediaeval[1] book of devotions. In so saying he 'demythologized' the supernatural world and gave it a concrete earthly significance. The same thing may be found in reasoned form in Luther, when he opposes to the 'gross and clumsy notions' of his contemporaries about God and heaven a different, spiritual view, though this was bound to appear to them as mystical:

> That gross mind [he means Zwingli] knows not what it means to be in heaven and will chop logic upon the subject. For when I said that Christ was in heaven while he still walked upon earth [in his interpre-tation of John 3.13, which speaks of the son of man being in heaven], God help us, how he did begin to argue and juggle with words! How, says he, could Christ then be in heaven? Does one eat and drink in heaven? But go to, thou fine adversary! Let any devout Christian tell

[1] Before 1420.

me if it is not higher and greater that man should be in God, nay, should be one with the person of God, than that he should be in heaven? Is God not yet higher and more glorious than heaven itself? Now Christ's manhood was from his mother's womb higher and more deeply in God and in the presence of God than any angel. For what is in God and in the presence of God is in heaven. . . . If, then, Christ can at one and the same time suffer and die on earth, although he is one person with God and within the divine Godhead, why should he not still more be able to suffer upon earth while being also in heaven? . . . Yea, more: not only was Christ in heaven while upon earth, but so also were the apostles and so are we all, even while on earth and mortal, if we do but believe in Christ.[1]

Where does the peculiarity and uniqueness of the Christian message lie? Certainly not in the fact that in the stories of the Bible supernatural forces intervene in the historical world – phenomena of this kind may be found in all the ancient religions – but in the way in which God and heaven are designated, in concrete terms, here on earth. The origin of this concrete designation, the source of 'revelation' in Christianity is, however, a particular earthly person. 'He who has seen me has seen the Father' (John 14.9). What kind of man is this? Who was Jesus?

A question of this kind can be investigated with the help of the historical method. Just because the real object which kindles Christian faith is in the midst of the real historical world, Christianity need not be given up for lost when the supernatural phenomena of religious tradition fall victims to historical criticism.

Moreover, even the supernatural phenomena are not simply annihilated *per se* by criticism. For in the course of critical investigation it emerges that they mean something different and something more than that which was generally recognized and criticized in the realistic thinking of modern times. The temporal extension of the historical context both in the direction of a creation and a primeval period and in the direction of an end-time, had a motive beyond the naïve attempt to explain and visualize the origin and end of the world in the external sense. Similarly the spatial extension in the directions of a heaven and a hell beyond the stage on which earthly events are played out, was not merely designed as a speculation about what lay above the clouds or under the earth. Neither an external historical nor an external geographical interest was

[1] *Bekenntnis vom Abendmahl Christi* (1528), *Werke, Kritische Gesamtausgabe* (Weimar, 1833ff.), 26, 318–345; see also E. Hirsch, *Hilfsbuch zum Studium der Dogmatik* (Berlin and Leipzig, 1951), p. 39.

the decisive motive – if this were so, nothing would be left, after a scientific rectification of these naïve assumptions; but when creation was talked of, the central question was what, according to the nature of his being, man was created for, intended for and called to; and in what relationship he stands to the world of nature. Again, when judgment, the resurrection of the dead and the coming rule of God was spoken of, men looked forward to the goal of history, the victory of divine righteousness, the elimination of evil, the comforting of those who suffer – in short, the fulfilment of the nature of historical man. And when men spoke of heaven, it was not in essence a locality in space that they meant, although this was present to the imagination; but heaven is the sphere where God rules and whence he intervenes decisively in world history. Hell is correspondingly the sphere ruled over by Satan. Man is in heaven when he lives in the presence of God and in God, in complete harmony with his destiny; hell on earth is where he is alienated from God and that destiny. The two words 'sky' and 'heaven' which are used to distinguish between the natural phenomenon and the mental horizon in which man really lives, in the light of his calling, makes clear the specific meaning of the mythical statements of the Bible: they are neither scientific nor historical in the descriptive sense; they are theological and anthropological statements about the nature and goal of human existence in history; they say what man is, should be and can be – man including his world.[1]

Since biblical statements are of the kind we have suggested, it is doing them no essential injury if today the mythological pictures of space and time are peeled away, leaving the design without accretions.

[1] A similar transference of function was present to the poetic mind long before there was any conscious 'psychologization' of heaven and hell. Cf. Marlowe:

Mephistoph: Hell hath no limits, nor is circumscrib'd
In one self place; but where we are is hell,
And where hell is, there must we ever be.
(*The Tragical History of Dr Faustus*, III ii.)
And Milton:
The mind is its own place, and in it self,
Can make a Heav'n of Hell, a Hell of Heav'n.
(*Paradise Lost* I, 1.254f.)
But heaven and hell do not continue to be mere attitudes of the inner self of man: they become influential in shaping the external world. Because men e.g. 'make life hell for each other', as we say, the scenery of hell once again acquires firm outlines in objective reality. Now hell is no longer the supernatural place of mythology, but a condition made by men for others here and there in the course of their history. Cf., for example, the transference of function as Brecht uses it in his *Hollywood-Elegie I*:

'Das Dorf Hollywood ist entworfen nach den Vorstellungen
Die man hierorts vom Himmel hat. Hierorts

This process, whereby the Christian intention is separated from the worldly form of the image, is far from new and is not even alien to the Bible itself. 'You shall not make for yourself a graven image, or any likeness . . .' (Ex. 20.4) – the oldest theological sentences in the Bible already ward off the material fixation of God.

God is 'the living one'. He 'comes'. Unlike the pagan nature-gods, he does not live in one special place in the cosmos, nor is he fixed once and for all in the images and concepts of human language. He is 'closer than breathing' and yet unimaginably unapproachable and remote. His word brings 'light' and 'life' – not physical brightness but the light in which man finds the right way leading to salvation; and not an endless prolongation of physical existence but true life in the knowledge and fear of the Lord, as Psalm 1 describes it.

These indications may serve to show that a relativizing treatment of the Bible is not necessarily an abrogation of its 'uniqueness' but may even lead to a new discovery of that uniqueness. Admittedly, a judgment of this kind is differently based from the dogmatic judgment of faith. The historical method places the Christian mind in a basically new situation, drawing everything into the whirlpool of criticism. Nothing has validity any more merely on the grounds of tradition or of institutions hallowed by authority. Everything must show the reasons why it has a claim to acceptance. No special privileges for Christianity – equal rights for all!

Troeltsch rightly says of the historical method: 'anyone who has given it an inch must give it an ell', and adds that for this reason it seems to have a kind of similarity with the devil, from a purely orthodox point of view.

It means a complete revolution of our thinking, just as modern science meant a revolution against the ideas of the ancient and modern worlds. Whereas science contains a new attitude to nature, history contains a new attitude to the human spirit and its ideas. The older

Hat man ausgerechnet, dass Gott
Himmel und Hölle benötigend, nicht zwei
Etablissements zu entwerfen brauchte, sondern
Nur ein einziges, nämlich den Himmel. Dieser
Dient für die Unbemittelten, Erfolglosen
Als Hölle.' (*Gesammelte Werke*, 10, p. 849)

'The village of Hollywood is designed according to the ideas that people here have of heaven. Here people reckoned that when God needed heaven and hell he did not have to design two separate establishments. Heaven was enough; for heaven serves as hell for the underprivileged and unsuccessful.'

absolute and dogmatic mode of approach considered certain states of affairs and certain notions to be a matter of course and absolutized them to unchangeable norms. Everywhere this attitude is being ousted by the historical approach, which views even what seems to be most self-evident and even the forces whose power is most far-reaching as products of the stream of history.[1]

But such expressions did not keep Troeltsch on his side from giving endless thought to the question of how – now that the content of Christianity had been reduced, in principle and methodologically, to the level of universal history – the peculiar character of the Christian religion could be newly defined; and how, even in the midst of historical relativism, one could still speak of something like 'the absolute character of Christianity'. Although he was acutely conscious of the existing contrasts between the historical and the dogmatic view of history, Troeltsch held the firm conviction – being passionately interested both in historical truth and the truth of Christianity – that by a consistent application of critical investigation, the peculiar character and the divinity of the Christian religion would show itself in a new light. 'Then and only then will our minds be freed from the heaviest of the present apologetic loads and we will be able to see the glory of God in history more freely and more impartially than ever before.'

In the next two chapters we shall sum up the results that have been achieved up to now by the historical-critical examination of the miracle stories in the Gospels.

[1] Troeltsch, *op. cit.*, pp. 734f.

5 Advances in Historical Reflection

Willi Marxsen: We must recognize the tendency with which passages were written

Of what ultimate use is the critical approach to the Gospels? What emerges as the total result? And who is served by that result? The contemporary person who is interested in the Bible and who only gets to hear about individual results of critical exegesis (and that mostly in a negative form) has the right to confront the professional theologian with this blunt question.

'Now Jesus did many other signs in the presence of the disciples, which are not written in this book; but these are written that you may believe that Jesus is the Christ, the Son of God, and that believing you may have life in his name' (John 20.30f.). The final words of the Gospel of John (a second conclusion was added later) reveal the aim that lies behind the writer's story, with its many miracles: the events which he relates are designed to inspire the reader's personal engagement, to awaken faith; and this means that the reader is to find a new life through his encounter with them.

But to read the same stories with the historian's eye means to establish what really happened at the time. It means that reading the texts – irrespective of the writer's intention – as if they are historical documents and examining the narrative on this assumption. What did Jesus really, say and do?

The historical approach is not competent to evaluate the discovered facts (in this case Jesus' words and deeds). But this is what Christian faith is doing when it declares these facts to be significant and unique, when it finds 'truth' in them, when it proclaims them as bringing 'salvation' – in short, when it says that here God is in action. In other words, the historical method is, strictly speaking, not competent to make a subjective interpretation and evaluation of the historically ascertained facts. Hence what the historical method wins from the text seems to the mind of the believer to be pretty scanty and somewhat damping to sanguine religious expectations.

One can take up a positive attitude to the historian's reserve, however, and say that he is not interfering with matters which are not his job. He leaves free scope to subjective faith to behave with regard to the facts as it thinks fit; he leaves the reflective theologian every opportunity to ponder over the subjective interpretations of faith, to express them dogmatically and to develop a creed of one kind or another on their basis; and he does not forestall the preacher whose purpose is to proclaim to others in suitable form what is significant in these stories.

But one could then go on to ask: if what is really decisive is still ultimately a matter for faith, if faith – or, put it more generally, subjective human interpretation and decision – is the real court of appeal for these stories, why does the historian not leave them alone? Of what use is he? Before the critical method was discovered things went on all right – perhaps even better and with less friction than today. Is it not possible to avoid all the complications which arise between the different spheres of interest belonging to faith and scholarly investigation by admitting that the latter is superfluous and, moreover, inappropriate? Can we not get on without it?

In answer one could simply point to the theological history of modern times and say: the question is of purely academic interest. We have developed the method with toil and sweat and we should not have gone to so much trouble if we had not been driven forward by some urgent necessity. We are therefore bound to use it. But this answer is not satisfactory. We have developed other things with toil and sweat which we would sometimes now gladly dispense with. Why should one not retrace faulty steps?

We must therefore find an explanation which is immediately convincing to ourselves if the method is to be further retained. Moreover, the answer must not only satisfy the interests of the 'outsider'; it must not only convince those whose angles of approach are not those of faith – the student of comparative religion, the literary scholar, etc.; it must be an answer which also satisfies faith and can be accepted within the Church.

An answer of this kind can only be found if we realize what the particular achievement of the method is and to what extent this achievement is of importance for faith. Its achievement is, as we have said, to establish as exactly as possible what actually took place historically speaking – entirely without assessment, soberly and objectively. Is it important for faith to learn what really happened at that time? Is faith interested in 'historical facts'?

It is usual in theology today to belittle the value of facts for faith. It is the kerygma, the proclamation, that is important. Anyone who is at all familiar with present-day theology knows that this belittlement must be understood as being, among other things, a reaction against the undue importance ascribed earlier to facts and belief in 'the facts of salvation' – an over-estimate which later became recognized as questionable. There are therefore indications that faith is deeply interested in the question of the facts – either in a positive or a negative sense. The heated theological discussion of the question also brings out the point that certain groups stress particular facts as being of special importance for salvation which are disputed by other groups, either completely or in their importance for faith.

All this shows that the point really in dispute is what should be recognized as a fact and what should not. And one sees confirmation of what was said at the beginning: that Christians do not speak objectively or with indifference about these facts but become heated to a degree which would be unthinkable among historians.

But if controversy exists about what is to count as a fact and what is not, one would suppose that the situation simply cries out for an expert to decide, without taking sides and as objectively as possible, what can really be established. He could decide on the facts and the theologians could then come to an agreement about the meaning of these facts for salvation.

It is this that the historians among the theologians have tried to do in the history of New Testament studies, but instead of earning gratitude they have come into constant collision with the teachings of the Church. For easy though it sounds in theory, in practice it is a difficult matter. The reason, as everyone knows, is that the four evangelists report things in the most matter of fact way which today neither historical scholarship nor general opinion can accept as facts, but to which the Church none the less clings when in its creed it proclaims that Jesus was conceived by the Holy Ghost, born of the Virgin Mary . . . rose again from the dead, ascended into heaven . . .

Yet side by side with such unusual events, the Gospels, as we know, tell of others which do not lie outside the scope of 'normal' historical writing in the same way. They tell how Jesus went about preaching and teaching and healing the sick; how he gathered a circle of disciples round himself and excited the masses through his preaching; and how in the end he was put on trial by the ruling authorities and was executed by the occupying powers.

One can therefore follow and distinguish two different series of events in the telling of the story of Jesus: one set of events is historically not unusual in principle, though perhaps unusual here and there; but there is another set of absolutely unusual events which the historian, through analogies, assigns to the realm of myth and legend. To this latter group belong the miracles (in the strictest sense of the word) which are ascribed to Jesus, and also the amazing phenomena which surround his person between his birth and his ascension. Theologians of the Early Church interpreted these facts by saying that in Jesus two different natures were united, a divine and a human. The doctrine of the two natures is still occupying theological thought today.

Let us look closely at the Gospels and put together all the additional information which we have elsewhere in the New Testament; and let us then ask, what do we know about Jesus' life according to the first group of facts and what do we know according to the second? We shall discover that the events belonging to the two groups sometimes even contradict one another. On the one hand, for example, Jesus is born in Bethlehem, on the other in Nazareth. On the one hand he is accounted son of God in the physical sense, on the other son of Joseph. On the one hand he is the son of a virgin, on the other 'born of woman, born under the law' (Gal. 4.4). On the one hand he refuses to perform signs and points to his preaching as the only sign which is to be given to 'an evil and adulterous generation' (Matt. 12.39), and yet on the other hand he performs signs and miracles in abundance. Occasionally the texts suggest that the contradictions in the transmitted material gave rise to discussion (John 1.45f.; 7.40–43, 52) and that later manuscripts subsequently tried to harmonize the contradictions. This can be seen, for example, in Jesus' family tree in Matthew and Luke (which according to its original meaning witness to the fatherhood of Joseph) and in the numerous variants of Matt 1.16 (the sentence which describes Mary's position).

If the history of Jesus himself is not a double one, which is impossible, then at least a double history has been written about him. On the one hand he is an undoubtedly remarkable but entirely human person; on the other he is a heavenly being who has entered the earthly sphere, one who was with God before his birth – indeed since the creation of the world – and returned to his eternal kingdom after his earthly death and sits at the right hand of the Father. How can this remarkable phenomenon of the double history of Jesus be explained?

There is an explanation, which has been discovered through the un-qualified and consistent application of the historical-critical method. Criticism means separation, division, and also distinction. Those ele-ments which are probably historical are divided and distinguished from the unhistorical ones according to the standards of our present know-ledge and in analogy with the experience which is general in historical scholarship as a whole.

After one has put a question mark against the historicity of certain stories, one examines them from other angles which may throw light on the texts. What meaning can a narrative text have if it cannot be accepted as a simple historical account? To put the question in another way: if the reason for the telling of such stories was not that they were factually true, how did they creep into the Gospels? To take an example, if Jesus was not, to the exclusion of an earthly father, con-ceived by the Holy Ghost and born of a virgin, how can the rise of the story be explained? Again, if it is historically established that there was no census at the time of Jesus' birth, and that Luke here uses a later event as motive for the holy family's move to Bethlehem, *why* should the evangelist think it so important for Jesus to be born in Bethlehem?

An indication may be found in the 'scriptural proof' so often appended to the stories – evidence for the virgin birth, for the significance of the city of David, Bethlehem, in the salvation-history, for the signs of the messianic end-time, etc. 'All this took place to fulfil what the Lord had spoken by the prophet.'

It is immediately evident that a theological interest was attached to Bethlehem as birth-place. Certain scenes out of the Gospel of John may serve to make this clear. Let us first look at a passage out of the calling of the disciples in ch. 1: 'Phillip found Nathanael, and said to him, "We have found him of whom Moses in the law and also the prophets write, Jesus of Nazareth, the son of Joseph." Nathanael said to him, "Can any-thing good come out of Nazareth?" Phillip said to him, "Come and see." ' (John 1.45f.). Nazareth is an unimportant place in the north of Palestine, in Galilee, far from Jerusalem. It plays no part in Old Testament pro-phecy. Is it surprising that this simple, insignificant piece of information about Jesus' historical origin should soon have been silted over by the people's expectations about the saviour and by messianic preaching? A Christian missionary made it clear to his Jewish hearers who Jesus was by telling a story of his birth in the city of David. Another passage reflects the surprise which Jesus' origin excited:

217

> When they heard these words, some of the people said, 'This is really the prophet.' Others said, 'This is the Christ.' But some said, 'Is the Christ to come from Galilee? Has not the scripture said that the Christ is descended from David, and comes from Bethlehem, the village where David was?' So there was a division among the people over him (John 7.40ff.).

'Search and you will see that no prophet is to rise from Galilee' (John 7.52). With this argument the Jewish scribes reject Jesus' claim. The pressure of contemporary ideas about salvation was so strong that the unexpected and new could only penetrate with difficulty and was again soon silted over and finally almost pushed out of the consciousness altogether by reminiscence of the idyllic and marvellous prophecy of Micah, a prophecy which had acquired classic status:

> But you, O Bethlehem Ephrathah,
>   who are little to be among the clans of Judah,
> from you shall come forth for me
>   one who is to be ruler in Israel (Micah 5.2).

Jesus' actual birth-place is replaced, so to speak, by a theological one.

The motives which underlie the story of Jesus' conception by the spirit of God and his virgin birth are not quite so transparent. The story only crops up at a late stage in the transmission. The earliest witnesses, Mark and Paul, are not familiar with it. It was supported by no wide Old Testament tradition: the prophetic 'proof' from Isaiah which Matthew includes in his story (1.23) rests on a wrong translation of the original Hebrew text which Matthew found in the Septuagint, the Greek translation of the Old Testament. The verse in Isaiah 'Behold, a young woman shall conceive and bear a son' (Isa. 7.14) probably referred originally to a particular woman known to the prophet. A more broadly based Jewish tradition was backed only by the somewhat modified idea that the births of certain important men in the history of Israel were not entirely natural and often involved an especial divine initiative. This was so, for example, in the case of Abraham's son Isaac, the bearer of the divine promise, or the prophet Samuel or John the Baptist, the forerunner of Christ. But most scholars see the complete elimination of earthly fatherhood as a non-Jewish and specifically Hellenistic motif. The demigods, the Greek heroes, were often derived from the union of a god and a human woman and legends about divine origin are told about a number of important heroes, emperors, poets and philosophers. According to the belief of the first Christians, Jesus was 'God's son'. In the

Greek-speaking world (and it was for this world that the Greek-educated author of the Gospel of Luke was writing) this belief could be expressed in an easily understandable way by the telling of a story about Jesus' physical descent from God and his consequent physical endowment with a divine 'nature'. Jewish thought, on the other hand, did not associate the title 'Son of God' with the idea of physical conception but with that of calling and 'adoption'. The 'son' is not associated with God through the bond of a natural relationship but stands before him as a responsible office-holder. Since Mark did not yet know the nativity stories, a calling of this kind plays a part in the structure of the Gospel of Mark, when at the beginning of Jesus' activity, at his baptism, the voice from heaven says: 'Thou art my beloved Son; with thee I am well pleased' (Mark 1.11; cf. Ps. 2.7; Isa. 42.1). One might sum it up by saying that in the introductory stories of Matthew and Luke a natural origin and birth is replaced by a theological account of Jesus' spiritual parentage. Jesus acquires a theological father.[1]

Starting from these examples, in which the doubling of the history of Jesus is particularly obvious, we can make some important observations about the evangelists' attitude to history.

1. The Gospel stories about Jesus are always at the same time stories about Christ. This means that they are by their very nature something other than pure factual accounts, which only record outward events; for they simultaneously have something to say about the meaning of their subject for the salvation-history. They say: Jesus is the Christ, the long-expected Messiah, the Saviour, the son of God. And they do not only say it; they proclaim it. These stories spring from a particular attitude to history. The narrator is not in a position to give the sober and objective rendering of the facts which one expects today from a historical account, because from the very beginning he is passionately interested and subjectively involved in his subject. This attitude to the story colours his mode of approach; the interest in salvation is dominant in such a way that different, unusual forms of presentation develop. One can speak here of a proclaiming or *kerygmatic* presentation, in contrast to all types of purely descriptive statement.

2. The unusual forms of presentation come into being through the activity of *reflection*. That is to say, the witnesses couple their account of Jesus with an account of what they themselves perceived and believed

[1] For the rise of the kergymatic stories, see W. Marxsen, *Das Neue Testament als Buch der Kirche* (Gütersloh, 1966), ch. II, 2, 3; also, by the same author, *Die Auferstehung Jesus als historisches und als theologisches Problem*, 4th ed. (Gütersloh, 1966).

and what they thought when looking back from the standpoint of their Easter experiences. Jesus is hence encountered in this type of narrative not as a purely historical phenomenon but surrounded by a shell of interpretation. In the course of this process reflection can travel a considerable distance from the historical subject, as we can see from the nativity stories. We shall return to this point.

3. The biblical witnesses to Christ do not generally express the ideas of their faith in new and original language. They take over already existing images and concepts of salvation. Jesus is either depicted as one who fulfils the hopes of Old Testament prophecy, or as one who meets the Hellenistic longing for a world-redeemer and peace-bringer. Jesus is depicted in these traditional forms although his real activity was so different from all preconceived notions that his people condemned him as a blasphemer. How can this be explained? An answer can be found when one understands why and how the process of reflection was arrived at.

At the beginning stands the encounter with the unusual words and acts of an unusual person. He appears as a breaker of the Law because he heals the sick on the sabbath and sits at table with the ceremonially impure, tax-collectors and sinners. He puts himself on an equal level with the highest authority – indeed above it – by contrasting the Mosaic law, given by the patriarchs, with a new proclamation of the will of God. He makes the claim to speak and act, directly and without mediation, in the name of God and presents his contemporaries with the ultimatum of making a decision about his message: he who is not with me is against me. The content of his message means that the end-time has now arrived. Judgment is now, and the rule of God on earth is now beginning. He takes account of the already present expectations and hopes of Israel, but in such a way that he refashions them and focuses them on this historical moment. *Now* it is possible for sins to be forgiven; *now* there is an offer of new life; *now* a decision must be made on which everything of ultimate importance depends.

What the new opportunity of living before God looks like is taught by the behaviour of parable-like figures. The guest accepts the invitation; the watchful man notices what hour has struck; the man who finds treasure in the field or a costly pearl risks everything for it. Tales like the story of the Good Samaritan and the Last Judgment are more precise: the service of God takes place in everyday life, in the unremarkable moment. The sayings of the Sermon on the Mount are also more precise: the decisive moment can only be perceived by the man who is free from concern about himself, free from the compulsion simply to react to the good and evil in his environment, according to the old Law – an eye for an eye, a tooth for a tooth. But it is Jesus' own behaviour which shows most clearly the new opportunity for understanding the meaning of life: as freedom from all 'rule' and as life lived for others without reservation, independent of earthly destiny.

The unusual nature of Jesus' behaviour roused people to wonder who he was. Two answers lay to hand in tradition. Either he was a blasphemer and a false prophet, who was deserving of death according to Jewish law, or he was the final and authorized messenger of God, the Messiah or 'the Son'.

Most surprising of all was the experience of his adherents, that his claim to complete authority did not seem to be refuted by the theological condemnation of the religious authorities and that even the snuffing out of his physical life by the secular powers could not affect what he was; indeed, once freed from the early confusion caused by the misunderstandings that still remained, his influence rose more than ever into an activating power of unsurpassed strength.

Who was this man? Or rather, who is he? This is the question that everyone is bound to ask who enters the orbit of his story. 'Are you he who is to come?' 'What do you think of the Christ?' At this point reflection begins. Reflection means mental assimilation. Names have to be found and the exciting and provocative event has to be interpreted for oneself, that is to say it has to be brought into relationship to one's own reality. Since the fact of Jesus was of ultimate, religious importance, since it affected the whole meaning of life, only an interpretation framed by the religious outlook came into question. What was easier than to use the names which already lay ready to hand for the highest and ultimate event?

> In many and various ways God spoke of old to our fathers by the prophets; but in these last days he has spoken to us by a Son, whom he appointed the heir of all things, through whom also he created the world. He reflects the glory of God and bears the very stamp of his nature, upholding the universe by his word of power. When he had made purification for sins, he sat down at the right hand of the Majesty on high (Heb. 1.1–3).

Such is the programmatic form in which the opening sentence of the Epistle to the Hebrews formulates the result of reflection. Jesus is set in relation to Israel's sacred history and not only that: he is set in relation to the world and its history in general.

In forming their concepts of faith the first preachers and theologians fitted Jesus into the total structure of their already existing reality, which had always been determined by a religious interpretation. They defined his functions within the framework of the fundamental ideas which had come down to them from the depths of history – ideas about the meaning of being and destiny, salvation and damnation, present and future. His role is determined for him. That means in concrete terms that his form is re-adorned with all the available symbolic titles and dignities which were reserved as expression for the highest divine power: Messiah and Son of David, Lord and King, Servant of God and Lamb of God, or (on the Hellenistic side) Saviour, Son of God and son of a virgin.

But the titles which say who Jesus is do not suffice. With them certain more or less fixed ideas about the typical circumstances of life, typical behaviour and typical destiny are associated. The long-awaited Messiah will come from the house and lineage of David and will be born in Bethlehem. The expected prophet, the second Moses and second Saviour of his people, is persecuted as a small child by a wicked king, is again called by God out of Egypt, gathers his people in the wilderness, proclaims from a mountain the law of the new covenant, repeats the miraculous feedings which belonged to Israel's primeval period during the first journey through the wilderness, and recapitulates and surpasses the miraculous signs of the ancient prophets Elijah and Elisha, to give only a few examples.

Thus in the presentation of the story of Jesus we constantly come across features which may be traced back to pre-existing types and images in Jewish and Hellenistic tradition. The transference of motifs to the actually existing Jesus of Nazareth from images formed about the expected redeemer must in part have taken place unconsciously when the message of salvation was passed on by word of mouth; this is frequently the case when popular legends are built up. In part, however, the first Christian missionaries and evangelists used these links deliberately, in order to make clear to their hearers in the Jewish and Greek-speaking worlds the status of the Jesus of Nazareth whom they proclaimed.

To sum up: the accretions which in this way crystallized during the course of reflection on to the original, actual history alter the whole picture completely. Whatever remains as the characteristic achievement of the Gospel account, as compared with normal secular history, is from beginning to end a spiritual superstructure, which in some places gives the impression of being a duplication of events, with the interpretative picture obviously diverging from its historical basis. The greater the distance from the historical sources, the greater the superstructure and the more self-contained and complete it is. Finally the curve sweeps from heaven to earth and back again; the Johannine Christ hardly touches earth at all. He no longer has any earthly or human traits and speaks only the language of reflection – or of self-reflection: I am the Bread of Life; I am the Light of the World; I bear witness to myself (6.35, 48; 8.12, 18; etc. There are more 'I' sentences in John than in the rest of the New Testament put together). The earthly Jesus seems to have been transformed into a purely spiritual Christ.

The climaxes or focal points in the graph traced by this supra-history are the miracles ascribed to Jesus, both those which he performs himself and those which happen to him. Anyone who views these miracles as simple reports of facts (a constant temptation because of the artlessly direct mode of narrative) is making a fundamental mistake. In reality they are complicated structures of reflection to which much has contributed: memories of scenes in the life of Jesus, experiences that the disciples had with Jesus before and also after his death, the immediate needs of the Primitive Church; and all this is interpreted within the frame of the prophets' messianic experience of history and is poetically intensified into a symbolical and expressive story. But the fact that these symbolic narratives take the form of genuine history leads to a big difficulty. Fact and reflection are welded indissolubly together on the same level. In retrospect one can no longer tell from the stories themselves how they came into existence. One unintentionally takes later statements, which only came into being on the basis of reflection, for early and original ones.

Willi Marxsen, whose writings have drawn particular attention to the factor of reflection, has formulated a principle which can serve as a rough guide or rule of interpretation for all the miraculous and supernatural stories: 'We must recognize the tendency with which passages were written; they must then be interpreted in the light of that tendency and may be used only within its context.'[1] If this rule is ignored, what were originally statements of reflection may be changed, almost without our noticing, into firm historical facts. This process, which was undoubtedly already at work in the transmission of the stories about Jesus, is called by scholars later or secondary historization. The ultimate result of the process is that the actual history of Jesus is shrouded in an apparent history; but this apparent history is hard to penetrate or to dissolve into its component parts in its present fixed and dogmatic form.

[1] W. Marxsen, *Das Neue Testament als Buch der Kirche*, p. 115.

The dogmatization involves the greatest danger; for what is dogmatized as being allegedly historical truth (or at least as being *also* historical truth) and is thus removed from all further questioning and discussion contains, as we have seen, human beliefs which transfer to Jesus all manner of temporally conditioned ideas of salvation belonging to the history of religion. In the past such dogmatizations have led to divisions within the Church, and the pressure of this inheritance is still a burden on the Church today. Because of it some Christians try to compel other Christians to 'believe', as truths necessary for salvation, particular ideas about the divine origin of Jesus or about his resurrection.[1]

In modern times, however, since the Enlightenment, the problems contained in the dogmatization have become acute in a different respect. For now it is not only historically conditioned *beliefs* which are made obligatory for Christians of later times; it is now becoming clear for the first time to what extent *actual historical untruths* have been enjoined as truths on believers by dogmatic faith.

What is the purpose and use of the historical-critical method? Is it in fact necessary or would it be better to do away with it on the grounds that its method of approach to the Bible stories is alien to faith? This was the question we asked at the beginning. The method's achievement can now be seen and evaluated. It consists of a disentanglement of the twisted threads of real history and non-historical interpretative history. That is to say, the historical-critical method separates from one another the different kinds of material (both historical and literary) in the texts. It offers a key to the interpretative or reflective stories – so difficult of access to us today – by showing how they came into being, what their purpose was and what the images and ideas they make use of really mean in their context in the history of religion, and what they mean when transferred to the person of Jesus. The method releases us from the necessity of believing the incomprehensible and improbable out of devotion to the Church; for it makes proper understanding possible.

In all this it only provides the foundation without taking over the task of faith or anticipating the believer's own subjective interpretation. The most important part of the preliminary work it performs is that it brings to light the real character of the subjects with which faith has to do: the early Christian proclamation and the historical 'facts' which preceded this proclamation, forming its ground and its inspiration. Just because the historical approach clings unswervingly to its simple opening question – the desire to know what really happened at the time: what Jesus

[1] cf. *Ibid.*, pp. 123–144.

really said and did, before all the kerygmatic interpretations – it offers contemporary man an opportunity which earlier times did not have in the same way: an opportunity to look behind the interpretations of early Christendom to Jesus himself. Should a Church which for nearly 2,000 years has proclaimed the message that the Word became flesh, that God became man, fail to be interested in the real appearance of the earthly Jesus of Nazareth?

6 The Meaning of Jesus' Miracles: An Exegetical Approach

All things are possible to him who believes

Anyone who makes a claim must substantiate that claim, for the world is full of false prophets.

In Israel people demanded visible signs from a prophet as proof that he was not speaking on his own authority but that God was present within him. A divine action had to follow the prophet's word. If a prophet appeared with the claim to speak in God's name and his prophecy remained unfulfilled, he had to die, according to the law of Moses (Deut. 18.18ff.). A legitimation miracle of this kind is told about Moses himself. When Korah and his company rebelled, he spoke to the assembled congregations of Israel:

> Hereby you shall know that the Lord has sent me to do all these works, and that it has not been of my own accord. If these men die the common death of all men, or if they are visited by the fate of all men, then the Lord has not sent me. But if the Lord creates something new, and the ground opens its mouth, and swallows them up, with all that belongs to them, and they go down alive to Sheol, then you shall know that these men have despised the Lord' (Num. 16.28–30).

He had scarcely spoken these words, so the saga tells, when the ground opened and the earth swallowed up the whole company, together with all their possessions.

In view of this background it is not surprising that Jesus too should have been asked for signs. Several times the evangelists report events of the following kind. Some of the scribes and Pharisees come to Jesus and say: 'Teacher, we wish to see a sign from you.' But he answers them, 'An evil and adulterous generation seeks for a sign; but no sign shall be given to it except the sign of the prophet Jonah' (Matt. 12.38f.). Jesus rejects the demand for signs in the form in which the scribes understand it. The mysterious words about the sign of the prophet Jonah is given a double interpretation in the text. According to the Old Testament saga, the prophet Jonah spent three days in the belly of a great fish. 'So will the Son of man be three days and three nights in the heart of the earth,' says Matthew, thus suggesting that the cross and resurrection are the only signs which are to be given in the case of Jesus. The second interpretation probably accords with the original meaning of the saying. Jonah preached to the men of the city of Ninevah and these men 'will arise at the judgment with this generation and condemn it; for they repented at the preaching of Jonah, and behold, something greater than Jonah is here.' According to this, the sign which Jesus gives his contemporaries is his preaching. They should believe because of that, and that will be the touchstone to decide their destiny for salvation or damnation.

How, now, does this saying rejecting signs fit in with the fact that in spite of it numerous miracles are told about Jesus in the Gospels and that after his death it could be said of him that he was a prophet 'mighty in deed and word before God and all the people' (Luke 24.19) or, even more unequivocally, 'a man attested to you by God with mighty works and wonders and signs' (Acts 2.22)? In his Whitsun sermon Peter draws the attention of his hearers to something which is supposed to have happened in their midst. What was it? Was Jesus perhaps inconsistent?

So it would seem at first glance. Scholars are generally agreed that Jesus healed the sick and 'expelled demons'. Healings and exorcisms are hard to differentiate, for in the ancient world most illnesses of unknown cause were regarded as a form of possession. Of course we do not think today that all the miracles of healing reported in the New Testament really took place in reality exactly as they are reported to have done. We have already seen the manifold reasons and occasions which caused the narrator to stylize his story theologically or to give it an entirely symbolic form. But we cannot in general deny the possibility that Christian faith, from which a liberating influence radiated, also led to liberation from physical ills in certain predisposed cases. What was here possible or impossible can hardly be decided in detail as long as psychosomatic medicine is still in its infancy and as long as the interrelations of the mental and spiritual with the physical being are still insufficiently clarified. That a new faith, which gives new hope and the opportunity for a new life, is also capable of renewing the physical powers and can give men the impulse to unsuspected achievements is, in varying degrees, a common experience and science is familiar with the most

surprising examples. Such 'miracles of faith' have occurred again and
again during the history of Christianity, especially at the focal points of a
particularly intensive religious life, for example, in the circle of the
Swabian pietist Christoph Blumhardt or at Lourdes. We may also come
across similar 'miracles' outside Christianity. Everywhere in the ancient
world stories were told, in more or less magical and fantastic form, of
miraculous healings and the expulsion of demons. Roman emperors,
Hellenistic miracle-workers and even Jewish rabbis were the authors of
deeds of this kind, not to speak of the miraculous cures which are said
to have occurred at the shrines of the god Asclepius, especially in Epi-
daurus, the Lourdes of the ancient world.[1] Yet the miracle stories in the
Gospels stand out clearly, both in number and content, from the general
background. They have a particular tone and stand in a particular context, of which we shall speak later. The widespread dissemination of
'acts of power' of this kind at least, make it understandable why the
scribes and Pharisees were not satisfied with them and demanded of
Jesus additional, special 'signs from heaven'. Acts of power are ambigu-
ous, for they do not show in whose name they take place. The lying
prophets and false Christs, whose appearance was expected in the end-
time, were also to perform mighty signs and wonders, which could even
lead the elect astray (Matt. 24.24).

Power and might – the Greek words are *dýnamis* and *exousia* – must
have been possessed by Jesus to an extraordinary degree. For his contemporaries the only question was whether his power came from God or
from the devil, as we hear from the Pharisees' angry saying that he cast
out demons by Beelzebub, the prince of demons (Mark 3.22. par.). For
people today the driving out of demons is one of the most embarrassing
features of Jesus' work; here his mode of activity desplays itself in the
concrete material offered him by another era. But even today these
obscure stories show one thing at least: that the immediate consequence
of his appearance was a de-demonization of the world, that disarming of
all the forces of evil which Jewish faith expected to take place only immediately before the coming of the kingdom of God, in the Last Days.[2] 'I

[1] Religious-historical material may be found in the following books among
others: O. Weinreich, *Antike Heilungswunder* (Giessen, 1909); R. Herzog, *Die
Wunderheilungen von Epidauros* (Leipzig, 1931); G. Mensching, *Das Wunder im
Glauben und Aberglauben der Völker* (Leiden, 1957). On the possibility of a
medical-psychological interpretation of miracles see in particular E. Liek, *Das
Wunder in der Heilkunde* (Munich, 1951); W. Bitter (ed.), *Magie und Wunder
in der Heilkunde. Ein Tagungsbericht* (Stuttgart, 1959).

[2] Evidence in W. G. Kümmel, *Promise and Fulfilment* (Studies in Biblical
Theology 23, London, 1957), ch. III.

saw Satan fall like lightning from heaven' – this is Jesus' response to the joyous account his disciples give him of their first mission: 'Lord, even the demons are subject to us in your name' (Luke 10.17f.).

Where did Jesus' proclamation derive the power to judge the world of his day in this way and, as John puts it, to cast out the ruler of this world (John 12.31)? Anyone who is not a contemporary of Jesus and sees himself confronted today, through the mediation of the texts, with all those (actual or believed) acts of power, is bound to ask the question: what really lies behind them? What did Jesus really say and do which was for the one of overwhelming and liberating effect, whereas for the other it seemed to be a danger to the whole order of society? Anyone who seeks to understand what is really at issue in the acts of power must not look at them in isolation, for they are part of the proclamation in whose retinue they are invariably to be found.

First, the unusual or extraordinary, which made people marvel, also showed itself in the whole nature of Jesus' activity. Jesus does what he thinks right, undisturbed by the customs of the country, that is to say, by the political and religious laws in force: for example when he does not observe the regulations about ritual purity at meals; or when he heals the sick on the Sabbath, the day of rest strictly regulated by Mosaic law; or when he associates with tax-collectors and 'sinners', the religiously and socially despised members of society; or when he shows in a parable that the Samaritan, even though he is regarded as racially and religiously inferior, has a real grasp of the commandment about loving one's neighbour, whereas the official expert in the law neglects it.

The unusual expresses itself above all in a characteristic which may be called the absence of religious ties. Jesus not only criticizes the ruling customs and the way in which the religious leaders of the people fulfil their office, but he does what no-one in Israel did and what was the equivalent of a breach with the Jewish religion: he calls in question the authority of the law given through Moses and sets up his own words in the place of Scripture. 'But I say to you.' His criticism is radical. Against what standard does he judge the existing laws? This emerges from the many disputes which are reported about healing on the Sabbath: he tests the laws and the behaviour of the guardians of the law to see if they really represent the will of God, and that means testing them to see if they really serve men. He himself acts with complete freedom, since he knows what is good for man, having a direct knowledge of the will of God.

This freedom from religious ties corresponds to Jesus' lack of social prejudice. His love of men ignored social classification and knew no limitations, which was highly unusual in the slave-owning society of the ancient world. His particular attention was directed towards those who needed it especially – the poor, the sick, the despised, women and children.

Strongest and most astonishing of all was the effect of what he said. This was the mode of activity peculiar to him; many deeds which we are told that he did have a demonstrative meaning and only serve the purpose of drawing attention to some decisive saying. The sovereignty and certainty of his words shows itself particularly in the disputes with the scribes and Pharisees, when he demolishes the arguments of his opponents with a saying or a counter-question to which there is no further answer. When he speaks publicly to the people it is reported later that 'they were astonished at his teaching, for he taught them as one who had authority, and not as the scribes' (Mark 1.22; Matt. 7.28; Luke 4.32). The scribes, who were also lawyers (since the religious law was also public and civil law), appealed in their doctrinal decisions to the legal code and made use of the official commentaries. They did not lay down the law on their own authority but on the basis of their own legal legitimation. Jesus is different from them because he appeals to no pre-given authority except the authority of God himself, and because he behaves as one who is himself the law-giver.

Of course the scribes and Pharisees could not simply accept illegal behaviour of this kind, especially when it even reached out to the temple itself and began to undermine their own authority. They were bound to dispute his legitimation and to put the question, 'By what authority are you doing these things, and who gave you this authority?' (Matt. 21.23. par.). They want Jesus to present his credentials. His answer is to put a puzzling counter-question: 'The baptism of John, whence was it? From heaven or from men?' The law offers them no answer to this question, which demands a personal decision with regard to John's call to repentance. They say, 'We do not know' and Jesus answers, 'Neither will I tell you by what authority I do these things'.

Why did Jesus reject in every form the usual Israelite demand for some visible authority for his words and deeds? One of his parables may give an indication: the story of Dives and Lazarus, which is told in Luke 16. When the rich man is suffering the torments of hell he begs the patriarch Abraham to send the dead Lazarus to his brothers' house, to entreat them to avoid coming to the same place of torment. But Abraham answers: 'They have Moses and the prophets; let them hear them.'

Dives goes on imploring: 'No, father Abraham; but if some one goes to them from the dead, they will repent.' But Abraham replies, 'If they do not hear Moses and the prophets, neither will they be convinced if some one should rise from the dead' (Luke 16.27–31).

This story says the same thing as Jesus in his answer to the 'evil and adulterous generation'. They have his preaching and should listen to that. Their conviction should rest on what he says and it is on this basis that they should decide whether he is speaking the truth, i.e., whether he is of God or not. External miracles do not take one any further in this matter, indeed they distract from the real point at issue. Inner conviction through the truth of his words is the only criterion which Jesus has to offer in response to the question as to his credentials. This means, however, that Jesus throws the question back to the questioners. They have to decide for themselves.

Assent to what he says is not to be reached under the compulsion of irrefutable external acts of power, or on the basis of formal laws or under the pressure of habit. It must come from a free act of will and on the basis of individual conviction. In the same way, rejection of what he says must be a substantiated rejection. 'If I have spoken wrongly, bear witness to the wrong,' says Jesus in the Gospel of John to a servant of the high priest who has reprimanded him because of his bold behaviour before the high office; 'but if I have spoken rightly, why do you strike me?' (John 18.23).

According to the Gospel accounts, Jesus had the upper hand in the intellectual debates or discussions with his opponents. What he said was so immediately convincing that they had nothing with which to answer him. His condemnation as blasphemer was not because he had been refuted theologically; it was an act of institutional force. His *exousía*, his power of conviction, lay in the power of his arguments, in the truth of the position he defended.

If one describes Jesus' views, as reflected in his rejection of the demand for signs, from the point of view of the history of thought, it may be said that his proclamation liberated man's personal power of judgment by appealing to his personal conviction and individual conscience. In this way Jesus declared man to be of age, autonomous. Traditional belief in the truth of the written law, which Paul characterized as faith in the letter of the law, was, like faith on the basis of external signs and miracles, an externally motivated and heteronomous faith; people believed because it was written in the Scriptures, because it was asserted by other people who ought to know. The faith in God which Jesus preached springs from the inner conviction and recognition that God is right. Such a faith was not basically new in Israel, having already been indicated in the prophets' proclamation:

> This commandment which I command you this day is not too hard for you, neither is it far off. It is not in heaven, that you should say, 'Who will go up for us to heaven, and bring it to us, that we may hear it and do it?' Neither is it beyond the sea, that you should say, 'Who will go over the sea for us, and bring it to us, that we may hear it and do it?' But the word is very near you; it is in your mouth and in your heart, so that you can do it (Deut. 30.11-14).

Man is to turn to God 'with all his heart' and it ought not to be difficult for him to do so because these words do not say anything that is alien to him.

Because it encouraged an independent judgment towards the official interpretation of the law, the proclamation of Jesus meant that the individual was set free to criticize the institution. It was this which made Jesus' preaching seem dangerous to authoritative Jewish quarters. John records the resentment roused by his preaching's claim to complete authority. 'Is not this Jesus, the son of Joseph, whose father and mother we know? How does he now say, "I have come down from heaven"?' (John 6.41f.). And in his native town the people took offence because he had no outward legitimation for his teaching and his actions. 'Where did this man get all this? What is the wisdom given to him? What mighty works are wrought by his hands! Is not this the carpenter, the son of Mary and brother of James and Joses and Judas and Simon, and are not his sisters here with us?' (Mark 6.2f.) But among those who believed in him, his activity meant liberation. The poor people especially, unversed in the law, who rubbed along from day to day, resigned to life and knowing nothing of the way of salvation, experienced this liberation as a new opportunity to live before God. The disciples who followed Jesus were for the most part fishermen from Galilee, from the Lake of Gennesaret; even a tax-collector was among them.

Jesus' actions did not need any additional legitimation either, and hardly any additional explanation. 'Go and tell John what you hear and see: the blind receive their sight and the lame walk, lepers are cleansed and the deaf hear, and the dead are raised up, and the poor have good news preached to them. And blessed is he who takes no offence at me' (Matt. 11.4-6). His actions – formulated in terms related to the promises of Isaiah – are to speak for themselves and end the puzzled guessing about his mission. See, hear, be attentive, be awake to the meaning of all that is happening – then you will understand yourselves who I am and what hour has struck! In this way Jesus throws the question of his credentials back to his questioners.

Although he therefore rejected the demand for legitimation, Jesus behaved, to take Luke's description, as a prophet mighty in deed and in word. One can sum it up by saying that his 'power' expressed itself as freedom from all human authority and as complete sovereignty. This sovereignty was not arrogance but was founded on his direct knowledge of the will of God, through a kind of inspiration. It expresses itself also as the power and capacity to see through earthly conditions and to make the will of God effective in them in spite of the resistance of the ruling powers. It came up against its limits where it could effect nothing as a spiritual and humane power: in the face of blindness, 'hardness of heart', lack of faith and brute force.

It might now be said that Jesus had this authority because he was 'God's son', not an ordinary man, and that it was reserved for him alone. But the original texts show that Jesus did not want to keep his power and liberty for himself. 'The sabbath was made for man, not man for the sabbath' (Mark 2.27). This is a general reversal of standards which does not apply only to the Son of Man. (Admittedly the saying was later felt to be so bold that the evangelists watered down its meaning or left it out altogether, Mark 2.28; Matt. 12.8 par.) Jesus' desire to draw the disciples into his own mode of being and to give them his own power shows most clearly in all the stories which have to do with the sending out of the disciples and their work in the world.

We are once told of a failure on the part of the disciples. A father brings his son to Jesus, begging him to have mercy on the boy because he is plagued by a demon and suffers from epilepsy: ' "I brought him to your disciples, and they could not heal him." And Jesus answered, "O faithless and perverse generation, how long am I to bear with you? Bring him here to me." ' Jesus rebukes the demon and heals the boy. But the disciples take him aside and ask, ' "Why could we not cast it out?" He said to them, "Because of your little faith. For truly, I say to you, if you have faith as a grain of mustard seed, you will say to this mountain, 'Move hence to yonder place,' and it will move; and nothing will be impossible to you" ' (Matt. 17.14–20).

It is obvious that Jesus wishes that they did not need him any longer. He positively thrusts them away from him; but in such a way that he gives them at the same time the certainty that they really do *not* need him, because the opportunity of faith is open to them: 'Have faith in God. Truly, I say to you, whoever says to this mountain, "Be taken up and cast into the sea," and does not doubt in his heart, but believes that what he says will come to pass, it will be done for him' (Mark 11.22f.).

Sayings of this kind give insight into the background of the phenomena of 'power' and 'might' in the New Testament – phenomena which appear strange and incomprehensible to people today: faith, allied to the almighty will of God and directed towards its goal with stupendous energy and concentration, may really bring about astonishing feats.

'Nothing will be impossible to you.' 'All things are possible to him who believes' (Matt. 17.20; Mark 9.23). These words cannot be surpassed in boldness. They ascribe to man what men had earlier believed was only possible for God. According to what we are told in the stories of the patriarchs, in the Psalms and in the prophets, it was God who 'alone does wondrous things' and for whom 'nothing is too hard' (Gen. 18.14; Pss. 72.18; 77.14; 136.4; Jer. 32.17). God is

> he who removes mountains, and they know it not,
>   when he overturns them in his anger;
> who shakes the earth out of its place,
>   and its pillars tremble;
> who commands the sun, and it does not rise;
>   who seals up the stars;
> who alone stretched out the heavens,
>   and trampled the waves of the sea;
> who makes the Bear and Orion,
>   the Pleiades and the chambers of the south;
> who does great things beyond understanding,
>   and marvellous things without number (Job 9.5–10).

With Jesus, faith in God's almighty power is not abolished; but the special thing about his message is that now men – both he himself and those who share his faith – can perform wonders in alliance with God. The miraculous power descends from heaven to earth.

Does this mean that now everyone can perform physical miracles through faith, as those people must assume who want to hold fast to a literal interpretation of the faith that moves mountains? Just as Father Malachy in Bruce Marshall's novel moves a dance hall to the Bass Rock, in order to teach modern unbelievers a lesson? Anyone who thinks about the content of Jesus' proclamation and the meaning of his actions realizes that this is a grotesque misunderstanding which need not long detain us, because it distracts from everything which is important in the Biblical message. The 'miracles' which Jesus performed in the world, and which his disciples are also to perform according to his will, are of an entirely different kind. Even the Old Testament, from which the evangelists have taken many pictorial ideas for their miracle stories, did not think of God's wondrous activity in such simple terms. When in the Psalms God's almighty power is depicted through images of his rule over the elements of nature, the psalmist's purpose is clearly to proclaim, praise or call upon God's sovereignty in the world of history:

> The Lord reigns; let the earth rejoice;
> let the many coastlands be glad!
> Clouds and thick darkness are round about him;
> righteousness and justice are the foundations of his throne.
> Fire goes before him,
> and burns up his adversaries round about.
> His lightnings lighten the world;
> the earth sees and trembles.
> The mountains melt like wax before the Lord,
> before the Lord of all the earth.
> The heavens proclaim his righteousness;
> and all the peoples behold his glory (Ps. 97.1–6).

God's righteousness is to be revealed on earth in the history of the nations, and God's will is to conquer. This is the great vision of prophetic faith, rising out of the darkest moments in Israel's history. The power of God rests on his justice. The clearer the believer's consciousness of this God's justice and righteousness, the more intense his feeling of the earthly contradiction, the crass contrast which exists between the power of God and the injustice of present world conditions. The contradiction is unbearable and itself demands its own abrogation, for God cannot, for his own honour's sake, resign himself to the conditions of world history; he would be neither power nor righteousness, let alone love and mercy, if he were simply to look on for long at the dealings of the world. The day must and will come in which he will root out unrighteousness from the midst of the peoples and set up a kingdom of peace:

> For behold, I create new heavens
> and a new earth;

and the former things shall not be remembered
　　or come into mind.
But be glad and rejoice for ever
　　in that which I create;
for behold, I create Jerusalem a rejoicing,
　　and her people a joy . . .
no more shall be heard in it the sound of weeping
　　and the cry of distress.
No more shall there be in it
　　an infant that lives but a few days,
　　or an old man who does not fill out his days. . . .
They shall build houses and inhabit them;
　　they shall plant vineyards and eat their fruit.
They shall not build and another inhabit;
　　they shall not plant and another eat;
for like the days of a tree shall the days of my people be,
　　and my chosen shall long enjoy the work of their hands . . .
The wolf and the lamb shall feed together,
　　and the lion shall eat straw like the ox;
　　and dust shall be the serpent's food.
They shall not hurt or destroy
　　in all my holy mountain,
　　　　says the Lord (Isa. 65.17–25).

It is in the dimension of history that the power of God is at stake, one might even say, the dimension of world history, for the choosing of Israel serves a universal purpose. Israel is the Servant of God who will carry his 'light' to the nations, the tool which God uses in order to achieve the salvation of the world.

Turn to me and be saved,
all the ends of the earth!
　　For I am God, and there is no other.
By myself I have sworn,
　　from my mouth has gone forth in righteousness
a word that shall not return:
　　'To me every knee shall bow,
　　　　every tongue shall swear' . . .
For thus says the Lord,
who created the heavens
　　(he is God!)

who formed the earth and made it
  (he established it;
he did not create it a chaos,
  he formed it to be inhabited!) (Isa. 45.22f.; 18).

In reminiscence of this promise, an early Christian hymn which Paul inserts into his Letter to the Philippians describes how Jesus, the obedient Servant of God, is raised from his humiliation on the cross to be ruler of the world (Phil. 2.5–11). Jesus himself understood his own activity entirely against the background of the universal messianic hope: 'The time is fulfilled, and the kingdom of God is at hand; repent, and believe in the gospel.' (Mark 1.15.) His acts of power are also to be interpreted as messianic signs, according to all the evangelists. In their view a transformation of earthly history into the royal rule of God is reflected in the New Testament miracles. An essential difference compared with the Old Testament hope is that Jesus no longer points merely to the future: 'The kingdom of God is not coming with signs to be observed; nor will they say, "Lo, here it is!" or "There!" for behold, the kingdom of God is in the midst of you' (Luke 17.20f.). Men must not wait for a divine intervention from heaven sometime in the future, says Jesus. God is entering into his kingdom in his, Jesus', own words and actions; and he will continue to do so from now on, wherever men accept and follow his words and deeds. Men are called to be co-workers with God (I Cor. 3.9). God reveals himself in human actions, first in the deeds of Jesus and then in the acts of those who are inspired by his spirit.

Thus, considered in their context in 'salvation-history', the miracles of Jesus, as well as his preaching, have an important theological significance. They draw attention to the fact that Christian faith is not merely an inner comfort for the soul, as it is frequently misunderstood to be; it actually changes external reality into salvation and life. The difference between the miracle as an arbitrary magical trick or display, or even between this and the legitimation miracle in the Jewish sense, is obvious. Even when Jesus' actions assume particularly miraculous features in the evangelists' accounts, their purpose is a purely human one. Whether he is visiting tax-collectors and sinners or driving out demons or healing lepers – the purpose is always to help, to change a situation, to break some inner fetter, and to open up new opportunities for living: 'the old has passed away, behold the new has come' (II Cor. 5.17). The decisive thing about Jesus' actions is not their miraculous form. This may even be totally absent and diminishes increasingly in the course of time, as the early Fathers already noticed; the spirit of love for humanity constantly creates new forms of expression. The really astonishing and miraculous thing is the promise to his brethren, his co-workers and co-heirs of the kingdom, that they had the power to conquer all earthly evil and could perform miracles *here, in the real world of history*, if they only believed and did not doubt, in the face of all appearances, that all things are possible to him that believes. 'Behold, I have given you authority to tread upon serpents and scorpions, and over all the power of the enemy; and nothing shall hurt you' (Luke 10.19).

But does not a promise like this sound even more magical than mere magical acts? If one really considers what this would mean in specific situations of everyday reality, is not such a faith pure illusion, simply wishful thinking? Faith performs a giant and humanly impossible task. Resistance melts like wax in the face of its terrific energy. It undertakes, and undertakes successfully, what is apparently hopeless. But is the basic experience of Christians in the world – in the face of overpowering difficulties, superhuman tasks and the hopeless suffering of others – not the very opposite of power? Is it not a consciousness of extreme weakness?

The story of the stilling of the storm (Mark 4.35–41) is often interpreted today as a symbolical story deriving from the Primitive Church. It describes the critical situation of the first Christians who – apparently left alone by Jesus – see themselves confronted with the overwhelming storm of dangerous persecution and begin to despair of their mission and to lose confidence in their faith. The ship of the Church, threatened by the stormy elements of the wicked world – this was the early allegorical interpretation which crops up again and again in art and literature. Woken by the disciples' cry for help, Jesus comes to their rescue, not without reproach: you of little faith, why are you so afraid? Have you no faith? Then he himself performs the saving miracle, stilling the raging elements through his word of command. People marvel and ask: 'Who then is this, that even wind and sea obey him?'

The story of Peter's sinking beneath the waves has a similar meaning. Jesus again appears as saviour to the faith which has lost its power in the face of threatening reality and is in danger of losing its ascendancy (Matt. 14.28–33). Both stories show, in the Old Testament manner, the divine sovereignty of Jesus by demonstrating his authority over the natural elements (Pss. 89.10; 104.6f.; 107.23–32; Job 9.8). Both also show the nature of the disciples' calling. Jesus wants their faith to be independent and strong; but in practice the disciples are fearful and helpless and constantly need new encouragement through the sight and the word of Christ, who is ever encountering them afresh.

Faith is not the magic talisman of fairy-tale. It is no guarantee against weakness, suffering and death. We are told that Jesus himself was 'in an agony' at the prospect of the cross and needed strength from heaven. And who is Jesus, the preacher of faith that moves mountains? He was humanly speaking completely unsuccessful. And in his preaching the warning of suffering stands in direct juxtaposition to the promise of victory. How can these two things be reconciled?

At this point the real miracle comes into view which distinguishes the faith of the Old and New Testaments from other forms of belief in gods and the divine. The Jewish-Christian faith is, from the very beginning, in the strictest sense *faith in opposition to sight* and *faith based on hope*. 'Faith is the assurance of things hoped for, the conviction of things not seen': this is its classic definition (Heb. 11.1).

Many of Jesus' sayings and parables have as their subject the promise that that which is now small, insignificant and concealed will later be revealed in all its glory. A tree where the birds of the air nest grows out of the tiny mustard seed; he that suffers now is called blessed because he will inherit salvation, etc. That is to say, faith has the greatest endurance of all; nothing in the world can defeat it. Even the death of its author and his witnesses cannot touch it. For it is based with complete certainty on a sovereign truth and effective power which is bound to man by covenant and works for him within the real world of history. 'Thy kingdom come,' says the prayer of faith and 'who shall separate us from the love of Christ?'

Although faith has no incontrovertible, objective proofs of its justification and its truth, a series of 'signs' may be found in the history of the past and the experience of the present which comfort and direct it throughout its trials; if it looks back to the history of the patriarchs from the time of Abraham, it finds itself surrounded by a great 'cloud of witnesses' (Heb. 11–12). The clearest token, the ultimate manifestation of the coming rule of God meets us in the story of Jesus of Nazareth. Wherever he appeared he brought light and life, as the Gospel of John puts it. In spite of appearances, his death on the cross could not silence his voice. He 'is alive'; he gives us his spirit as comforter and support; he is the pattern and forerunner for his own; he confers no magical powers but offers instead the possibilities of patience, endurance, purposefulness and ceaseless activity in ever-new hope and courage. Paul's unbelievable strength in the face of weakness (II Cor. 6.4–10) shows the way in which

Jesus Christ goes on acting in history. It is his image which never grows pale:

> Therefore, since we are surrounded by so great a cloud of witnesses, let us also lay aside every weight, and sin which clings so closely, and let us run with perseverence the race that is set before us, looking to Jesus the pioneer and perfecter of our faith, who for the joy that was set before him endured the cross, despising the shame, and is seated at the right hand of the throne of God. Consider him who endured from sinners such hostility against himself, so that you may not grow weary or faint-hearted (Heb. 12.1–3).

Finally, be strong in the Lord and in the strength of his might. Put on the whole armour of God, that you may be able to stand against the wiles of the devil. For we are not contending against flesh and blood, but against the principalities, against the powers, against the world rulers of this present darkness, against the spiritual hosts of wickedness in the heavenly places . . . (Eph. 6.10–12).

1. The language of the Bible suggests that Christians are inclined to view the real thing that concerns them in life as something to be looked at, something localized somewhere beyond this world, concentrated in mysterious centres of action behind the scenes, from whence it intervenes, divinely or demonically, in the everyday world. 'We have not to do with flesh and blood – there are other realities.' In this sentence fundamentalist circles place a sure finger on a text which sums up all the objections which they have to levy against modern theology and its programme of a 'worldly interpretation' of biblical ideas. It is worth while looking more closely at the text for which they have so particular a predilection.

In the first place, one can view it as a particular expression of a dramatically dualistic philosophy which was widespread in the Middle East. The cosmos is not a harmonious structure but is divided and torn apart by the conflict of two mighty powers. A kingdom of light is at war with a kingdom of darkness, which dominates the world. Satan, the prince of devils, has allies in the upper and lower ranks of a hierarchy of forces of darkness. The 'principalities and powers' frequently mentioned by Paul belong to this hierarchy and so do the spiritual hosts of the heavenly regions mentioned in our particular text. In certain systems of Gnosticism (an eastern doctrine of salvation which has certain similarities with Christianity) there are precise ideas about the realms belonging to the 'spiritual hosts of wickedness' which press in concentric layers on the world of men. These strive to prevent light and liberty from penetrating the world from above or souls from ascending into light. The Gnostic concepts of the course taken by the drama of redemption vary greatly in detail but the point is always to tear souls destined for the world of light away from the darkness; for example, when the warrior for light makes himself invulnerable by dressing himself in a heavenly garment or by arming himself with the weapons of light.

It is easy to see that in the Pauline and post-Pauline epistles basic concepts – not merely isolated motifs – have been taken over from ancient demonology and that the actual Christian content is so entwined with it that later periods could confuse a general basic philosophy belonging to the ancient world with the Christian message of redemption. The unique character of the New Testament text only emerges when one asks what *this particular* 'armour' against evil, which the Christian receives from his God, looks like.

> Therefore take the whole armour of God, that you may be able to withstand in the evil day, and having done all, to stand. Stand therefore, having girded your loins with truth, and having put on the breastplate of righteousness, and having shod your feet with the equipment of the gospel of peace; above all taking the shield of faith, with which you can quench all the flaming darts of the evil one. And take the helmet of salvation, and the sword of the Spirit, which is the word of God (Eph. 6.13–17).

We can grasp what lies behind words like truth, righteousness, peace, faith and so on, because these are comprehensible in terms of human experience. But who are the 'rulers of this present darkness' and the 'spiritual hosts of wickedness in the heavenly places'? Against whom or what is the Christian to be armed in this world?

This particular text – and many like it – gives no direct answer to this important question but only one shrouded in myth which is a puzzle to contemporary understanding and is hence totally unsatisfying. We call it mythical because the evil experienced in the real world (what it consists of is not plain) seems personified or hypostatized in a series of independent and actually existing beings. Even Luther constantly talks of 'the devil and his angels', as if he were speaking of a physical being who admittedly generally carries on his activities through the medium of evil souls in the world who are in his power but who can also appear directly. One can make an appointment with the devil and the devil can literally wring one's neck at the same time.

Today we talk differently about evil. Let us think of cases where the word comes to our lips: human callousness, brutality, selfishness, the exploitation of others, destructiveness, the ignoring of human rights, crimes against humanity – evil is always behaviour practised by men or groups of men against other men or living creatures, behaviour in which both the one who acts and the object of his action are alienated from their natures and their well-being. 'Evil' can conceal itself in triviality, stupidity and arrogance; it knows endless nuances between mental and physical brutality; its possibilities can be discovered in the most subtle manner within the human personality itself, and it can pollute the whole atmosphere in frightful collective manifestations (as it did in the anti-human ideology of National Socialism), issuing in orgies of human hate and mass annihilation. Anyone who thus runs over in his mind the way in which evil is thought of in contemporary speech and the how and where of its manifestation in reality notices a two-fold difference from the ancient view. First, we do not trace back the manifold manifestations of evil in historical life to supernatural extra-worldly beings; and, secondly and consequently, we are ceaselessly concerned to find concrete causes in the world of experience and to combat these with effective means. For example, we have established that the reason for the severe mental malformations and mis-developments of character which lead to crime are often to be found in deprivations in childhood or social life in general; psychologists speak of frustrations, meaning that something has been lacking which was essential for a favourable development of the person's good characteristics – perhaps love, care, a happy family life, a good upbringing, decent work, and so on.

The history of medicine shows graphic examples of the struggle for that exact, concrete diagnosis of disorder which is the prerequisite for a reasonable therapy; this struggle can be observed in all fields of empirical research since the beginning of modern times. As long as people believed that illnesses were due to the intervention of evil spirits, the sick were treated by exorcism, by magical spells or, in the case of Christians, through prayer and the sign of the cross. But it was not Beelzebub, the Lord of the Flies (according to Goethe's *Faust*), who was dangerous but the flies themselves, in as far as they carried the bacteria or viruses which were the germs of illness. As soon as this was recognized, new and quite different methods of healing had to be developed. Scrupulous cleanliness was now of more use than exorcism.

The abuses of social and political life are much more obscure and harder to diagnose than the illnesses of the body. Today we are sufficiently familiar with the processes of nature, and hence we no longer see demons in storm clouds or in the human body. But the field of historical life is for many people still a sphere of irrational 'forces' inaccessible to human understanding. It is ruled by 'providence' or 'fate'; it is determined by 'god-sent' leaders, and now and again by demons let loose from hell. National Socialism, especially, gave a new impetus to the non-rational interpretation of history; partly because its theory was itself irrational, but partly also because it let loose behaviour of which one could later say: that was humanly speaking inexplicable – demonic forces were at work. With a true instinct for evil, pietistic circles declared Hitler to be a manifestation of antichrist; and what he did was certainly anti-Christian. But Hitler and those like him were neither demons of the underworld nor fateful mythological figures. Anyone who so views them can only see a phenomenon like National Socialism as something metaphysically pre-ordained which descended on unsuspecting and innocent people. Consequently he can even today do no more than hope and pray that nothing of the same kind will ever happen again. Apart from that he is powerless; he can learn nothing from history; he knows no way of pre-venting a particular development, for he believes that every event is mysterious and incapable of being influenced, being a decree concocted in the world beyond. The case is instructive in many respects: knowledge of the true connections of cause and effect only begin to penetrate when the seats of the accused in the great trials are occupied, not by demonic characters, but by citizens with quite ordinary faces, husbands and fathers of respectable appearance, excellent subordinates with a keen sense of duty, loyal comrades, decent little people who have acted in good faith and done what they thought best for their country. And again, true knowledge only begins when the analyses of historians, students of ideologies and social psychologists tell us what everyone could have discovered for himself if he had examined his own experience honestly: that it is possible to name the historical factors which pave the way for the rise of an ideology; that one knows the pattern of thinking which moves the sheep-like masses helter-skelter in a particular direc-tion ('what's good for the country is good for us' etc.); that psychological propaganda tactics know how to make use of all the discontent and rankling resentment which is at large and how to direct it into its own channels. When this research into causes is systematically carried out and thoroughly publicized, it must be possible to re-evaluate the past and to learn from it. Hoping and praying is not enough.

Of course these are statements which hardly anyone would quarrel with directly. But do not many Christians through their traditional, conventional religion frequently give the world the impression that they would prefer to leave the necessary affairs of reason and politics to God?

Today it is more possible than before to discover the roots of colonial wars, social revolutions and other struggles for power in society, and the interests that lie behind them. Consequently it seems to the thinking person a curious 'mystification' of the real causes, a sort of smoke-screen, when in Christian services of intercession for peace or the like God is called upon to play the role of a kind of cosmic fire brigade, whereas generally only imprecise and ineffective appeals, couched in highly general terms, are addressed to men. In what way is God involved in these processes? This is completely unexplained and it is a matter to which we would do well to devote some thought in the interests of the suffering people in the world.

In many respects Christians give non-Christians the impression of not really sharing in the realities of the world, as if they had not yet recognized, in this field at least, the radical nature of their responsibilities as well as the immanent possibilities of salvation. Their activity could be far more effective, in the interests of brotherly love. But a thorough thinking-through of these ideas will remain lacking so long as Christians still think that questions of this kind are 'merely secular' and hence somehow secondary in importance; because *really*, in matters of faith (which is where they themselves feel most 'engaged' and where they believe themselves to be personally at stake) one is dealing with 'completely different realities'.

2. Whatever may be said about the manifestations of the devil applies equally to the manifestations of God. If one thinks abstractly about the former one thinks abstractly about the latter. The man who fails to notice the demonic at work in the scenes of everyday life will also fail to find the signs of God's presence in specific situations. Christians who are always waiting for special revelations or dispensations or leadings from a heavenly world often prove to be blind towards the real world. The man whose gaze is directed towards a supernatural history and who looks for miracles and 'facts of salvation' is in constant danger of losing his eye for 'normal' history. It does not occur to him to expect divine revelations on the level of profane everyday happenings (in a political event, for example), or to encounter the Absolute in his day to day comings and goings – perhaps in a street incident. Yet it was one of

Jesus' main purposes to maintain precisely this, through word and deed and through the devotion of his whole life.

Paradoxically, this purpose of Jesus' was subsequently threatened by the mythologization and hallowing of his life and work, a transformation which silently took place in the language of the proclamation and later in all the details of institutional religion. Contrary to its original intention, the glorifying language of the first preachers, which exalted Jesus into heaven and declared him the supernatural son of God and man of miracles, is for contemporary people a distortion of the real heart of the message rather than a clarification of it.

Does anything in the real world depend on the way in which one interprets the miracles in the Bible or, more generally, the supernatural salvation history or, more generally still, God's whole activity? It is a reasonable question; for the whole 'miracle problem' could in the last resort turn out to be of complete indifference (at least for people in general) if the widely held contemporary view that this is a 'purely religious' matter, and consequently the private affair of the individual, were true; that it is an internal theological squabble, to put it in somewhat unfriendly terms, whose result is completely lacking in interest for real life. This view certainly reflects the judgment of the contemporary mind, which believes that the miracle question is finished and done with; but it is an improbable solution, because belief in miracles crops up again and again as a question and a possibility in a religious tradition which today influences the behaviour of millions. How can this religious tradition belonging to the past (the earliest biblical writings are, after all, nearly 3,000 years old) be taken into and absorbed into the present without contemporary life being restricted by it, yet so that the essential human experiences preserved in it are not lost? That is the leading and still unanswered question which runs through the criticism and interpretation of miracles in modern times.

If any one insight can be said to have been gained from the historical development of the problem it is this: that we are dealing with what is certainly a religious question, but one which is not remote or specialized, being a matter of one's attitude to the world in the widest sense. Hence the question of miracle has always also had a scientific, anthropological, even a social and political dimension, as well as one belonging to the history of thought. This is evident when we trace the ideas which run from Spinoza to Feuerbach and Bloch. Where, in the whole range of our experience of reality, is the absolutely important and determining factor of our human existence? There are multifarious things and events between heaven and earth, but what is *really* real? This is the religious, philosophical, practical and basically human question to which faith in a supernatural God and miracles gave an answer. In certain events in the history of Israel, and finally in the event of Jesus of Nazareth, *true* reality was experienced. But the answer which was arrived at on the basis of experiences of this kind formulated the decisive events in the visual forms of a world outlook which is today a thing of the past: Jesus ascended into heaven. These visual forms were dogmatized at the same time as the essential events themselves. Hence in later times they became a double problem. First, they blocked the further development of the general experience of reality and kept this in its old state: this was the problem of the Enlightenment. Secondly, however, they are also a hindrance to a new experience of that particular reality which is vital to religious faith – at least they are a hindrance to the understanding of it; this is the chief problem of modern theology. For both reasons one may say that in actual reality much depends on the way in which Christians interpret the miracles of the Bible.

In both the Old and New Testaments miracles were *revelations*, that is to say, something was visible or experiencible in them which had been hidden before; the people involved recognized and understood something which was of the greatest importance for their whole lives. When Peter saw how the nets broke under the weight of the fish, he fell at Jesus' feet and said, 'Lord, depart from me for I am a sinful man.' Miracles were interpreted as signs, just because they contained something which had to be understood. They were signs of the presence of God in the world at that particular moment. Today many Christians decide with an effort of will to believe that miracles are word for word true, because they are in the Bible, and struggle for an 'obedient' or even a 'joyful' profession of faith in them. But they find nothing in miracles, they understand nothing from them, and certainly nothing that is of prime importance to them at that particular moment. Where today do we wonder – in the full biblical sense of the word – over the signs of the presence of God? That is an open question.

3. Finally, the example of a great preacher and theologian may serve to show how the miracles of Jesus can be so understood that even today they *reveal* something. Here is the text from the Gospel of Mark:

And again, departing from the coasts of Tyre and Sidon, he came unto the sea of Galilee, through the midst of the coasts of Decapolis.

And they bring unto him one that was deaf, and had an impediment in his speech: and they beseech him to put his hand upon him. And he took him aside from the multitude, and put his fingers into his ears, and he spit, and touched his tongue; And looking up to heaven, he sighed, and saith unto him, Ephphatha, that is, Be opened. And straightway his ears were opened, and the string of his tongue was loosed, and he spake plain. And he charged them that they should tell no man: but the more he charged them, so much the more a great deal they published it; And were beyond measure astonished, saying, he hath done all things well: he maketh both the deaf to hear, and the dumb to speak (Mark 7.31–37 AV).

Here are Martin Luther's comments in a sermon preached in the year 1538:

That Christ hath healed this man – over this they are amazed. But that they themselves can hear, over this they do not wonder. Through this small miracle God will stir us up to recognize the greatest of miracles. The whole world is deaf, that they do not comprehend this. ... Hence he says 'Ephphatha', that is to say, 'Be opened!' If we had eyes and ears we would be able to see and hear how the corn cries to us 'rejoice in God, eat and drink, use me and serve thy neighbour! I will see to it that the barns are full!' And if I were not deaf, I could not but hear how the cows say as they wind in and out of the byres, 'Rejoice, we bring butter and cheese; eat and give to others.' The hens say, 'We will lay eggs,' and the birds say, 'Be glad, we will hatch other fledglings.' Likewise do I hear the sow grunting with joy because she gives pork and bacon. All creatures speak to us. And every man should say in his heart: I will use what God hath given and will share it with others.

But the Devil keepeth the people from listening and they cry only 'more, more'! Greed will not rest till the rust has gathered on the coins. And if a man can sell his neighbour a bushel for a gulden more, he will do so. So is our joy spoilt with care and greed, so that we dishonour our Lord God. . . we are not worthy to hear a bird sing or a sow grunt.[1]

As we have said, the quotation comes from a sermon, not from a strictly exegetical lecture. In the many sermons which Luther preached in the course of his life on individual Gospel passages, he reserved for

[1] Luther, *op. cit.*, 46, 493–495; quoted in E. Mühlhaupt (ed.), *D. Martin Luthers Evangelien-Auslegung* (Göttingen, 1953), pt. 3, pp. 25ff.

himself the liberty of accentuating sometimes one point and sometimes another. Here the stress is one-sided and, according to modern exegetical interpretation, not even correct. The story is really relating a typical messianic miracle of the kind expected in Israel, since the time of the prophet Isaiah, for the end-time:

> Then the eyes of the blind shall be opened,
>   and the ears of the deaf unstopped;
> then shall the lame man leap like a hart,
>   and the tongue of the dumb sing for joy (Isa. 35.5f.).

The miracle prefigures the new world on earth. And yet – does not Luther's interpretation carry Jesus' intention a stage further? What does life in the new world mean? How ought we to imagine it? The Old Testament texts say clearly that it is not an alien, supernatural state of being which must be expected, but the fulfilment of earthly and human destiny. Earthly and human salvation is to take the form of the removal of evil. The origins of evil, however, lie in sin – sin which expresses itself, for example, in a darkening of the atmosphere in the world of men or, in the case of individuals, in 'hardness of heart', that is to say, in failure to know God and a false orientation in the world. Luther says about these things:

> But the Devil keepeth the people from listening.
> Our house, farm, field, garden and all else is full of [the message of] the Bible, for God does not only preach through his miraculous works but also opens our eyes, stirs up our senses and sends his light straight into our hearts.[1]

Men do not give sufficient attention to the circumstances in which they live because they take everyday life as a matter of course. 'Nothing out of the way,' they say. They want the sensational. Miracles, even the miracles of Jesus, once served the same purpose; consequently we see Luther constantly concerned in his Gospel exegesis to correct the naïve belief in miracles and to draw his hearers' attention to the 'true and high miracle' which 'Christ brings about, and brings about unceasingly, in Christendom through his divine almighty power'. But the deeper reason why man does not hear God speaking to him in the voice of creation lies in the fact that he is shut in within himself or – as Luther says in his 1516 lecture on the Epistle to the Romans – *zurückgekrümmt*, twisted back into himself. He does not accept the gifts and opportunities offered by the

---

[1] *Ibid.*, 49, 434, 16–18; quoted in *Luther Lexikon*, p. 435.

world and when he does accept them he uses them brutally and selfishly. Through his false greed he ruins the beauty of creation and at the same time becomes the slave of earthly things, instead of ruling over them in reasonableness, liberty and responsibility.

Christ's work of redemption (which is just as often described in myths and formulae as the works of the devil) means that he overcomes the power of sin in the heart. We must cease to listen to and marvel at the story of his words and works, life and death, simply as external facts and must instead (as Luther says elsewhere) 'draw them deep into our own flesh', that is to say, absorb them into our own lives. Then the natural-supernatural 'distortion' will disappear and the causes of the world's blindness will be removed together with all cramped and self-absorbed egoism. Christ opens all the senses to the realities of the world. A Christian understands the language of creation.

LIST OF MIRACLES WITH INDEX

BIBLIOGRAPHY

Augustine, Collected Works in: J. P. Migne, *Patrologia Latina* (MPL), vols. 32–47. Texts on the problem of miracle are collected in F. Nitzsch, *Augustinus' Lehre vom Wunder* (see below).

Bahrdt, Carl Friedrich, *Briefe über die Bibel im Volkston. Eine Wochenschrift von einem Prediger auf dem Lande* (Halle 1782f.).
Ausführung des Plans und Zweks Jesu. In Briefen an Wahrheit suchende Leser (Berlin 1784ff.).
Bavink, Bernhard, *Science and God*, ET (London 1933).
Becker, Ulrich and Wibbing, Siegfried, *Wundergeschichten* (Handbücherei für den Religionsunterricht 2, Gütersloh 1965).
Bitter, Wilhelm (ed.), *Magie und Wunder in der Heilkunde* (Conference report, Stuttgart 1959).
Bloch, Ernst, *Das Prinzip Hoffnung* (two-volume edition, Frankfurt am Main, 1959).
Religion im Erbe (selected articles), ed. J. Moltmann (Siebenstern Taschenbücher, 1967).
Bohr, Niels, *Atomic Theory and the Description of Nature* (Cambridge, 1961²).
Bornkamm, Günther, *Jesus of Nazareth* (London 1960 and New York 1961).
Bultmann, Rudolf, 'The Study of the Synoptic Gospels', in: R. Bultmann and K. Kundsin, *Form Criticism* (New York, 1962).
The History of the Synoptic Tradition (New York and Oxford 1968²).
Jesus and the Word (London and New York 1958).
Primitive Christianity in its Contemporary Setting (New York 1956 and London 1960).
Das Evangelium des Johannes (Meyers Kommentar, Göttingen 1953¹³; ET in preparation).
'The Question of Wonder', in: *Faith and Understanding* (Collected Essays, London and New York 1969), pp. 247ff.
This World and the Beyond (London and New York 1960).

'New Testament and Mythology' in: H.-W. Bartsch (ed.), *Kerygma and Myth* (London 1953 and New York 1961); see also *Kerygma and Myth* II (London 1962).

Delling, Gerhard, 'Botschaft und Wunder im Wirken Jesu', in: H. Ristow and K. Matthiae (eds.), *Der historische Jesus und der kerygmatische Christus* (Berlin 1961²).

Dibelius, Martin, *From Tradition to Gospel* (London and New York 1934).
Jesus (London 1963).

Ebeling, Gerhard, *The Nature of Faith* (London 1961 and Philadelphia 1962).

Eddington, A. S., *The Nature of the Physical World* (Cambridge 1928).

Fascher, Erich, *Kritik am Wunder. Eine geschichtliche Skizze* (Stuttgart 1960).

Feuerbach, Ludwig, *The Essence of Christianity* (London 1853, New York 1957).

Fuchs, Ernst, *Studies of the Historical Jesus* (London 1964).

Fuchss, Heinrich, *Hat die Bibel recht? Ein Streifzug durch die Geschichte des Kampfes der Theologie gegen den wissenschaftlichen Fortschritt* (Leipzig and Jena 1957).

Garaudy, Roger, *From Anathema to Dialogue* (London and St Louis 1967).

Gunkel, Herrmann, *Das Märchen im Alten Testament* (Religionsgeschichtliche Volksbücher, Tübingen 1921).

Gutbrod, Karl, *Die Wundergeschichten des Neuen Testaments* (Stuttgart 1967).

Harvey, Van A., *The Historian and the Believer* (New York 1966 and London 1967).

Hegel, Georg Wilhelm Friedrich, *Lectures on the Philosophy of Religion* (London 1895).

Heisenberg, Werner, *The Physicist's Conception of Nature*, ET (London 1958).

Heising, Alkuin, *Die Botschaft der Brotvermehrung* (Stuttgarter Bibelstudien 15, Stuttgart 1966).

Hennecke, E. – Schneemelcher, W. – Wilson, R. Mc. L., *New Testament Apocrypha* 2 vols. (London and Philadelphia 1963, 1965).

Herrmann, Wilhelm, *Der Christ und das Wunder* (1908; reprinted in Schriften zur Grundlegung der Theologie, part II, Munich 1967).

Herzog, Rudolf, *Die Wunderheilungen von Epidauros* (Leipzig 1931).

Hume, David, *The Philosophical Works of David Hume* (Edinburgh 1826).
also R. Wollheim (ed.), *Hume on Religion* (London and New York [Fontana] 1963).

Käsemann, Ernst, 'Wunder im Neuen Testament', *Die Religion in Geschichte und Gegenwart*[3], VI (Tübingen 1962).
Jesus Means Freedom (London 1969; US title *Was Jesus Liberal?*, Philadelphia 1969).

Klein, Günter, 'Wunderglaube und Neues Testament', *Das Gespräch*, vol. 28 (Wuppertal-Barmen 1964).[3]

Korch, Helmut, *Das Problem der Kausalität* (Berlin 1965).

Kümmel, Werner Georg, *Promise and Fulfilment* (London 1956).

Lewis, Clive Staples, *Miracles* (London and New York 1947; Fontana 1960).

Liek, Erwin, *Das Wunder in der Heilkunde* (Munich 1940[4]).

Luther, Martin, *Werke, Kritische Gesamtausgabe* (Weimar 1883ff.).
K. Aland (ed.), *Luther-Lexikon* (Berlin 1956).

March, Arthur, *Das neue Denken der modernen Physik* (Hamburg 1957).

March, Arthur and Freeman, I. M., *The New World of Physics* (New York 1962).

Marshall, Bruce, *Father Malachy's Miracle*, rev. ed. (London 1947).

Marx, Karl, *Marx-Engels-Studienausgabe*, 4 vols. (Fischer Bücherei 1966).

Marxsen, Willi, *Der Streit um die Bibel* (Gladbeck 1965).
Das Neue Testament als Buch der Kirche (Gütersloh 1967[2]).
'The Resurrection of Jesus as a Historical and Theological Problem', in: C. F. D. Moule (ed.), *The Significance of the Message of the Resurrection for Faith in Jesus Christ* (London 1968).

Mensching, Gustav, *Das Wunder im Glauben und Aberglauben der Völker* (Leiden 1957).

Nitzsch, Friedrich, *Augustinus' Lehre vom Wunder* (Berlin 1865).

Olshausen, Hermann, *Biblischer Commentar über sämmtliche Schriften des Neuen Testaments* (Reutlingen 1834[2]).

Paulus, Heinrich, E. G., *Das Leben Jesu als Grundlage einer reinen Geschichte des Urchristentums*, 2 vols. (Heidelberg 1828).

Planck, Max, *Scientific Autobiography and Other Papers*, ET (New York 1949).

Reimarus, Hermann Samuel, *Fragmente eines Ungenannten*, ed. G. E. Lessing, in: K. Lachmann (ed.), *Gotthold Ephraim Lessings sämtliche Schriften*, vol. 12 (Leipzig 1897[1]).

Renner, Rudolf, *Die Wunder Jesu in Theologie und Unterricht* (Lahr/ Schwarzwald 1966).

Rohrbach, Hans, 'Biblische Wunder und moderne Naturwissenschaft', in: *Naturwissenschaft und Gotteserkenntnis* (Mannheim 1965[6]).

Naturwissenschaft, Weltbild, Glaube (Wuppertal 1967).

Schweitzer, Albert, *The Quest of the Historical Jesus* (London 1954[3]).

Spinoza, Baruch Benedictus de, *Tractatus theologico-politicus*, R. H. W. Elwes (trans.), rev. ed., 2 vols. (Bohn's Philosophical Library, London 1900).

Spülbeck, Otto, *Der Christ und das Weltbild* (Berlin 1957[4]).

Stallmann, Martin, *Die biblische Geschichte im Unterricht* (Göttingen 1963).

Stock, Hans, *Studien zur Auslegung der synoptischen Evangelien im Unterricht* (Gütersloh 1967[4]).

Strauss, D. F., *The Life of Jesus Critically Examined*, 3 vols. (London 1846).

A New Life of Jesus (London 1865).

Thomas Aquinas, *Summa Theologiae*, Latin text and English translation, Thomas Gilby and others (eds.) (London and New York 1964ff.).

Troeltsch, Ernst, 'Historische und dogmatische Methode in der Theologie' in: *Gesammelte Schriften*, vol. II (Tübingen 1922[2]).

Weinreich, Otto, *Antike Heilungswunder* (Giessen 1909).

Wendland, Johannes, *Der Wunderglaube im Christentum* (Göttingen 1910).

Zimmer, Ernst, *Umsturz im Weltbild der Physik* (Munich 1961).